Mr Singh, Kashmiri greengrocer to South Kensington, looked Justine Hardy in the eye over a cabbage. He began to rage, quietly and in a polite fruit-and-vegetable sort of way, about the state of his former homeland, India, and the irresponsible and inaccurate coverage by the world's press: 'You are a journalist. You should be writing on one of our great newspapers. Then you will be starting to understand us.' So Justine Hardy goes to work for *The Indian Express* in New Delhi.

Memories of Kipling's 'seven years' hard' as a reporter in India haunt her as she travels to Assam and finds the shadows of terrorism stalking the tea gardens. Her landlord, an erstwhile Rajput prince with a fondness for exotic fish with frilly tails, offers advice on all things vital, from choosing face-packs to getting a dowry. Her rickshaw driver picks his way gently through her inadequate Hindustani as he takes her from the city's slums to the manicured playing fields of the polo set. In the High Himalayas she meets the Dalai Lama: under the strobe-lights of Delhi's discos she witnesses the passage of AIDS through city society.

Scoop-wallah is an idiosyncratic, funny and sad tale about writing as an outsider on the inside of a country where the newspapers are still printed on hot-metal machines and deadlines are missed because of cows at rush-hour. India's clash of past and present continues to wrong-foot Justine as she tries to get her story in order.

Justine Hardy was born and educated in England, trained as a journalist in Australia, and has worked on newspapers and magazines both there and in India. Her most recent book, *Goat: A Story of Kashmir and Notting Hill*, is also published by John Murray.

She continues to write for newspapers in America, England and India, and presents on television. She lives in London and India.

SCOOP-WALLAH

JUSTINE HARDY

John Murray
Albemarle Street, London

For Gautam
and another side of India
as it tries to find
its voice

The author and publishers would like to thank A.P. Watt Ltd on behalf of The National Trust for Places of Historic Interest or Natural Beauty for permission to reproduce extracts from the Kipling Papers (pp. 17, 191 and 249); Rudyard Kipling, *Something of Myself* (pp. 46, 72, 120, 126 and 145); and Rudyard Kipling, *Kim* (p. 91).

First published in 1999
by John Murray (Publishers) Ltd,
50 Albemarle Street, London W1X 4BD

Paperback edition 2000

A catalogue record for this book is available from the British Library

ISBN 0-7195-6148 5

Typeset in 11.5/14 Goudy by Servis Filmsetting Ltd, Manchester
Printed and bound in Great Britain by The Guernsey Press Company Ltd

Contents

ACKNOWLEDGEMENTS

THIS BOOK IS about people. It relies on them for its flesh and blood. The risk I take in putting them down on paper is that no one likes to see themselves in black and white. If you say they are beautiful they will say you are a liar. If you say they are ugly they will sue. You can't win, so you just have to cross your fingers.

In India I was welcomed in so many places. Thank you, Sourish and the gang at *The Indian Express*; Rani Sahiba and Maharaj Sahib at Hailey Road; Vijai and Rani Lal in Delhi and Pragpur; Billy and Alka Singh in Assam; Mr and Mrs Krishna at Jangpura Extension; and Reggie Singh in Simla. My love to Paddy and the boys in the office, Tarun, Dev, Manoher, Yaatendra and Sashi, to Gita for your enthusiasm and to Rajiv, my lifeline. Thank you, Arvind, for the polo views, and the Delhi Polo Club for the horses and afternoons of sanity. Readers interested in DRAG can write to: DRAG, 75 Paschimi Marg, Vasant Vihar, New Delhi 110057 (tel: 00 91 11 614 2383).

In England there is one person who started all this – Peter Hopkirk – because he said that I could not possibly work on an Indian newspaper and not write about it. My gratitude to Gail Pirkis at John Murray for rebuilding me. Thank you, Kamin, for being the go-between, and Adie for your resilience. A big thank you to Will Curtis for his pictures of Assam and Spiti on pp. 58, 97, 107, 112 and 125.

My greatest debt, however, is to two people – my mother and Raj Kumar Yashwant Singh, the Prince of Hailey Road. Carry on regardless.

The Kashmiri of South Kensington

Sourish Bhattacharyya
Associate Editor
The Indian Express   2 April 1996

Dear Mr Bhattacharyya

I am an English journalist and will be based in Delhi for the next
year. I wonder if there might be some writing that I could do for
you at *The Indian Express*? May I come and see you?
 This is not an April Fool as you will see from the date at the top.

Yours sincerely
Justine Hardy

Indian Express Newspapers Ltd
9 & 10 Bahadur Shah Zafar Marg
New Delhi 110 002

10 April 1996

Dear Miss Hardy

I would like to give sincere apologies for not replying to your letter
at an earlier date but I have been attending a family funeral.

I am most intrigued to have received your letter. I do not believe that we have had an English journalist working on the paper for quite some time.

You must come in and see us.

I am not quite clear on your point about the April Fool; perhaps an English habit that we somehow failed to adopt. You will, no doubt, be able to explain it to me.

Sincerely
Sourish Bhattacharyya
Associate Editor

India and I are inextricably linked. When I am in India I do not think of England, but when I am in England I think of India. Family and friends, those I love, are separate islands that float between the two places. When I cannot sleep in London I have waking dreams peopled by the characters who inhabit my life in Delhi, and I get up and write about them. When I cannot sleep in Delhi it is either too hot to dream or the sound of the monsoon drowns out all thought as it empties itself over the city. And so I get up and write about it.

For ten years I had come at India from different directions: first as a newspaper trainee from England, then as a fully fledged reporter from Australia, then again as a features writer from London, but always from the outside. Now I needed a change of approach. Inspiration came from an unexpected source.

I had gone out to buy a cabbage at a greengrocer's in South Kensington. The shop is owned and run by a family from the state of Jammu in North India. Father Singh came to England after the blood-letting of Partition, when the two wings of the Indian sub-continent in the far east and west were lopped off to form Pakistan. The death toll of Partition is put by some at a million and a half: others estimate that half a million people were slaughtered in the desperate exchange of Hindus and Muslims. The state of Jammu, riding the new India–Pakistan border, became a tinder-

2

The Kashmiri of South Kensington

box. Mr Singh, the soon-to-be South Kensington fruit and vege-table merchant, saw only bloody destruction for his family if he stayed. He took the boat to England.

His nephews now run the shop and are English in all but name and facial hair. Father Singh lurks in the background wearing his looped moustache, the badge of his cultural past and the ensuing bloodbath that made him flee his homeland.

The cabbage was huge. Could I have just half? Father Singh nodded and beckoned me to the back of the shop. There, in front of a sympathetic audience, he began to rage in a polite fruit-and-vegetable sort of way about the state of his former home and the irresponsible and inaccurate coverage by the world's press. He shook an old hunting-knife to make his point before wielding it on the cabbage. He told me that I should be out there writing about it. He was unmoved by my explanation that I was not a foreign correspondent.

'Oh, I do not mean on a *farangi* newspaper,' he said. 'You should

3

be writing on one of our great Indian papers, then you will really be starting to understand us.'

Speech delivered and cabbage halved, he took my purchase to the till and totted up the amount. He charged me half – half a cabbage, half a bill. One of his nephews raised a questioning eyebrow.

'You will say nothing. This young lady is with us. She will be writing for one of our papers so as to learn the way we are thinking and feeling about our country.'

His nephew wiped his nose on his sleeve.

Thus the order was given. Father Singh led me out on to the street, into the throng of clip, clip South Kensington ladies. He sent me forth, tap, tap, with his hunting-knife. The glossy ladies tripped on by, knowing nothing of the half-cabbage or the rivers of blood that had flowed on India's station platforms in 1947.

There are three main English-language newspapers in India: *The Times of India*, *The Statesman* and *The Indian Express*. *The Times of India*, founded by an English proprietor in 1838, has grown into a group of eleven dailies published out of Ahmadabad, New Delhi and Bombay. *The Statesman*, also founded by an Englishman, began life as *The Calcutta Statesman* in 1875, branching out in 1930 with another edition published out of New Delhi. *The Indian Express* was launched in 1932 in its first incarnation as a small daily in Madras. In 1950 the paper was bought by the entrepreneur Ram Nath Goenka. He built it into a well-muscled newspaper empire. Goenka died in 1991 but the group is still run by the family.

Since Independence the vernacular and regional-language newspapers have grown apace. But in a multilingual society it is the English-language papers that predominate, even though their founders packed their bags over half a century ago.

English is still the currency of the social establishment. The socialites of Calcutta, Bombay and Delhi may swirl their saris and stand proud in their national dress of white *churidar* trousers and black, high-necked *shervani* jackets, careful copies of the sartorially patriotic Nehru, but still they speak English. Their feet are silent speakers too, shod in English shoes, black Oxfords to match the aspirations of language. Every word contradicts India's passionate attempt over the past fifty years to expunge lingering traces of the Raj, as if by using English, they can separate themselves from the common man.

More tellingly, English is also still the lingua franca of the press élite and some areas of politics, and it dominates the business world. In a country driven by the desire to build companies, go global and make billions, English shapes the deal.

The Kashmiri of South Kensington had decreed that I go for one of the great papers. That meant one of the big three. A *Times of India* report on English football supporters made me suspect that that paper might not welcome an approach from a female English journalist looking for work: 'How strange that such a supposedly civilized nation can cultivate such a pure breed of hooliganism. Times have changed. It will be remembered by some old geezer or nostalgia-maniac that the bare-footed boys of Bengal used to beat the booted *babus* of the Raj. Perhaps that is how the English rationalize India's rather low position in the world soccer rankings. They like to think that we still just have not quite got the hang of putting on boots.' *The Statesman* too was clearly keen to shake off its Raj origins. That left *The Indian Express*.

The Indian Express has perhaps the most relaxed style of the three, and it also has a reputation for grabbing a story and shaking it until the controversy rattles out. It is a terrier paper, one of the first to turn the vituperative pen of investigative journalism on the politics of India. The scale was tipped by a friend from Delhi.

'I will always choose *The Indian Express* first for a reason of loyalty. During the dark days of Mrs Gandhi's so-called State of Emergency it was the one that defied her. So many of the papers were asked to bend and they were so weak they not only bent, they crawled. Goenka and *The Express* did neither thing. That paper came out every day wearing its great black spaces of censorship. To me it was Goenka and his press mourning the freedom that they had fought for. I call that brave journalism and I have supported the paper every day since.'

Goenka had taken risks throughout his publishing career. During the Quit India struggle in 1942 he had helped to print clandestine literature on his presses, befriending underground workers at the risk of losing his lucrative government advertising contract. He waved the flag in the face of censorship once again during the Emergency of 1975, printing messages of defiance between the lines of the editorials. Goenka said publicly that he did not mind sacrificing everything that he had created so long as he did not have to face the day when there was no voice to challenge Mrs Gandhi's authoritarianism.

So I wrote to *The Indian Express* and then set about applying for a visa from the Indian High Commission in London. I filled out the visa form, happy to give details of my father's profession, his domestic arrangements and his dog's name. Then I waited. No word came. I rang.

At the other end of the line someone shuffled papers, mispronounced my name perfectly every time and then submitted me to an endless rendition of 'Jingle Bells', seemingly played on frayed knicker elastic and milk-bottle tops.

At last I was told to come in and talk to a Mrs Modi.

It was raining when I went to see her. Those waiting for visas sat in a long grey line, their faces pallid under the neon glare. The rude white light made Mrs Modi's electric-blue sari trip the light fantastic when she appeared, but there was no smile to match.

She did not like my idea at all.

'You see, you will be taking work away from an Indian,' she said, hitching up her sari by way of emphasis.

I agreed with her but explained that I would be writing and commentating on India as an outsider, something that would be hard for an Indian journalist to do.

'It is of no importance what standpoint you are coming from, you are still going to be standing on an Indian.' The lady was not to be moved.

I gave an impassioned speech about my love for India. It fell on deaf ears. Mrs Modi picked her fingernails and plucked at hairs on her sari that were not there. At last, worn down by my purple prose, she gave in.

'You must realize that this is not normal procedure. I am hoping that you will respect this. It will become most apparent if you abuse this privilege in any way.'

She got up to indicate that the meeting was now over.

'Enjoy my country,' she said with an almost smile.

A Head-stand

THERE WAS NO shipboard romance, no starry nights spent draped fetchingly in chiffon over the weather rail, discussing the East with close-clipped young men bound for the Indian Civil Service. I was fifty years too late and confined to fighting a path through a check-in queue of huge boxes held together with fraying string, televisions being taken home by every returning Mr Corner Shop King. He, his family, all his worldly chattels and I were travelling cattle class on Indian Airlines.

The Muslim gentleman on my left was drunk before the busy flashing route map even had us over Frankfurt. He had a loud argument with his friend or brother, or possibly neither, about whether the prohibition of Islam applied 33,000 feet up. The air hostesses paid no attention. It was only when my neighbour, now very drunk and dribbling freely, lunged at my bosom that help finally came in the shape of a steward. He moved the merry Muslim and did his best to clean me off with a moist paper towel.

At Delhi airport I took a rickshaw. On the way into town we stopped in the traffic beside a building site panelled in corrugated iron and splashed with political slogans and lurid posters advertising Hindi movies – tits-and-arse subcontinental style in startling shades of lycra and silk. Beyond the posters a donkey carried sandbags up and down an earth ramp. Delhi looked confused, the present pushing and shoving wherever it could, with the past sitting heavily on its shoulders.

It felt a bit like coming home, a strange sensation to have about a city that is neither my birthplace nor my home.

The rickshaw driver looked in his various mirrors, tilting the one closest to him to check if there was any leg or better on show. All this was familiar. Rickshaw drivers have tipped their mirrors to get a better view of their female passengers ever since the rickshaw and the wing mirror first teamed up. No dice today. His spoilsport passenger was swathed from head to foot.

The traffic began to move. An old Ambassador taxi cut us up and a cow wandered into the middle of the road, a half-chewed blue plastic bag hanging out of her mouth; fag in mouth, bag in mouth, the same look. The traffic darted around her in a disjointed, shrieking ballet, constantly just missing her as she made her way towards another spot that might yield up a further plastic tidbit. Brakes yelled and a bus shot straight across our path. The rickshaw driver swerved, bouncing off the kerb before continuing on his previous course. I clung to my luggage, the only buffer between this life and the next. I knew I would get used to this again. Or perhaps die.

We turned off into a quiet side road. We were in fashionable Delhi, a few minutes from Connaught Place or, as it had recently been renamed in a particularly energetic fit of anti-Raj fervour, Rajiv Chowk. Chowk means square, a curious choice for a large circle within another circle that is famous around the world for being, well . . . a circle.

The rickshaw stopped opposite a *chai* stall in front of an ugly high-rise building, not a usual sight in this area of town where elegant white stucco bungalows predominate. There was a crowd of rickshaw drivers around the stall, some squatting on the pavement involved in a card game, others hanging out of their rickshaws, small glasses of sweet, light-brown tea in hand.

Piece by piece I unloaded my bags from the rickshaw until there was a mound on the pavement. The last thing was a box of books that had cost me £100 in overweight baggage. I made as much noise as possible dragging it out of the rickshaw. The *chai* drinkers looked on unmoved. I began the performance again, lugging each

Passing Rajiv Square, famous for being a circle

bag to the entrance of Jodhpur Apartments, which was to be my home in Delhi. By the time I got to the box of books I had lost interest. I crossed the road to the *chai* stall.

The owner was a fat man in greying *kurta* pyjamas, the top draped over his balloon belly. He raised an eyebrow and called out to Mataji, his mother. She stuck her head out over the counter to see what was going on. In contrast to her son's rather grubby clothes, her sari was spotless, her white hair scraped back into a neat bun, her skin draped across her cheekbones. She smiled, her dark brown eyes melting into the folds of creased skin, and held out a glass of *chai*.

Returning to the box of books I sat down and slowly drank. The *chai* drinkers drank even more slowly and stared. Mataji was watching. As I finished she sent a boy across from the stall to take the empty glass. I kicked the box of books most of the way into the hall. The lift boy seemed annoyed that I had so much with me. With a pained expression he put his foot out to jam the lift door open. I was now soaked in sweat but he waited while I loaded the luggage. He waited while the lift door closed in on the dense heat. He waited as we stopped at each floor for no one. Then he turned on the lift fan as we reached my floor.

Jodhpur Apartments, the name was on a brass plaque above the curlicued metal-work of the elegant front door. It was not an address picked at random but a carefully crafted destination involving a cross-cultural marriage, tenuous family links, and several erstwhile princes. My cousin had married an Indian. One of their great friends had become my best friend in India. He was an erstwhile prince and so he arranged for me to stay at Jodhpur Apartments with more erstwhile princes. Even if I was defying convention by working for an Indian paper, at least I had the right address.

Someone was shouting behind the doors, now in Hindustani, now in English.

'You bloody fool, *jao*, *jao*, you are making me sick, *jao*.' There was no reply to this fulsome insult.

The shouting stopped and someone trotted off down a corridor. I rang the bell and waited. Nothing happened.

There was a long pause.

The same footfall finally trotted back towards the door. It opened to reveal a boy of about eighteen with a beautiful face and sleep in both eyes. He stared, his eyes moving leisurely up and down, and then he stretched slowly, arching his back to reveal a smooth, dark belly.

Someone else was shuffling down the corridor out of the interior darkness of the apartment. It was an old man who only came up to the shoulder of the boy, his eyes sunken in, his cheekbones thrust out. He was probably just over five feet but even this was

11

diminished by his stooping posture. Dhan Singh, the senior family retainer at Jodhpur Apartments, snuffled against his sleeve and waved me through the door without much enthusiasm; a welcoming committee of sorts.

My room was white and sparse: two beds, a suffering sofa, a view over a dusty garden, the roar of an old air-cooler. The bathroom was next door – a loo, a shower, a basin, and buckets for Indian-style baths.

Dhan Singh shuffled back with a signing-in book. We settled on one of the beds amidst the luggage to start the process of filling-in, a rehearsal for the months ahead of forms in duplicate, triplicate, full of personal details and domestic arrangements, all vital information to be tied up carefully with string, filed away and stacked to create more piles, in more offices, to feed the bureaucratic monster that lies at the heart of India, an organ of manila files and fraying string.

Satisfied with my form-filling, Dhan Singh retired, bent reverentially over the book.

The apartment returned to silence. The bed was hard. The cry of a knife-grinder came up from the service road below, a tree-shaded lane that runs behind the houses of Hailey Road. This was where the merchants used to bring their goods to supply the households of the British, insulated behind their white colonnaded exteriors.

Sleep came as the knife-grinder passed on down the road, his voice a sheer rasp as he reached the end of each cry: 'Come to the grinder, bring your knives, tools and weapons. I will give you blades to cut the air, wood or life.'

*

Just around the corner of one end of Hailey Road there was a newspaper stand. Of course it did not just sell newspapers. A *chai* pot stood on one side. Slots in the walls at the back were stacked with brightly coloured packets of *biris*, the leaf-rolled smoke of the Indian on the street. A pile of glossy betel leaves lay surrounded

Dhan Singh, a welcoming committee of sorts

by silver pots containing the aromatic concoctions that go into the greatest Indian hobby of all, the chewing and spitting of *paan*, the mildly narcotic tonic that fills the lower lip of India.

Underneath all this was a patchwork of magazines. A bulldog politician frowning from a news journal nestled beside a generously cleavaged beauty spilling from the front cover of a movie magazine, one of the hundreds that fuel the gossip machine of the constantly churning Bollywood film industry. *The Hindu* lay next to *The Muslim Voice*, a moment of peaceful religious cohabitation restricted to the news-stand. *Femina*, the sometimes-thinking glossy aimed at the new class of female professionals, sat cheek by jowl with the news magazine *India Today*. The cover of the former flagged the inside track on sex and the single woman, the latter a report on female infanticide in Rajasthan. The magazines spilled off the stand and on to the pavement. Here I found the resting place of the newspapers, Delhi's big three lined up at the front, *The Times of India*, *The Statesman* and *The Indian Express*.

To Indian eyes the modern English broadsheets are so full of air it is a constant source of amazement to them that we manage to fit in all the news. Indian papers have an antique look to them. They are printed in classical fonts that are tightly packed almost to the point of illegibility. The photographs in the news sections often have that furred black-and-white haze that you find in the yellowing papers wrapped around your grandparents' china in the attic. In them politicians predominantly stick to traditional dress, adding timelessness to the printed page. The sports sections show polo ponies at full gallop, lean heroes swinging gracefully at the camera, and cricket players all in white; the ugly shell-suits of the one-day internationals somehow seem to feature less. The past sits on the pages until you reach the features section. Then all hell breaks loose in an explosion of Western fashion spreads, over-coloured recipe pictures, glossy with *ghee*, and those perennial lifestyle tales of what the rich and nearly famous eat for breakfast and how they juggle parenthood with almost fame (not a mention of the serried ranks of nannies and servants).

The difference in style between the news sections of the papers and the features is a journalistic canyon. Every Indian journalist has the right to claim a personality disorder. Take an average day with four simultaneous stories covered by one reporter: the first on the visit of the German Minister for Overseas Trade (not read by many); the second, on a multiple-death train crash in Bihar (read by everyone in Bihar); the third, the news of a Bombay film star's split with her boyfriend of two and a half minutes (read by everyone); and, finally, a report on the increase in monkey homosexuality in the hill station of Simla (big monkey area) and its effect on the monkey population (read by those with simian interests). This is as it has always been. Kipling constantly found himself reporting on floods, outbreaks of cholera, the colour of the Vicereine's frock at a formal reception, murders, divorce trials and the fine performance of Captain Fortescue's fragrant young wife as Yum Yum in *The Mikado* at the Gaiety Theatre in fashionable Simla (less simian and homosexual then).

A contemporary Indian paper even feels antique. It is not just a case of fingers becoming smudged with print. Whole articles transplant themselves on to shirt fronts, particularly during the monsoon when the humidity pulls the print off the page with damp zest. For those who have never had the chance to experience an Indian newspaper at first hand, a flavour can be found in *The Asian Age*, the paper proudly printed simultaneously in New Delhi, Calcutta, Bangalore, Bombay and London. *The Age* is directed at the Asian community overseas. It has a stronger grip on international news than the home-grown variety but the smell of India still rises off its pages amidst tales of government corruption, indefinite rail strikes, Sikh dramas, Hindu grievances, Muslim complaints and, in the top right-hand corner of the front page, the promise of *The Asian Age* to its readers, a promise that so much of India still trusts:

Reading
is
Believing

Certainly Dhan Singh, the major-domo of Jodhpur Apartments, and Ram Kumar, second-in-command to Dhan Singh and cooker-of-the-books, believed what they read. Every morning, sitting on the bench outside my room, they would bury their heads in the newspapers. Dhan Singh read the Hindi papers. Ram Kumar, an unabashed social-climber from the tip of his large nose to the soles of his much-mended black Oxfords, read the English papers. As far as they were concerned every word was the honest-to-God truth and they would quote chunks of articles to each other in defence of their arguments. Ram Kumar's busy little moustache would bounce up and down as he pontificated on some new corruption scandal. Dhan Singh would stand up to make his point. Ram Kumar would then get up and go on getting up until he stood almost a foot above Dhan Singh. The old man would wave his finger in the social-climber's face, his neck cricked back, while Ram Kumar would look down with the kind of oil-slick smile that needs to be slapped right off a face. Their arguments would rage all day, interrupted only by the all-important periods of mid-morning, midday and mid-afternoon sleep.

The greatest difference between English and Indian newspapers, however, has little to do with news coverage, Bollywood lives or even the progress of the adulated national cricket team, on or off tour, but in matches and dispatches Indian-style. First there are the matrimonials or, as *The Indian Express* so pithily calls them, Lifemate on Sunday: '*Tall, slim, beautiful, adjusted, co-operative, submissive, homely (employed, unemployed), B.ed bride from respectable middle class family for handsome Punjabi executive 26, 174in, salary Rs. 40,000 annually, going places fast. Medical history of bride of main consideration. No demands, no bar. Write to Box No.*' Hardly an equal opportunities advertisement.

Under Grooms Wanted the requests tend to be a little more humble: '*Double Postgraduate employed (Rs. 3400 p.m.) woman 34 (looks younger) seeks suitable lifemate. Widowers also considered. Simple marriage preferred. Caste, no bar.*' In spite of the great steps made by professional women in India it is still rare to see an advertisement for a groom making quite the same demands as are made of potential brides.

And so to death. In the Memorial section, *'Our beloved Sardani Inder Kumar left for her heavenly abode on such and such a date'*, is followed by the heading *Grief-stricken* below which unfolds a long list of the mourning family members, scrolling down like film credits, the closest relatives obviously taking top billing. Below the roll-call of the mourners we are reminded of *'The 16th Anniversary of Shri Narain Dass Khundar who left us on this day but whose words, actions and memories are still with us evergreen. Hard work alone triumphs. We continue to march in your golden path.'* There are pages and pages of such small advertisements and within these nuptial and funereal lines beats the pulse of India. The matrimonial advertisements call across the states, from Kerala in the deep south to Himachal Pradesh near the Tibetan border, drawing the one united map of the subcontinent; and the bereavement and anniversary announcements speak of a country where death is accepted as part of life.

But it is the culture of the arranged marriage that cuts through to the heart of India in these sections of the press. Whatever political or ethnic wars rage, the sons and daughters of India still abide by the rules. Across the classes, from Delhi drawing-rooms to dusty desert village market-places, contracts of marriage are drawn up between suitable boys and girls. Each day, over millions of cups of tea, the financial futures of countless couples are slotted into place by fathers, uncles and brothers, while the women start making lists of the lists that they will need to make for the wedding. The great nuptial machinery cranks up, its catalyst those two or three black-and-white lines in the newspapers.

For ten years I had seen this world from the outside. Now I hoped for a different view. Perhaps I felt a little as Kipling did when he wrote to a friend in 1883: 'I am in love with the Country and would sooner write about her than anything else. Wherefore let us depart our several ways in amity. You to Fleet Street (where I shall come when I die if I am good), and I to my own place, where I find heat and smells and oils and spices, and puffs of temple incense, and sweat and darkness, and dirt and lust and cruelty, and above all, things wonderful and fascinating innumerable.'

Kipling had worked on the *Civil and Military Gazette* in Lahore for five years in the 1880s and then on the Allahabad *Pioneer*. Over a century separated us, not to mention a great many rungs on the literary ladder, but still, like him, I wanted to dig into the sweat and darkness, to see things wonderful and fascinating innumerable.

Yashwant Singh, my landlord, a Rajput prince dispossessed by modern politics of his birthright but making do as the Prince of Hailey Road, arrived at my door in the middle of a Delhi dust-storm. I had jet-lag, he was hung over. We introduced ourselves. He was pale and interesting, aristocratic, elegant and effete. He draped himself around the doorpost, surveying the scene of disgorged bags.

'Why have you come to India?'

'To work for an Indian newspaper.'

'My God, you must be joking. They are all rubbish.' He stuck out his tongue and examined it down the swoop of his nose.

'I look too awful. Have you ever seen anything so disgusting?'

I offered some Vitamin C.

'This might help. I think you look fine.'

'How would you know? You have never seen me before. I was once so beautiful. How old do you think I am?'

I was on trial.

'Oh, I am so bad at this, maybe thirty-six?'

'I think I may come to love you. I am forty-two and have lived such a life. But you could be lying, so it may be just a passing affair.'

He waved the topic away.

'You cannot possibly write for an Indian newspaper. You will never be able to work in Fleet Street again.'

'Wapping,' I said.

'Whatever. My God, what is the matter with you people? No

more Fleet Street. You will shoot your Queen next. That will teach you.'

The dust whirled and spun outside the window.

'You cannot go out in this storm. I forbid it.'

There was no choice. I had an appointment at *The Indian Express*.

The visibility on the street was down to a few feet. I stood on the pavement, trying to tie a scarf around my head, face and mouth. The grey dust licked at every exposed corner.

Bushan came to me out of the swirl. He was the rickshaw driver attached to Jodhpur Apartments. He was to become my king of the road, my hero of the rickshaw, the brightest face in the crowd of rickshaw drivers at the *chai* stall. Yashwant's mother, the Rani Sahiba (Mrs Prince, so to speak), had told me that I was only to use Bushan. He was the rickshaw driver adopted by the family, to be there whenever they needed to get around. It was bad enough that they had been forced to use rickshaws. Their great Bentleys and palanquins now fill the curio areas of the palaces of their former lives. Their gilded era as the Maharaja class, protected and petted, enamoured of so many things British, at least all the things within a mile of Savile Row, has passed. Even so, it was still an honour for Bushan to be the personal rickshaw driver to a royal family.

He was an obvious choice. He was always clean-shaven, his shirt crisp and his hair oiled. He stood out from the other rickshaw drivers with their stubble and *dhal*-stained *kurta* pyjamas.

'Where to, Mem?' Bushan asked through a mouthful of dust.

'Bahadur Shah Zafar Marg.'

Bahadur Shah Zafar Marg, New Delhi's answer to what Fleet Street once was. Many of the papers still use hot-metal printing and their editors still chain-smoke and get heart-attack fat. It is a wide boulevard, a constant sea of people, but it is not the usual riot of Delhi streetlife with its hawkers, jaywalkers, beggars, shoppers and passers-through. On Bahadur Shah Zafar Marg the crowd comprises journalists rushing in or out of buildings on the trail of a scoop. A two-headed pig in Gujarat, a crying Vishnu sculpture in a temple in

Cooch Behar, a woman who has given birth to a goat in Haryana (her husband, the cuckolded goatherd, standing proudly by), the baby boy who sings erotic songs in his sleep, the woman who concocts wedding banquets from three lentils and half a spoonful of *ghee*, every tale has to be told. It is the job of the scurrying journalists to bring these vital stories to the attention of the people.

The *Express* building rears up from the street, a monstrous grey concrete bunker. The marble steps leading to the entrance are pock-marked with blood-red betel stains, the fresh ones arterial in colour, the older ones a more venous hue.

Bushan stopped on the other side of the road. I assumed this was because the central reservation prevented him from crossing to the front of the building. I was wrong.

'Not so good for Mem driving in rickshaw. Not too tip-top.' Bushan pointed to the rows of new Maruti tin-box town runarounds parked up in front of the building.

'No one will see in the dust,' I said.

'They will look, they will see.' He waved towards the building.

A stream of smart young men and women in new jeans and Ray-Ban sunglasses ran up and down the steps, cocooned in their English-language degrees and designer beer confidence. I hung around the rickshaw for a moment, discussing with Bushan exactly where he would wait, how long I might be and whether he should go and come back if time dragged on. As I talked he kept brushing the dust off me. Realizing the hopelessness of his task he waved me away. He would wait as long as I needed him but he pointed out that he could not start waiting until I had gone.

The reception area of *The Indian Express* was a scrum, architecturally spacious but now filled with a series of encampments, small groups of protestors sitting under limp banners. There were some women, a sheet stretched out over their heads, complaining of some miscarriage of justice that they felt should be championed by the paper. Their picket was half-hearted. They were brewing up *chai*, breast-feeding babies and chattering to each other and the security guards; more tupperware party than protest.

A man was dancing around by one of the doors that barred the

A monstrous grey concrete bunker

way into the inner offices. The guard was beginning to lose patience and shouted at him. The man promptly stopped dancing and stood on his head, holding his hands in the prayer position in front of his chest. The guard ignored him.

21

The woman behind the reception desk was imprisoned behind a thick screen and a grille. I had to shout three times before she heard who it was I had come to see. She gave me an identity badge with a scrawl in one corner. She did not know how to find the associate editor of *The Indian Express*.

The security guard at the main door did not know much more. I was going to see a big paper cheese but no one knew where his office was. I headed off along a corridor, past the man still standing on his head.

Half-way down was a large stone sink with a single tap sticking out of the wall above, the kind that you find in old sculleries, where vegetables from the walled garden were once washed. A young man was at the sink assiduously washing his hands. I asked him in bad Hindi where I might find Sourish Bhattacharyya. He gave me a pained smile.

'I work with Sourish. I will take you there if you just hang on a second.' He had an American twang and a Ralph Lauren shirt.

'We are an English-language newspaper, you know.' He peered at my identity badge.

'What is your name? It says Mr Head. This cannot be right. Such terrible writing. People are so ignorant.' He shook the water from his hands, careful not to spray his shirt or jeans.

'It's Hardy.'

'Like Thomas. Such a smashing writer,' he said smugly.

I laughed apologetically.

'I'm afraid I do not speak terribly good Hindi now. I was at college in England, at Bangor, you see.'

'I'm not sure that the Welsh would thank you for that.'

'Perhaps so, but mostly Indians are not understanding about Wales. I think some people are thinking it is a college at Oxford University. I have friends who were at Oxford.' He rolled the learned town around his mouth like a boiled sweet.

'A degree by association then.'

He shrugged and set off down the corridor.

We walked down more corridors and past other sinks and taps before reaching an open-plan office stacked with computers, printers and photocopiers. A man in a very dirty green uniform was inside a photocopier, his legs the only part of him not battling with wires, paper trays and cartridges belching black toner. The desks were microcosms of India today: ancient typewriters, the keys sprung on elegant arched metal legs, next to computers droning from behind flickering green screens, both instruments still in use, side by side, past and future.

A girl sat in one corner bent over a computer, a telephone cradled against her ear. She was shouting at someone in Hindustani and most of her conversation was abusive. I looked at The Twang.

'Well, of course we sometimes have to speak our mother tongue. This is India after all.'

Sourish Bhattacharyya was sweating. He had a towel in one hand to mop his forehead and flannels were wrapped around his wrists to protect his computer keyboard from the rivulets running down his arms. The air-conditioning was not working in his tiny office. He shook the flannels from his wrists before shaking my hand.

'Please, do sit down.' He looked around. There was only room in the office for his desk and chair. I was standing on the other side of the desk with my back touching the glass partition wall.

He waved his hand and sat down. I perched on the desk, my legs dangling.

'So, you will have to tell me about April Fool's Day.'

He leant forward, his belly spilling above and below the table. I tried to explain but it didn't sound very funny.

'So everyone plays jokes on each other on that particular day?'

'Only until midday.'

'Oh, oh, I see, only until midday. So you all know that you are going to play jokes on each other for a few hours once a year. Very English, very strange. But then so is your request to come and work for us. You are about fifty years out of date.' His tone was not so much sarcastic as bemused.

He rocked back in his chair, allowing his belly to regroup.

'I think I quite like the idea, though I am not so sure about April

Fool's Day. If everyone knows they are going to have a joke played on them then there can be no point.' He picked up the book that I had put in front of him.

'You have managed to have a book published, so apparently you can write, though that is not so much of a guarantee nowadays. Journalism does not seem to have so much to do with writing at the moment. Are you most interested in the dating habits of Hindi movie stars?'

But of course; such a question to ask.

'Well, I will talk to a few people and we'll see if we can find you some work.' His chair groaned a little and he gently eased it back on to all four legs.

'I have to say that this is unusual. Is it so very hard to find work in England now?' He smiled.

'Yes it is, but that is not why I am here. I would just rather be working in India, Mr Bhattacharyya.'

'I am Sourish. It is much easier to pronounce than Bhattacharyya.' He flicked through some of the articles slotted inside the book.

'I don't see that you will have any problem writing for us. It might be interesting for us to have a view that we are not perhaps used to. All of us Indians are sometimes a little too Indian, if you understand my meaning.' But he was worried that I might have difficulty in writing in the house style.

The strange mixed language of English-speaking India uses a vocabulary that is extinct unless you are a frequenter of some of the more rarefied prep-school playgrounds of England's shires. It is difficult to reconcile the Levis, the designer shirts, the degrees from Bangor and the mid-Atlantic, *masala*-flavoured accents with the curiously antique phraseology of the English-language newspapers as found, for example, in a contemporary Bollywood news round-up: 'I find myself in the most onerous position of having to pass on this news to the good citizens of Delhi. Oh, such crying there will be on Lodhi Road near the residence of the delectable Delhi born and bred star, Miss Sonya Devi. The divine Miss Devi has told this miserable reporter that she is to take her leave of the silvery screen. Oh evil day in the history of modern India.'

Surely this was satire of a movieland kind? Miss Devi was, after all, a second-rate actress who had never even managed to make it into a one-on-one disco, belly-dancing love scene in a Hindi extravaganza. The Divine Miss Devi had only had five blink-and-you-miss-them roles before she decided to retire. In Indian terms, where actors are often working on up to ten films at the same time, this was not even getting off the movie starting-block.

Sourish gave me a selection of the Sunday lifestyle sections from the paper to mull over.

On home ground English newspapers take some beating when it comes to the art of the punning headline. Indian papers take this game to undreamt-of heights. A cross-section from one week's Indian Sunday lifestyle sections makes the English tabloids look like amateurs: 'Any Which Way But Beating' – a piece on the fall-out of unsuccessful heart surgery (health section); 'Check Before Chopping' – how to decide whether to circumcise your baby boy (another health piece); 'Revenge of the Killer Bimbos' – are Indian women newscasters being pigeon-holed as brainless sari hangers? (*Voice of the Women* section); 'Mexican Yum Yum Kidney Beanz Meanz Good Stuff' – a rundown on tacos and trimmings in the cookery column.

Sourish wanted to know whether I was up to this. I promised to be a quick learner. After all, he was talking to a girl who had written for the ladies-who-lunch glossies back home. Surely there was no better training-ground?

He also wanted to know what I planned to write as an introductory piece. I had thought about going up to Assam in the north-east to see how the tea-planters survived in an area that was in a constant state of civil unrest.

Sourish massaged his temples hard as if he was in pain. He felt that might be a bit intense as a kick-off topic. I suggested that as so many Indians did not really seem to know very much about the north-east, this might be an article that would catch the public interest. He was not convinced.

'How are you going to get there?'

'I'm going to try and fly. The tourist office said they would help with some of my flights since I am researching for the BBC as well.'

Sourish rolled his eyes.

'I am thinking that this is unlikely. You should not count on it. But be sure that *The Indian Express* cannot pay for any of your travel expenses.'

There had been no mention of money until this point.

'How much will I get for each article?' A nonchalant question, popped in as an afterthought.

'Each article should be coming out at about 1,000 words plus any practical information that needs to be given at the end. You get Rs. 1,000 for each article and about Rs. 250 for each of your pictures that we use.'

Rs. 1,000 was about £16. That meant five articles a week just to pay the rent. Sourish was making up a bundle of back copies for me to take home for house-style prep. I was trying to do some mental arithmetic.

'Will there be a limit on how many articles I can write for each issue?'

'No, you can write as many as you like. Do you still want to do it?'

'Of course.'

'I look forward to seeing your copy then. Do you think you will be able to find your way out again?'

I made my way back down the corridors, navigating by the sinks and taps.

There was a shout from behind me. Sourish was jogging down the corridor. He did not look happy about the turn of speed.

'You forgot something.' He waved a capacious green handbag.

I blushed, stuttered, began to apologize, accepted the proffered bag and thought how nice it would be to climb inside it and snap it shut.

'Are you sure you were offering me work?' came a sort of inside-bag voice.

'Oh, oh, now I see how English you are. Of course I was, if that is what you want. The handbag . . .' he shrugged, 'I would always be forgetting it if I had one. Blessings on pockets I think. *Acchhā*, now go and write me a story.' He turned and set off back down the corridor at a more leisurely pace.

The headstand man had just abandoned his protest in the reception area. He was lying down quietly, recovering from the lengthy inversion. He must have been balancing on his crown for about forty minutes. That constituted a reasonably serious protest. A blue-jean and T-shirt journalist was crossing the hall. He stopped to speak to the no-longer-upended man. It seemed to be a polite conversation, though it would have been hard to argue from a horizontal position after forty minutes of being upside-down.

I asked the journalist what the protest was about. He replied that the headstand had been in aid of circus performers who had been trying to form their own union so that they could demand a minimum rate of pay. Delhi's Municipal Council would not allow it because the authorities felt that the circuses would charge more and then the poorer people would no longer be able to afford to go. Once the poor were priced out the audience would dwindle and die. The council felt they were acting in the interests of the circus performers in banning a union.

'But why is he protesting here?' I asked.

'Because we did not write about it.'

Reason enough for a forty-minute headstand.

As I left a security guard was dispatched in hot pursuit. It wasn't hard to find me – I was the only European in the crowd on Newspaper Marg. The guard was slight and fit but he seemed exhausted by the chase. He pointed to the identity badge on my shirt. I gave it back, thanking him for his trouble. He waited, panting. I scrabbled about in the green handbag for some change. He looked at the coins without smiling, stopped panting and loped off. Two men had been pushed to give chase in just ten minutes. It did not seem a particularly auspicious start to life on the edge of Delhi's press pack.

Bushan was waiting, as he had promised, under a frangipani

bush. He had picked some of the blossoms and laid them across the front shelf of the rickshaw. He gave me one of the flowers, its scent soft and lush, then stood with a question-mark face.

'We will go and have a cup of *chai* to celebrate.'

He smiled broadly and punched the roof of the rickshaw with a victory cut. It was touching. I had only known him for a few hours.

Cocktails for the Blind

MY FIRST WEEKS in Delhi coincided with the unenthusiastic trudge towards a general election. In Assam the mood of the terrorists was volatile. Over a hundred villages were torched and seventy people murdered in a bout of pre-election violence. It was not a good time to head for the north-east frontier. I had to go and find another story.

Delhi was bored by the election. The capital had been worn down by months of high-voltage corruption that had tainted virtually every minister.

Yashwant hissed when I asked him about it.

'We are so tired of it all. Boring men, rotting in their political stink, unable to look beyond covering their own backsides with corruption money. Look at them all, they are ancient, ridiculous old fools and vast, bossy women. Have you ever known a country run by such a bunch of octogenarians?'

'China.'

'Don't be ridiculous. Deng Xiaoping is way beyond that. He must be a hundred and ten at least. Anyway he has been dead for years. When did you last see him walking and talking without all those politico *wallahs* propping him up?'

I shrugged.

Yashwant had a view of his own. He could see no earthly reason why the reins of power should not be handed over to his safekeeping in Hailey Road. They were all getting it wrong. He would get it right. He felt that it was merely his lack of motivation that stopped him from running the country.

'Except that the boredom of the whole thing would drive me insane, but perhaps I am there already. Madness now appears to be the only prerequisite for a political career.'

Yashwant is a Raj Kumar, a prince, the son of a raja, another prince. His cousin is the Maharaja Gaj Singh of Jodhpur, known across the world (though not always to his face) by his pet name, Bapji. The family seat of sorts is Umaid Bhawan, a great domed party piece of the art deco age that was started in 1929 by Yashwant's grandfather at a time when the state was in a trough of famine and drought. For thirteen years the Maharaja gave employment to 3,000 of his people by building a palace to rival Lutyens' New Delhi. It is vast, more akin to a cavernous nineteenth-century factory than the familiar desert palaces with their filigreed balconies and hidden courtyards. The architect, H.V. Lancaster, designed the whole building, all 3.5 hectares of it, as a series of interlocking sandstone blocks, like a gargantuan child's Lego set that could be dismantled and reassembled on an oversized royal whim.

In the years leading up to Independence, the next Maharaja, Yashwant's uncle, held to ransom both Jawaharlal Nehru and Mohammed Ali Jinnah, the leaders-in-waiting of India and Pakistan, in a show of political petulance designed to get the best possible terms of accession for his beloved people of Jodhpur. His *coup de grâce* was to whirl a fountain pen from his coat, flick the end to transform it into a .22 pistol, and hold it to the head of V.P. Menon, Mountbatten's constitutional adviser and the only Indian on the Viceroy's senior staff. With a theatrical flourish the Maharaja cried out, 'If you betray the starving people of Jodhpur you will be shot like a dog,' causing the generally rock-like Menon to shake uncontrollably for several hours.

This same Maharaja, with his sparkling eyes and jig-dancing eyebrows, was also the first Indian to become, like Mountbatten, a member of the Magic Circle. The last Viceroy was so impressed by his fellow amateur magician that he squirrelled away the confiscated fountain pen/revolver, later donating it to a grateful magician's club with a flourish and the tale.

The Maharaja went on to take, as his second though unofficial wife, a nineteen-year-old Scots nurse called Sandra McBryde. She changed her name to Sundra Devi, took to saris and whisked her new husband home to meet the family. He was most impressed by her brother Dennis, a travelling salesman from Stoke-on-Trent. The newly-weds stayed at Claridges and Sandra was to be seen around town in jewel-encrusted silks and chiffons. At the same time the Maharaja's first wife was giving birth to his son and heir, Bapji, in Jodhpur.

Two years later the Maharaja was killed when a bullock cart rumbled into his path as he was landing his private plane. Bapji succeeded to the title. Sandra McBryde packed up her saris and headed home to catch up with Dennis and resume her nursing career in the Midlands.

Yashwant's father is the younger brother of the magic- and nurse-loving Maharaja. He has a famous moustache that glows with love and attention. He sees the world through the eyes of an old hunter, his catalogue of tiger-shooting tales his armoury against the horrors of the modern world. His wife, Yashwant's mother, the Rani, is tall and beautiful, her patrician face etched with years of family intrigue. She too is from a royal family, the eponymous, dazzling and doomed house of Patiala.

Yashwant is the elder son and heir. Though born nearly a decade after Independence, by which time the maharajas already carried the prefix 'the former', he grew up in palaces, fussed over, cherished and petted by queues of *ayahs*, aunts and cousins. He was well cast for the role, delicate and fine-boned, prodigiously bright and outspoken from an improbably early age. He claims to have given lengthy diatribes from his pram to rapt audiences on his constitutional rights and preferred baby outfits. And all this before hitting his second birthday.

As a small child he was seldom given the opportunity to walk. One servant after another carried him from room to room to be crooned over by female family members desperate to press on him

The Rani in chiffon and pearls, Maharaj Sahib in whiskers and Yashwant in his element

a little more *ghee*, another sweetmeat or just one more sliver of cake. Yashwant grew up in a sea of oestrogen, his sharp and destructive wit honed by their hilarity at his childish and petulant antics, played out in high pantomime along the echoing marble corridors of royal palaces.

No child could emerge unscathed from such claustrophobic overindulgence. A sense of balance and proportion was not among the qualities deemed necessary for a young desert heir. Yashwant was nurtured on hyperbole and the superlative. There was little in his world to make him aspire to anything as proletarian as a job. The people worked while the maharajas, 'former' in name only, were the dream fodder of Everyman.

When I suggested going out on to the streets to gauge the mood of the largest democracy in the world as it prepared to go to the polls, Yashwant was disgusted. He assured me that I would catch a disease. Failing an audience with the Prime Minister, he decreed that I should attend the clubs and dinner parties of Delhi to take the pulse of the intelligentsia. I pointed out that neither my wardrobe nor my ideals were really up to it. Yashwant went into a sulk.

Beyond my window was the balcony where Yashwant's great green parrot lived in splendid isolation amidst a riot of waxy-leaved plants. As we talked of politics and gin gimlets I could see one of the houseboys levering himself up on to the flimsy outer railing of the balcony. He seemed distracted; understandably so since he was up on the fifth floor. He teetered as he stood up, then held out his hand for something just out of view. A rope was passed over and the young man threw one end through the railing of the balcony above and secured it before tying a noose around his neck, giving the knot a good yank to test it. He leant out from the railing and looked down.

'Yashwant, someone is about to kill himself.'

He had his back to the window and was looking through my dictionary.

'Who?' he asked without looking up.

'I don't know. Do something.'

He turned and looked at the boy swaying on the railing.

'Hardly defenestration, dear. He is doing some repairs.'

I opened the window to get a full view. One of the cleaning girls was handing a small bucket of cement and a grouting knife to the boy.

'What if he fell?'

'He would hang himself.'

When I broached the idea of a day-to-day diary piece on the political feelings of the people across the full social spectrum of Delhi, Sourish was similarly unenthusiastic.

'Some industrialist will give you a lecture on politics of such boredom as you are not believing and the man in the street will not care. He probably won't even vote.' For Sourish elections came and went. Film premières, the fodder of features, only happened once.

'What about covering a film opening tonight? Of course none of the stars will really be there, just the guy who has two lines in the last scene. How about a piece on how you view the Indian film industry in comparison to your British one?'

'Perhaps I could ask some of the actors what they think about the election?'

'Oh, oh, stop now. We are not producing political analysis in *Better Living*. Leave that to the front pages and the television. We can't compete with CNN. We do views, you know, viewspaper.' He thought about it for a bit, liked the idea and said it again.

'Viewspaper, yes, yes. Now off you go and find some stories.'

There were two other people with us in the tiny hot office. One had come to repair a computer. He wore an overworked expression and rolls of multicoloured sticking-tape braceleting his arms. The second, another journalist, was going through his article on the erosion by urine of so many of Delhi's Mogul landmarks.

Just the four of us in Sourish's equatorial shoebox was a low head-count by Indian standards. If the shoebox had been bigger there would have been a larger crowd: a couple of other journalists with queries, perhaps a picture editor huffing over some bad prints, a young copyist with a girlfriend problem, some friends from Uttar Pradesh with a college son grasping at all strings to get Golden Boy a job. An Indian newspaper editor is judge, jury, marriage-guidance counsellor, provider of jobs, commissioner of tall tales, and an authority on taste and the social climate. In spare moments, he may have the chance to wield the red pen.

Sourish sighed. 'You are still sticking on the election. Come, we have a meeting. Get some ideas.'

The meeting took place in the one uncluttered space in the middle of the *Better Living* office. Sourish settled himself in a chair, a pile of copy on his knee. There was no one else there. He seemed unconcerned. A man walked in carrying a small rabbit hutch. Sourish ignored him. The rabbit hutch was a spare part for the disembowelled photocopier. The loud fitting process began as some other journalists wandered in. They greeted Sourish and one another. The bubbles of general chatter pipped and popped. Some people sat on the floor or propped themselves against the wall. The meeting was not called to order. Individual conversations continued, sometimes stretching across the gathering crowd to draw in someone else's opinion. There was a heated discussion about a top designer who was dallying with a toy-boy, another about the latest rage to hit Delhi, rollerblading. No one worried much about that. People were too lethargic during the hot season to start blading with any seriousness. It would hold over as a post-monsoon story when the pavements cooled. There was an update on the Delhi green belt argument, a perennial cause for concern. Naturally there was a buzz about who was sleeping with whom down in Bollywood. The chatter ebbed and flowed. Sourish sat flicking through the pile of copy on his knee. At last he raised his hand.

'Coffee, tea, anyone?'

In a single moment of unity, several gophers were dispatched. They returned with trays of coffee, tea and water. Everyone grabbed, gulped and left.

I looked at Sourish.

'A meeting?'

'Yes,' he replied.

'But no one said anything.'

'How odd, I heard all sorts of chat,' and he headed back into his shoebox.

'No one mentioned the election,' I said, pursuing him.

He laughed.

'Go away, go out into the streets and find a story.'

On the way back to Hailey Road, Bushan would not be drawn on the election. He told me that his parents, his wife and he would go and vote. That would be the end of it. He did not think he would be very interested to read the opinion of other rickshaw drivers. He had to listen to them at the *chai* stall every day. I pressed on. Was there anyone whose opinion on the election would interest him? No. Sourish was right. Elections did not make for very sexy features.

I asked Bushan what he *would* like to read. He shrugged and suggested that news should be good.

Why did the election not qualify as news? Bushan said that it was not interesting news. Then what constituted interesting news? It boiled down to the Indian cricket team and movieland, with a passing reference to the government perhaps throwing in a free health service. This last point was the topic of the moment. Delhi was in the grip of an epidemic of dengue fever, a tropical horror that was wiping people out in medieval fashion. It transpired that Bushan himself had recently had a bout of dengue and had hovered dangerously close to the edge of the abyss for several days, hence his skeletal state and the bruising beneath his eyes.

Our conversation was a mixture of pidgin-Hindi and drop-stitch English. Bushan was not only my king of the road, he was also my language tutor. It was safe practising with him. He did not laugh at my marmalade pronunciation, my fat English vowels distorting the clatter of the North Indian intonation. He would listen and sometimes pause as he attempted to unravel what I was trying to say. He worked backwards from the words that he recognized, laughing aloud at some of my mistakes – my request to go to the lady with big, fat, white arms when I really wanted to go to the big vegetable stall to buy ladies' fingers. He was patient and gentle with my frustration, sometimes pulling out of the traffic in order to give me his full attention and an instant grammar lesson.

There is sometimes confusion about the difference between Hindi and Hindustani, one of those basic questions that people often feel too embarrassed to ask, as if to do so would show up a basic lack of cultural understanding. Hindi is the more formal language, used predominantly by politicians and newscasters. Hindustani is less rigid, the mish-mash language that is spoken on the street and in the *chai* stalls and understood in most areas of North India. It is the language of the layman and it is easier to understand than the purer Hindi. When in doubt an English word is thrown in with just enough of an Indian inflection to give it parochial clout.

As in French, Hindi still has the elegant, almost courtly 'thou' form and the more familiar form for family, friends, juniors, orders and abuse. Insecure in my command of the language, I was never sure which to use so I stuck to the polite form for everything. I wended my way around Delhi 'theeing' and 'thouing' like a woman possessed. My first effort at the abusive 'you' form was enjoyed by a couple of rickshaw drivers who had taken me half-way across Delhi in the wrong direction. Bushan had thoughtfully furnished me with a dazzling battery of Hindi expletives for just such an occasion. They did not have the desired effect. Instead, the pair of them fell about laughing and called out to other rick-shaw drivers to give them a running commentary on the *farangi* woman's vulgar diatribe. This was possibly because Bushan had supplied me with genteel versions. The wicked rickshaw drivers were being accused in no uncertain terms of being naughty chil-dren. It was not a proud moment.

In the late afternoon Bushan and I set out to find a buzzing *chai* stall, the birthing-pool of the gossip on the streets. The hum of an early evening breeze curled the dust on the roads. The faces at the *chai* stall were half in shadow, as if they were about to be commit-ted to canvas in biblical oils. But they were just drinking *chai*, smoking, talking and waiting for the heat of the day to lift. In con-trast to the idleness around the stall was the action inside where a young man and his mother were at work, he less than she, as is the way. The mother wrestled samosa dough, juggled pans, heated a saucepan of milk and nudged the flies away from her face with a bony shoulder. Her son seemed absorbed in rearranging stacks of *biris* in elegant triangles on the shelves at the back of the stall. Squatting outside, a boy scrubbed potatoes and chopped them into large pots.

Bushan put out his hand, a barrier between the counter and me. He asked what I wanted, waving me away from the listless drink-ers. *Chai* and a packet of 501s, the king of *biris*. Bushan did not approve of my smoking nor did he like the idea of my sitting in full view of the other customers. He would have preferred me to return to the seemly isolation of the rickshaw.

The only audible conversation was between the mother and

son inside the stall. They were discussing the election. The government had granted a two-day holiday to encourage people to go to the polling stations, but they had overlooked the fact that the two-day holiday ran into a weekend, so providing a four-day fiesta across the land. The mother and son were ruminating on how best to spend the four days. Their plans bore little relation to the government's hopes. They were heading off to see their cousins in Jodhpur before the full weight of the hot season flopped down on Rajasthan. They had booked their train tickets months beforehand, realizing that most of the nation would use the opportunity to take to the railways and go a-visiting.

A story. What percentage of the world's greatest democracy were going to be abandoning their vote in order to enjoy a long weekend jolly? It was light but with enough of an undertone to satisfy my journalistic vanity; a grown-up story in a frilly dress. Sourish should let that slip through.

Greengrocers seemed to make good starting-points. I went to see my local Delhi man, less romantic than the Kashmiri of South Kensington though catering to just as select a clientele. He and his family are the grocery stars of Connaught Place, the larder darlings of the diplomatic set. They provide Jaffa Cakes, Marmite and quilted Andrex Supasoft lavatory paper to those expats unable to bear local kitchen and bathroom integration. The grocer, his wife and brother planned to shut up their shop and head for the hills to breathe some clear air and forget about mango orders and disgraceful mark-ups for a few days. The grocer swore blind that he had applied for proxy votes but said that he had not had any response. The manager of the Mercedes import company in Barakhambra Road was thinking about taking his wife and girlfriend to a palace hotel a few hours' drive from Delhi. He told me that his wife thought the girlfriend was his secretary. He elaborated by saying that sharing rooms would not be a problem as his wife had a condition that meant she did not wish to share a room with her husband, and anyway he was getting a hot-season discount for the two rooms. I did not probe. Miss Micro-Mini-Skirt, the latest Bollywood movie starlet, was going to stay at home, eat ice-cream with her boyfriend and watch racy films. *Close Encounters of the Third Kind* was on her list. I suspected they weren't quite the encounters she had in mind. A lunch delivery boy from the law courts on Janpath planned to break into one of the chambers that he delivered to in order to become computer literate over the four-day holiday, courtesy of the law firm's computers.

And then, at another *chai* stall, I met a group of young men who were proposing to set fire to themselves at various polling stations to protest against rumoured plans for a Hindu-only state that some believed to be part of the manifesto of the right-wing Bharatiya Janata Party. All of the young men were Muslim.

As they sat and talked about their dreams, one of them drew an outline in the dust with his long fingernail. It was the outline of India as it had been before Partition, the wings that became Pakistan and Bangladesh still flying free.

'We can never be one again because we no longer understand tolerance. I am not wanting to live in a place where my religious ideals are being spat on. I am not wishing to bring children to life in a place that will judge against them because their hearts are in Mecca. My life is better given as a sacrifice for change.' He clutched his head as he spoke.

I asked if he really meant to burn himself to death. He and his friends assured me that they did. But wouldn't their act, I suggested, be seen as a gesture of anger that contradicted their great desire for tolerance? The young man who had drawn the map silenced me and told me that it was his destiny. He was nineteen.

They were all students. None of them would give their names or listen to any attempts at reasoning. They said that the politicians were deaf when it came to the voices of the people and that action was the only thing that had a voice – an unbridled cry from the heart, the blinkered courage of youth. I asked them what would happen if someone told the police about what they intended to do. They said it would make no difference. The police would not take any notice.

The subject was changed. They began to talk about their families and their studies. One described his girlfriend, giggling as he spoke, fluttering his hands in front of his face. He started a story about the lengths he had gone to in order to shake off a chaperone on a recent cinema visit with the beloved. He had arranged for another friend to engage the chaperone in animated conversation as they queued for tickets. With the decoy in full flow, the young couple had planned simply to slip into another film – a chance to hold hands, to behave as teenagers without the cold wash of censure from middle-aged eyes, nothing more risqué than that. They had carefully chosen a topic of conversation for the friend to use in distracting the chaperone, not an easy task as she was a bossy cousin of middling years and middling interests. The story became convoluted, the friends joining in and adding to it, obviously having heard and enjoyed the tale before. I missed parts of it as the enthusiastic teller slid into Punjabi. They were all laughing, the storyteller so much so that he gave up the telling and just rocked backwards and forwards. This group of young men, teasing each other and shrieking with laughter, were the same group that were planning to set fire to themselves. Boys to men and back again, almost in the same breath.

I had my camera with me and asked if I could take a picture. They agreed. The *chai*-stall holder took a picture of us all together. As soon as the shutter clicked one of the group leapt up and grabbed the camera. He started to shout, calling me an animal, a cynical journalist who was trying to fool them into trusting me so that I could get a story and be called a newspaper heroine for stopping their protest. He shook the camera and started hitting it against a cherry tree. Some of the ripe fruit fell around him. Then he threw the camera at me, demanding that I give him the film. I told him that it was a picture for me, for my album, otherwise why would I have included myself in the group? I wanted to remember them. The words were useless. He spat in my face and told me I was a liar. I rewound the film and gave it to him. He threw it on the ground and stamped on it, shouting and encouraging his friends to do the same. They stood in silence, watching as he continued to jump and scream long after the film was obliterated in the dust. They looked very young and frightened. I left.

Both stories were written up. The one about the young men was spiked.

Election day in New Delhi fell on 27 April. The temperature had risen to 101°F. The streets were almost silent, every shop shuttered and clamped with rows of padlocks. It was impossible to get near a polling station. Guns were shaken at foreign film crews and journalists alike, regardless of whether they carried the relevant media passes or not.

There had been virtually no last-minute campaigning. The soon-to-be-former Prime Minister had been preening himself, basking in the success of electoral reforms that seemed to have resulted in a relatively quiet start to the series of polling days.

No traffic disturbed my walk across the centre of the Indian capital at eleven o'clock in the morning. On the dusty grass patch in the centre of Connaught Place a dread-locked *sadhu* in an orange loincloth was digging a deep hole in a rose bed. There was nobody about to stop him. All the government gardeners were on holiday. He finished digging, shook the dirt from his begging bowl, jumped into the hole and settled himself in the lotus position. A rose bush that had been partially uprooted by his digging drooped its yellow flowers prettily over his shaggy head. He put his begging bowl on the edge of the hole, just where it might catch the attention of passers-by. I asked if he was going to vote. He closed his eyes and started to chant. *Sadhus* do not vote. They are above such things.

New Delhi only managed a turn-out of about 40 per cent, hardly surprising considering the overloaded trains heading for the hills. By the end of polling the news was that there had been a handful of immolations by passionate young men unable to express their political beliefs in any other way. The Electoral Reform Commission declared the election a great success – just a few burnings and some easily controlled riots at the ballot box. It was the quietest general election on record.

The Indian Express gave some coverage to the burnings but it was not front-page news. The items were buried away in the home news section amongst stories of farming scandals and striking factory workers. I did not look for pictures. I was told that there were some, of bodies ablaze outside polling stations. Often the reason for their violent protest had not been clear to those who had witnessed the horror.

A few days later I returned to the *chai* stall where I had met the young men, perhaps hoping to see them there, still laughing about the chaperone and the film queue. There were a few rickshaw drivers around and a different man brewing the *chai*. I had some tuberoses with me, their scent beginning to cloy in the heat. I unwrapped them and put them beside the bench where we had sat. It was a useless act. I did not know what had happened to the boys. The flowers were an empty apology for something neither said nor done.

* * *

Yashwant was feeling ill and was not in the mood for this sort of maudlin behaviour. By way of light entertainment he suggested that I join him at an Alcoholics Anonymous meeting up the road at the Episcopalian church that evening. I agreed. Yashwant retreated back into the darkness of his room, groaning prettily.

On the way past the kitchen I looked in. Strong sweet tea might take away the bitter taste of loss. One of the houseboys was sitting on the kitchen floor trying to scoop up a pile of spilt sugar with a small fork. He wasn't getting very far. Dhan Singh hovered, directing the action and becoming increasingly excited as each small forkful of sugar fell through the prongs back on to the floor. I asked for a cup of tea. They both looked up then turned back to the sugar pile.

I filled the kettle and tried unsuccessfully to light the burner. Dhan Singh produced a lighter from his pocket, lit the burner and returned to the sugar. I could not find the tea. The water was not boiled for long enough. The teabag was put straight into a cup rather than into one of the elegant silver teapots ranged along the shelf. There was a floating film on the tea, and the cold milk bubbled up in lumps. I looked down at the cup with a sad face. Dhan Singh wheezed, took the cup and poured it into the sink, relit the burner and put some milk in a saucepan. He patted my arm.

'No, Mem, *chai* to bring.' It was the first time that he had spoken to me in English.

At twilight Yashwant's teetotal plans were forgotten. He had no intention of going anywhere near the Episcopalian church. He was going to have a cocktail party on the roof instead. It sounded rather grand. I protested that I had nothing to wear, nothing for the political cocktail circuit or even rooftop cocktails.

'How absurd. You are English, of course you have frocks.' He opened the cupboard in my room with a flourish – two dresses of sack-like cut, one brown *salwar kameez*, profoundly unattractive, one pair of jeans, slightly dirty. He shut the door.

'But you have to meet the fat cousins. They are so funny. You see we all have our weaknesses. I drink, they eat. We are none of us very good at just being ordinary. We none of us thought we would ever have to be. So come, come, sweet child, stop torturing me. The fat cousins never look smart. You will be perfectly fine. Wear jeans, we all wear jeans now. There is no glamour any more.'

We sat on the roof in the dark. I squatted on the bubbling asphalt and watched the ants climbing up my legs. The fat cousins were jammed into chairs that the houseboy had bumped up the stairs in an ungracious fashion. Their thin boyfriends sat beside them, one on an upturned dustbin, the other astride a whisky crate. There were a few other people scattered around the roof in the darkness. No one spoke as we waited for the recalcitrant houseboy to return with some soda and ice. Dhan Singh had refused to come up to the roof bearing anything that was going to contribute to the alcoholic content of the evening. He had been shuffling around in the apartment, muttering to himself as I set off for the roof, dabbing at the *dhal* stains on the front of his grubby shirt.

Yashwant was centre stage in a deck chair, immobilized by the pelican bill of the seat and an old back problem. The fat cousins were equally beached. Both of the boyfriends were quiet. Desperate to fill the silence I heard myself saying it was like a braille cocktail party since we were all having to feel our way in the dark. The remark was met with silence. Under the cover of a cackle of laughter from somewhere in the blackness, Yashwant hissed at me that one of the boyfriends was blind.

There had been a lethargic breeze at sunset, a faint break in the city haze, the sky rinsed by the twilight as it fell from the tops of the skyscrapers that punctuate Delhi's ceiling of trees. Now the breeze had given up. We sat limply on the rooftop, waiting for candles to illuminate the night.

The houseboy reappeared, backlit in the doorway, bitching as he tripped over a tangle of loose aerial wires. The pools of candle-light that he carried caught the faces on the roof. Beyond the immediate group of Yashwant's courtiers there were four others, a bearded man who constantly pushed his glasses up the bridge of his nose, a stocky woman in a tangerine sari that made her glow in the diluted light, Mangay, a beautiful young friend of Yashwant's, his face all angles and symmetry, and Gita, Yashwant's cousin-in-law, a curly-haired Punjabi beauty.

The light of the candles brought the two groups together. Yashwant introduced me namelessly and grandiloquently as an English writer. The man with the glasses rammed them against his nose with great force.

'Your country is dead,' he announced.

'Any overriding reason?' I asked.

'You have had no great writers since Orwell. Your literature was your country.' He crossed his arms.

'Is that a fact or a personal observation?' asked Yashwant.

'It is fact of course.' The glasses were given another shove.

'Of course,' replied Yashwant. 'Though I am personally of the feeling that I would have drunk myself to death years ago without the literary interventions of Amis, father and son, Julian Barnes and Michael Ondaatje.'

'Michael Ondaatje is a Sri Lankan, now living in Canada.' It was not a wise moment for me to undermine my ally.

'Whatever,' replied Yashwant, stung by my barb, 'but your Jeanette Winterthingy should be fed to the pye dogs, feminist *pish pash* thinly disguised as literature. It is disgusting. I would have thrown it out of my pram.'

He waved his empty glass for a refill.

'Dead, all dead,' shouted the opposition, his glasses fast descending his nose.

'Why?' I asked.

'For twenty years you have only recycled your small island complaints and called it literature. I am telling you that you must read Indian literature. We have found a new voice but you people are taking too long to listen.'

I countered with a long list of internationally acclaimed Indian writers and concluded with the latest star in the firmament, Arundhati Roy.

'All NRI,' he raged – Non-Resident Indian.

'Roy lives in Delhi.'

'You seem to know where they all live. We could have a literary soirée. Do you have their addresses?' Yashwant asked

The man with the glasses refused to be distracted.

'They do not speak with the voice of my country any longer. They have been away for too long. They have lost their sense of smell and taste. They sniff the exhaust fumes of expensive cars and forget the smell of tamarind and open sewers.' He paused for air.

No one spoke.

'So you have come here to try and learn to smell and see as we do, to drink out of our talent pool? Or are you going to write another of those revolting recycled books about how great and good everything was when your bloody Johnny sahibs were pretending to understand our country?' He tilted his head in such a way as to incite violence.

'She has come here to disappear for a while until the clamour about her has died down in London. Now pack it up and stop being so totally dull. And you obviously do not cook or you would know that tamarind does not smell.' Yashwant was bored with the subject.

There was a pause and then the fat cousins laughed long and loud. The evening resumed. The man in the glasses headed for the whisky bottle. As he passed he hissed in my ear.

'You go on and drink from our talent pool. You will drown.'

This was a full frontal attack on open ground, whisky talk with a touch of malice, tempered by cocktail rancour. The heat was beginning to spill bile into Delhi. I wanted to get out.

Kipling understood the effects of the hot season.

> One must set these things against the taste of fever in one's mouth, and the buzz of the quinine in one's ears; the temper frayed by heat to breaking-point but for sanity's sake held back from the break; the descending darkness of intolerable dusks.

The offices of the nineteenth-century *Civil and Military Gazette* had not enjoyed the clattering din of air-conditioning, but even that crutch of modern life is no guarantee of comfort. As the heat increased, the daily load on the heavily pirated Delhi electricity grid proved too much. We were thrown into sticky darkness in every artificially lit and cooled office while the pirates ran their companies off their ill-gotten volts.

The weather was not going to break. It was time to go to Assam.

The Garden of
Shades

TERRORISM IS A word that has lost its impact in India. Among a people who are constantly fighting for their little bit of space, a state of fear and submission is part of the daily round. The terrorists are shades. They flit from the shadows, take life and melt back into the darkness. In Assam they have perfected their art and in doing so have become a permanent part of life. Children in Assam are taught not to walk in the shadows.

The journey to the north-east began in the clippings library at *The Indian Express*. Sourish's assistant led the way there by a short cut, deep down, past the pissoir, under a huge pipe, through a dusty hole and past the print works. By law all printing machines have to be underground. The great Harris Graphic hot-metal machines of *The Indian Express* lurk in the bowels of the building like so many monsters. It was mid-afternoon and the presses were still. Some printers, their clothes and faces smudged grey with ink, sat around playing cards on broken chairs, their sharp bottoms poking out through the exhausted wickerwork.

We reached the library and Sourish's assistant disappeared. Two rows of desks were occupied by thin men and fat women barricaded in by mounds of newspapers. At the end of each row was a desk set slightly apart from the rest. Here was the important dividing line of seniority. There was a choice – a moderately fat woman in a brown sari wearing glasses on a gold chain or a very thin man in a grey suit. He too wore glasses but his were held together with peeling sellotape. The woman peered at me over her frames, a flicker of surprise at my colouring registering briefly.

I was sent to a desk in one corner, to perch on a broken chair and wait for the mound of cuttings to be delivered. After half an hour a very thin file arrived. Assam may be the major tea-producing state of India and the victim of endemic terrorism but it is clearly not considered very newsworthy.

Half-way through the slim selection it was time for tea. Glasses of *chai* neatly wrapped in baby-pink paper napkins were handed around to everyone. Almost everyone. The *chai-wallah* ignored my limp wave each time he came near the sad little desk in the corner. In the hierarchy of the library I was an outsider.

There were several articles that would be useful to keep for reference. I took them to the senior woman to ask if they could be copied. She waved me away towards a man in charge of photocopying, further down the pecking order of desks. Time passed in front of that desk. The man did not stir. I coughed. I wriggled. I flapped the articles at flies and then pushed them under his nose. With a languid wave of his hand he dismissed me, telling me the copying would take a few minutes. Back to Coventry corner and the drunken lurch of the broken chair. Another half hour passed. The cuttings were still sitting untouched on the photocopying desk. There was a copier outside Sourish's office. I picked up the clippings, told the man that I would do them myself and made for the door. Galvanized by my transgression of library law he raced me to the door and blocked it. I ducked under his arm. An ungainly tussle ensued, then a frantic chase down the dusty passages, past the card players, under the pipe, through the cloud of sour piss. The photocopy man glowered as I copied the articles, grabbing each one from the glass even as the green copy light made its sweep. Mine was behaviour in defiance of municipal orders.

Now I needed an airline ticket. Mr Rahul Mehta, the Mr Big of complimentary travel tickets, was very bored by life, in particular by the hand he had been dealt that afternoon. His office was at the end of a wide corridor, his door large, the interior very small. Four desks were crammed together. Four heads were bent over the desks appearing to work. One had his teeth gritted over a cross-word, the second was making a paper-clip chain, the third could have been given the benefit of the doubt. He may have been working but the flow of his handwriting seemed to give off a personal rather than a business air. The fourth was fiddling with a *tiffin* box, unclipping and reclipping the top as if the next hour and a half until the official lunch break was an eternity.

It was not clear which of the four was Mr Mehta. An introduction elicited no response. There was one spare chair in the room. Naturally it was broken. I sat down facing the man who might have been working.

'I am sorry if I am interrupting but I have come to see if you can help me get some domestic flights that were generously offered by your director in London. I think you have a file on me from your London office. I have a duplicate of the letter sent to you by the director.' I flourished the letter in front of the man.

He looked up from his frantic writing, smiled politely and turned his name board to face me: Sanjay Ravi, Assistant Director Tourism.

'You will excuse me, Miss Hardy. It is most pleasant talking with you but Mr Mehta is the gentleman who is seated to your other side.' He pointed to the man fiddling with the *tiffin* tin.

'How do you do, Mr Mehta.' He ignored my outstretched hand. I carried on regardless.

Mr Mehta nodded at the end of each sentence. The nodding then became more persistent, a mute accompaniment to the clicking of the *tiffin* tin lid. I turned back to his deputy.

'Do you find my English difficult to understand, Mr Ravi?' I asked.

'Please do call me Sanjay, Miss Hardy. I think you are speaking perhaps a little too fast.'

'Shall I speak more slowly or should I use Hindi? My Hindi is not very good but I can try.'

'No, no, that will not be necessary. Just a little more slowly if it is possible.'

'Thank you, Sanjay.'

'You are most welcome, Miss Hardy.'

'Please call me Justine.'

'You are most welcome, Justine.'

Mr Mehta stuck his finger in his ear and made a gurgling noise in the back of his throat as the subject of flights to Assam was raised.

An hour later the same question was still being posed and there had not even been the offer of a cup of tea. Finally, extracting his finger from his ear, Mr Mehta admitted that he was aware of my name, mentioned to him by the London director, but he was not at all sure about domestic flights. His travel budget had been frozen indefinitely.

'Mr Mehta, I appreciate the situation but my travel has been sanctioned by your London office. I was assured that I would be given all the help I needed. Is there perhaps someone else I could talk to, perhaps Mr Palva? Your director in London suggested that I should talk to him if I had any problems.'

This time Mr Mehta did not need a translation. The *tiffin* tin was abandoned, he barked something at the man fiddling with the paper clips, picked up his telephone and started to shout at someone else down that as well. Mr Palva was the Minister for Tourism and his boss: Mr Hire and Fire, the man who gave new meaning to 'frozen indefinitely'.

I was bustled out as the sacred lunch hour approached. Mr Mehta seemed to think that he might be able to do something.

Two days later he left a message. A budget had been found to get me to Assam and maybe even back as well.

Yashwant was unenthusiastic. He was being abandoned to the wrath of the hot season.

'You will be shot, you know. You are much safer staying in Delhi. You could write about us. You will have to talk to Gita. She will tell you not to go to Assam. Her father was a tea planter and she was married to one. She'll tell you how poisonous the whole thing is. Assam is so boring. It is just a bunch of tea planters and mad separatists.'

'That's exactly why I want to go.'

The plane shuddered and plunged. Several oxygen masks had been knocked free of their moorings and swayed above our heads. Nobody else seemed very worried. I knew I was going to be sick. I waved at one of the air hostesses. She ignored me for a while until I started to pant, a vital exercise in vomit control. She eyed me suspiciously.

'Baby coming?' she asked.

Pointing and flailing I made frantic gestures. It is hard to mime a sick bag with one hand. Indian Airlines did not seem to think that sick bags were necessary. I searched desperately in the seat pocket: inflight magazines, jolly pictures of a woman in a sari demonstrating lifejacket fastening, sticky, tightly twisted sweet papers (proof that I was not the only nervous passenger) and a nasty tissue housing something best left alone.

'It was only an air pocket. It is happening all the time in the hot season,' said the kindly Sikh gentleman sitting beside me. 'I think you will get used to it.' He offered me his half-finished cup of tea as a receptacle.

The odds against being sick into a small cup of cooling tea discreetly were too high. The roaring wave of nausea began to recede. I pressed my sweating forehead against the unsympathetic plastic window and saw Assam.

A broad beam of a river curled through the landscape, the Brahmaputra, the load-bearing dark chocolate roar that springs from Tibet. The Sikh gentleman leant across to peer through the window.

'If we were the other side of the aircraft I would be showing you my tea garden.' He patted my hand.

'Better now? Vomiting time passed?' He smiled.

The sympathetic Sikh was the manager of one of the largest tea estates in Assam. He had lived and worked in tea gardens for thirty years, twenty-two of those in Assam. Two years before, his neighbour, another garden manager, had been shot dead in front of his family on the steps of his bungalow by extremist Assamese separatists. The kindly Sikh said it had taken him years to get used to the violence but that he now saw death as part of the job, part of life in the gardens.

'You see we have no choice but to accept. We can build no fence so high or wall so thick that they cannot get us if they want to.' He stopped.

'Do not be alarmed, Miss. The gardens here are the most beautiful that you could see.' He patted my hand again.

The tea estate managers, their families and assistants are soft targets for the separatists who rage against those they regard as foreigners from other Indian states. The core of the separatist movement in Assam comprises the Bodo tribals, the earliest ethnic settlers of the area. Their fight is against the descendants of the great nineteenth-century influx of workers to the tea estates and, more recently, the cross-border migration of Bangladeshis. The latter situation came to a head in 1979 when Indira Gandhi officially opened the borders of Assam. Neighbouring Bangladeshis flooded in, claiming pockets of land as their own. Then the violence began in earnest.

To the separatists, the tea planters are bigger fish than poverty-line Bangladeshis. They are headline grabbers because they represent foreign tea companies in a system set up during the British Empire, the original thorn in the flesh of the Assamese tribal people. To the Bodo tribals Indian-owned tea companies are foreign, as are Indian owners from other states even though they may have owned their tea gardens for several generations. They are all outsiders.

The Assamese have always been a proud people. Their country is fertile and well-watered. They did not want or need to work for the foreign tea companies. So the estates brought in labourers from the famished plains of India, the vast dust bowls of cheap labour, Bihar, Bengal and Orissa, who were attracted by the promise of work and good living conditions. These labourers became immigrant communities, floating within the confines of the tea estates, isolated from the rest of the country, worshipping the gods of their home states, following their own customs and celebrating their own familiar festivals. Many of the workers on estates today are third- or fourth-generation migrant pickers who still speak Bengali, Marathi or even Telegu, a language of the deep south of India. In the eyes of the separatists these pickers are undesirable twice over; once for being outsiders and again for accepting pay from foreign overlords.

There are two main arms of the separatist movement, ULFA, the United Liberation Front of Assam, and NDFB, the National Democratic Front of Bodoland. Neither, of course, is to be confused with ALF, the Assam Liberation Front, or PLFA, the People's Liberation Front of Assam. These acronyms become a joke, a deadly game. It does not matter to the victim which way the letters are thrown up, they all come down in the same way, at the end of a sniper's bullet. Death is hardly softened by a bit of alphabetical juggling, Scrabble at flesh-piercing velocity. There is continual confusion. The acronyms share a common cause but there are still losses in almost friendly fire. Meeting in the shadows on their dark journeys they click off safety catches and bark initials at each other. A wrong letter and a trigger gets squeezed.

Assam is a region of anachronisms, the little kingdoms of each tea garden existing as oases of nineteenth-century colonial order. Beyond them the villages and towns of Assam bubble and fester with the separatists' bouts of action and violence. These passionate tribals are relatively new to the cruel, liquid rules of terrorism but they are learning fast, often given sharp lessons by their cousins-in-terrorism in Kashmir. The Bobos have learnt to move around the countryside between the isolated tea estates on bicycles, riding through the dusk like any other local making his way home. They slip into bushes and thickets on the edges of the tea gardens, then pedal through the tightly regimented blocks of tea to get to their targets sitting out in the evening cool or walking in the fruit orchards of their bungalows.

Tezpur is one of the main towns in Upper Assam. The streets are wide boulevards shaded by palms, the houses have verandas and shutters painted in pastel colours. There is a sense of almost Mediterranean comfort, an atmosphere of prosperity and fecundity absent in so many of the desiccated areas of India.

A train goes from Guwahati, the state capital in the south, to Tezpur. It has a smell more profound than the usual assault of spices, overflowing lavatories and stale bodies. I could not place it. The conductor had to be bribed to wake me at three in the morning to change trains at Rangapara North, an almost deserted station peopled only by an old beggar woman asleep on the platform and a security guard. When the guard saw me get off the train he prodded her awake with his rifle butt. She staggered up and lurched on to the tracks, squatting down and groaning through a stream of diarrhoea. The guard screamed and jumped down to kick her until she lay curled and motionless in a foetal bundle. The acid taste of vomit came into my mouth.

As I lay between the guard room and the public urinals for two hours, the flowers of an oleander tree fell into my hair and clothes. The security guard had refused to wake me when the Tezpur train came in. It was not part of his job. Was knocking old, sick women unconscious part of his job, I asked. He shrugged. I had asked in English, pretending to be brave by asking the question in a language that he would not understand.

I was woken by a boy up in the oleander tree. He was plucking the flowers and dropping them into a basket below to make temple garlands to sell. He had assumed that I was waiting for the train. Thanking him, I dropped some rupees into his basket. He called out. He told me that Lakshmi, the Hindu goddess of good fortune, would give me many sons. When I looked back to wave he was bouncing on a branch, scattering the flowers on to the platform below.

Tezpur station is a little over a mile from the centre of town. When the train pulled in the platform was still. There were no bobbing heads, no red-shirted porters barging into each other to get to the heavily laden passengers first, no *chai-wallahs* weaving their trays of glasses and tea amidst the throng, always just sliding or ducking away from a collision, no *pitha*-sellers, their fermented rice rolls wrapped in banana leaves, hollering through the train windows to the mass of bored, hungry passengers. This was not how a station was supposed to be.

No one else got off the train. One porter was curled up asleep under a table. He woke up and shooed me away. A young man appeared in the doorway of the station. He wore a pair of new blue jeans and a chunky watch, very much on display. He spoke a little English.

He said that the whole area was on an all-out, one-day strike, a *bundh*. It had been called by the separatists in retaliation for the recent murder of a high-profile Assamese journalist who was known to have been sympathetic to the separatists' cause. If the porter helped me to carry my luggage into town he could be shot for breaking the *bundh*.

Arrogance, thinly veiled as justification, made me believe that if I was with the porter he would be left alone. Eventually he was cajoled into helping me at ten times the going rate. The young man waved us off from the station, wet-lipped with the anticipation of a shoot-up downtown.

The porter chose to walk down the middle of the wide, lifeless streets, his eyes fixed straight ahead. A bad Curry Western, no Clint or clapper board to save the day. Every half-closed door seemed ominous. Shadowy figures flitted behind windows and across shaded verandas. That had been the smell on the train, the smell of fear. I caught it again on the porter's breath.

A yell from a side street. The porter began to run. There seemed to be noise all around us. We abandoned the main boulevard and cut into a side street, hopping back and forth across a narrow, stagnant canal. The porter stopped running. There had been no other sound apart from the yell. The rest had been my heart.

The porter sat down to readjust his load. He laughed, wiping some of the dirt from my bags with his red headcloth. We were both covered in dust, mine streaked by sweat.

On the marble steps of the only hotel in Tezpur that was open, the doorman would not allow the porter in. He sat down silently and put his head in his hands. Even after he had been paid, over and above the marked-up price, he remained there, silent head in silent hands.

The manager wanted to know if I had passed a pleasant journey. I sighed and slumped against the desk. He waited, tapping a smart pen on the desk in a steady rhythm.

'We have been expecting you, Miss Hardy,' he announced.

'Why?' I had not known where I was going to stay.

'We were alerted as to your arrival by the booking clerk at Guwahati. He told us that you had been most insistent on getting a ticket to Tezpur. It was the last train before the *bundh*. It is often most unwise to travel during a *bundh*.'

'Thank you.'

'You are most welcome. Your good friends from the tea garden have also been calling to be made aware of your safety. You have been a most effective strike-breaker, Miss Hardy. Will you be taking breakfast?' He handed me a key from a full board. I was the only guest.

The dining-room was huge, ugly and smelt of dead rats. Mildew made merry amidst the swirls of the carpet and islands of damp glistened on the walls. Every table was laid up with intricately folded brown paper napkins erect and uniform in smeared glasses. There was a small table in the corner for me. The manager hovered at the door and then ushered me from the corner to a long table in the middle of the room. He pulled out a chair.

Five waiters stood to attention against the wall by the service door. I opened the Tezpur newspaper that the manager had left and waited. No one moved. By the time I reached the sports section I had started to fidget, unravelling the sculpted napkin, rattling the cutlery. Eventually I called out. All five walked very slowly across the room. One unfurled a napkin and put it on my lap on top of the one already there. Another rearranged the cutlery. The other three hovered. I asked for a menu. The five disappeared through the service door.

A lengthy menu arrived with promises of Assam tea with lemon and fresh papaya with lime juice. Not possible. Fresh fruit, where fresh fruit grows, was out of the question. Assam tea in Assam – just not possible. But in a hotel in the middle of an all-out strike in the north-eastern tip of India, porridge, toast and marmalade were naturally available.

As long as the *bundh* lasted, I was a captive in the hotel. Out of boredom I sent all my dirty clothes to the *dhobi*. They returned smelling of boys' locker room. The *bundh* was taking its toll.

Alka Singh rang from the tea garden after the third re-run of Barry Norman and his film*fest* on the BBC World Service. Alka was the friend of a friend. Her call was one of salvation. Barry's busy pullover was beginning to cause mild hysteria in the dank hotel room.

Alka is married to Billy Singh, the manager of one of the oldest tea estates in Assam. She had taken it upon herself to look after me. She insisted that I must leave Tezpur as soon as possible and get to the tea garden. It was made very clear that the drive was only to be undertaken during daylight. She spoke to the hotel manager to negotiate a taxi, a commodity as rare as fresh papaya.

The taxi-driver arrived, a weasel in *kurta* pyjamas. He drove fast and well while we were in terrorist country, but as soon as he felt he was in a safe area he stopped the car and started to tinker with the engine. There was nothing wrong with it but the performance indicated it was time to renegotiate the price. It was not a time to haggle. Rupees bought daylight.

There was one more unprompted stop. The weasel, buoyed up by his mounting fare, thought that the rough state of the road might just be another point of leverage. He got a flat no and he took it quite well. We arrived at the garden just before twilight.

The drive up to Billy and Alka's bungalow was the main road from the tea workers' houses to the garden. The pickers were walking home, conical plucking baskets balanced on their heads, bright, thin cotton saris luminescent in the dusk. Here were the real live characters from the front of teabag boxes on supermarket shelves, the illustration that just cannot be true, it is too pretty, too out-of-date. Beyond the vivid animation of the pickers the

The garden of shades

garden stretched away, a sheet of green plucked into conformity, not a leaf straying above the smooth sheen. Here were thousands of acres of disciplined roots, picked by a thousand workers governed by one man – Billy Singh – a kingdom of green lapped by the shifting tides of the separatists.

Alka was waiting. The weasel became obsequious. Alka waved him towards the kitchen to find food and water for his taxi radiator. No one had been to stay at the garden for months. The separatists had been on a killing spree, burning out villages all around. Not a time for social visits.

Billy appeared on the veranda with the tea – fruit cake, slices of Welsh rarebit and Assam's green gold, plucked the day before, from the bush to fine porcelain in twenty-four hours. He was young for a manager, glossy and twinkle-eyed, one minute giving me a lecture about risking the terrorist-ridden streets of Tezpur, the next laughing about his psychedelic memories of college acid trips. I told him that I wanted to write about the estate. He became serious. He talked about his plans to introduce Girl

Guides into the workers' settlement to encourage the daughters of pickers to nurture ambitions beyond those of their mothers. The seriousness passed and he moved on to films.

Alka dropped in comments, sometimes berating Billy gently for his barrage of questions and sweeping statements. She stopped talking when it came to pouring the tea. She passed a cup and watched to see my reaction as I drank.

The rim hovered at my lips.

'Of course after Sean Connery no one could really compete with his Bond. He was the top. Roger Moore and that hair, and George Whatsit, my God, what were they thinking of?' Billy thumped the table. My cup jumped and hot tea shot straight down the front of my shirt. Billy laughed.

'Don't worry, we have plenty of that.'

Another cup, another rim. It was good tea. Alka smiled.

Their daughter, Simran, appeared from the bungalow. She stretched, uncurling from heavy afternoon teen-sleep. Alka fussed around her, calling to the kitchen for a banana milkshake and fresh toast. Simran took it all in good humour, moulding herself around her father, her head resting on his shoulder. Billy stroked her hair and his speech slowed and calmed. Alka leant her head on the back of the wicker chair, a studio study portrait.

It was almost dark, too late to swim in the pool as the mosquitoes rampaged. Billy took me to see the bungalow garden in the last hem of light; past the stubby pineapple plants, the orange and lemon trees, the lychees dragging down their branches, the tamarind tree, the cinnamon tree, its bark curling away, ready for the spice jar. He only stopped when we got to the vegetable patch. Beyond the *bhindi* plants and the green chillies he pointed to the potatoes and to his pride and joy, his Brussels sprouts.

'Such perfect Bubble-and-Squeak soon,' he said, stroking the precious green knobs.

At the end of the garden, opposite the gate into the bungalow compound, was a spreading frangipani tree, a canopy of blossom. Below was a sandbag bunker, inside a guard, his rifle levelled at the gate. Billy shrugged.

'We were being picked off by the separatists, manager by manager, one family after another torn apart. We had to do something to protect ourselves.' He tapped the polished letters on the shoulder of the guard's uniform: ATPSF, the Assam Tea Plantation Security Force. The young man beamed. I admired his hat, the shooting side pinned up with another shiny set of initials. He bustled about in the confines of his bunker, embarrassed by the attention. Billy led me away.

We waited for supper looking out into the black void through the mosquito-netted veranda. Billy was distracted. He would begin a story, jump up from his chair and start to ask why dinner had not arrived, where Simran was, why it was such a hot night. A mellifluous flow from Alka covered his staccato conversation. She talked about her work with local village women and her attempts to find a market for their tribal linen. She suggested that we might go down to one of the villages to see the women weaving.

Billy leapt to his feet again.

'You will not leave the estate!' There was silence.

A houseboy came out with the first of the supper dishes: rich Assamese fish curry with sticky rice, fried aubergines and *raita*, all to be eaten with the hands.

The conversation over supper centred on Michael Caine films and plans for a grand coconut and chicken curry the following night if Sukkuji, the cook, could be bribed to wring some necks and do some plucking. Films and food to chase away the silence that crept in through the tiny holes in the mosquito netting.

That day in a nearby village, a local *panchayat* (village council) representative had been shot. Troops were pouring into the area to try and suppress the agitation boiling amongst the separatists. On the heels of that murder, an assistant manager in a tea garden was shot at point-blank range by an ATPSF officer, one of the boys who was supposed to have been protecting him. There had been a misunderstanding over a television that had been promised to the security guards but had not been delivered. The local tea plantation community was on a security alert. The violence was coming from every direction now.

It was quiet when Billy saw me to my room at the far end of the bungalow. We agreed to meet at one of the blocks of tea on the other side of the garden the next morning.

A guard walked with me to the meeting place and waited as I examined the old section boards. Some blocks had been planted in 1914. As one crop was plucked in France, another took root in Assam.

There was a quick game of hide-and-seek. I had drunk too much coffee at breakfast and did not have a word of Assamese to explain the need for a moment of privacy. Nothing for it except to mime peeing, followed by desperate attempts to mute the flow. The guard had insisted that two metres away, behind a narrow tree, was quite far enough out of his sight.

The meeting in the tea garden was to see a *pooja*, a prayer-offering ceremony. A plot of new tea was being planted, the first to be put in for five years. There were to be 3,000 plants in all but Billy was there to witness the digging in of just the first lucky seven. A young plant stood next to the plot where it was to be bedded in. Beside it were five dark green betel leaves, each one with a burning incense stick, little mounds of chickpeas and glistening sweets, and a string of bright plastic flowers hung at a jaunty angle.

Billy ordered the first hole to be dug. The women, who had been carrying the plants to the section in circular baskets, gathered round. The first plant went in. Everyone clapped. The chickpeas and syrupy sweets were passed around. Alka stood under a tree, sheltering from the hot sun but lending her support. She applauded enthusiastically and talked to Billy's young assistants. The women pickers watched her, checking how she stood, how her hair was done, her clothes, her jewellery. She was after all the Burra Sahib's wife, an elevated and isolating role to play on an estate with a thousand workers. Alka was the closest thing they had to a Hindi movie star. She represented all things feminine and modern, all the things that they as women might want to be.

Alka left and Billy drove me out of the garden towards the factory on the edge of the estate. An old woman waved to us from the window of what looked like a gypsy caravan. Billy stopped the jeep. Even before he had opened his door, the two guards in the back were out and at his side, rifles raised.

The caravan was the tea garden crêche, the woman, a canny, cross-eyed, one-armed matriarch who watched over the babies of the women pickers while they worked. Billy asked her whether she was getting the right amount of milk and biscuits for her charges. Her eyes rolled and out poured the complaints. Billy jotted down her gripes and told her that he would attend to them. She put her one hand on her hip and gave him a hard look with each wandering eye.

'There are too many children in the crêche. She is always chewing my ear about more this and that,' he said as we got back into the jeep.

'How about family planning?'

'I try. I show them that Alka and I have just Simran and that it means that we have a good quality of life because we only have one child to support. But our lifestyle is so alien to theirs and I can't really change their cultural conditioning. As long as they have enough floor space in their houses for their children to sleep on they will go on having babies. I have to bully the women to make them take the twelve-week maternity leave that we insist on. They would work right up until full labour and be back picking the next day if they had the choice.'

As if to order two girls crossed the road in front of us. Each was laden front and back, full baskets of tea slung across their shoulders, almost full-term pregnancies jutting out in front. They could not have been much more than fifteen or sixteen.

'Every hour they spend out of the garden they see as money unearned. They find it almost impossible to understand that we are subsidizing their hospital and maternity leave. It means the one-armed bandit always has a full house.'

The two girls used their swollen bellies to push through into the next plot of tea.

Where the garden had been still, the factory roared: a giant building in constant motion, metal tubs of fermented leaves crashing in and out of drying bins, trolleys rattling up and down narrow passages piled with tea to be fired, thin, brown legs darting around the relentless movement of the hungry machines, lines of CTC (teabag tea) moving along belts, pouring in a continuous line, an unending trail of gunpowder, mugpowder, the dust swept into piles by stooping women with bamboo-frond brushes.

Billy talked and spat through the daily tea-tasting process. The cups were graded according to quality. He tilted the tea in the light to check the colour then sucked it across his tongue before spitting it neatly into a small pot. He talked about brightness, about the depth and copper tones of the leaves. The nuances were lost on me, though the varying shades of golden brown caught the sun, absorbing the light, becoming richer. This was the art behind the tea-break, behind pyramid bags and soggy mounds steaming on the draining board.

In the afternoon I sat with Alka on the veranda and talked about the tea life of Assam.

'You see I am alone. Simran is at school most of the time. Billy is out in the garden.' Her hands twisted through the thick ropes of her hair.

'Each time Billy is not back by the time he said he would be I start to worry and picture the ugly things that might have happened to him. I know how many distractions there are for him, how many people want to talk to him at the end of each day, but still my mind has him riddled with bullets every time. Those bloody movie channels full of all that horror and such. No wonder my mind plays these games.'

Did she feel lonely or unfulfilled? She and Billy had met at university where Alka had been studying French and philosophy. They were married before Alka finished her degree.

'Oh, I have so much to do all the time.' She looked out at the two *malis* on the lawn. One pushed a lawnmower from behind, the other pulled it from the front with a rope around his forehead. She waved towards her carefully nurtured rose garden.

'I have the garden to oversee, the house to run for Billy, the servants to look after. Sukkuji, the cook, and Rita, my *ayah*, they are like family to us.' She plucked at her sleeve.

'There is a lot to do. A Burra Sahib's wife has things to do.' Her voice went up at the end, more a question than an answer.

'It is so much better than when we first came. For three years there was no telephone here. Simran is at school thousands and thousands of miles away in Rajasthan, you see. If I wanted to call her or my friends in Delhi I had to drive two or three hours to the nearest town. It was desperate.' The hands were back, working the hair.

'On 26 January 1996 they finally put in a telephone on the estate. Can you believe that something so silly could change my life so much?' She clapped her hands in delight.

'Sometimes it takes me twenty or thirty attempts to get through but that does not seem to matter because I just remember what it was like before.

'Now I can call my friends in Delhi. We chatter away and I stop feeling, well you know, so far away from them all, from everyone. Simy can call me from school if anything happens. I can call her.'

Sukkuji appeared from the kitchen, his grey hair newly hennaed, slicked back and shaved around his ears and his neck to a regimental stubble. A snappy dresser, sartorial Sukkuji, and proud of his appearance. There was a short conference with Alka about the grand dinner. The chicken had obviously been successfully caught and wrung. There was a very serious discourse about the ice-cream that Alka had ordered from town for pudding. Sukkuji did not think that it would make it back in a solid state, but Alka had great confidence in her cool box. Sukkuji had taken offence that his repertoire of sticky puddings had been usurped by the popular pretender from town with its artificial this and that, toffee chunks and all.

Food: it fills the long days and the loneliness. The complications of a coconut and chicken dinner push the separatist clouds to one side while the much-planned delicacy is on the plate. Then there is always tomorrow's menu to be discussed, and the next day's.

'We all eat too much, you know,' Alka explained after Sukkuji had gone back to the kitchen, still puffing about the ice-cream.

'See how fat I have got. Billy and I plump up a bit more each year. I must show you pictures of us when we were at college. We were all young and thin then. All this sitting around just makes you fat.' She plucked at the flesh on her arm: Billy, Alka and the chicken, all fattened up for slaughter.

She said that it was not so long since the tribals of the north-east had given up cannibalism.

'They would do well with us and it would all be Sukkuji's fault.' She laughed.

'Sukkuji is a very important part of our life. He has been with us for years, moving from garden to garden as we have moved. My *ayah* Rita is the same. She came to us when she was just sixteen. We are her family. She is nearly twenty-five now and I would like to find a husband for her. Someone good and strong so that she can have her own family.'

She led the way back into the bungalow to see the old albums of when Billy and she had been young, slim students without responsibilities and *ayahs* to marry off. She pointed to a picture of Billy and her standing beside a river with a group of friends – Billy, dark and thin, clowning for the camera; Alka, head thrown back, laughing, looking very young.

'You see we left all that life behind when Billy decided to work in tea.' The album was closed.

*

The wail of an air-raid siren called the workers in from the garden. The ominous sound marking the end of the day filled the air with a sense of loss.

The road to the garden above the bungalow again filled with people. The women had taken off the thick aprons that protected their saris from the branches of the tea plants. A stream of colour flowed along the road, topped with bobbing baskets, many with the ubiquitous black cotton shade umbrella stuck into the wickerwork. Babies were carried by their mothers or slung across the chests or backs of their sisters. These were girls hardly old enough to go to school but already proxy mother figures to their siblings. The volume of chatter had increased since the midday heat among the bushes. This was the homecoming, the pickers moving from one area of the estate where they worked to another where they lived, to the homes that come with solar lighting and pumped water, a primary school with a permanent staff, a hospital with midwives and doctors. Here were all the ingredients of a nineteenth-century philanthropist's dreams. Terrorists and cerebral malaria are less discerning in their appraisal.

Sukkuji's chicken was good and rich, steeped in yoghurt and cardamom. We all had third and fourth ladlefuls, just in case the ice-cream had been sabotaged. It had not. Simran cheered the toffee chunks.

Would they like to go to another garden in a less volatile area?

Simran picked at her ice-cream and did not answer. Billy spoke for them all. They were very happy in the garden. It was rewarding and the quality of the lifestyle justified the risk. The subject was dropped, the ice-cream finished.

The conversation moved on to a football match that was coming up at The Club, the social centre in the lives of the tea garden managers and their families. It was a place where the innocuous tittle-tattle of life kept them amused, a place where, over gin and tonics and games of tennis, bonds were formed and gossip fizzed. Billy's team was fancied for the cup, inspiring the flutter of a few rupees.

A long discussion ensued on the travel arrangements for the day. Would it be better to take a couple of jeeps or a small minibus, to make a mid- or late-morning start? One thing was set in stone. Everyone would have to leave the big event before sunset to get back to their gardens before dark. With the twilight came the malarial aedes mosquitoes and the gun-toting shades.

In the tea garden the senses and emotions fly just above the ground, whipped about by the breezes that blow through the tidy rows of plants. The smell of rain on the bright tea is sharp and clean, with just the first edge of the aroma that comes from a cup. The backs of the pickers are burnt by the sun in the flailing heat, even in the shade of the black cotton umbrellas. Billy and Alka greet their visitor from the outside world with greater warmth and generosity than most hosts. The frangipani smells sweet and heavy above the sandbag bunker and the guard.

In the end it was not the weasel taxi-man but one of the estate drivers who took me away from the tea garden. Billy, Alka and Simran stood on the steps of the bungalow to wave, Simran dragged out of bed for the farewell, sleepy and draped once more around her father, Alka's hand in her hair. They all waved and smiled as the car bounced down the drive.

Even before the plane left the runway the tea garden had become another country; Sukkuji dyeing his hair while dreaming of syrupy recipes, Billy making teapot empire plans, Alka thinking of Delhi among the fragile roses. And beyond the smooth roll of the tea plants, the shadows.

This was the picture to sell to Sourish: a sweeping backdrop, a loving family, a state in ferment, men in uniform, death and violence, and some disastrously rich sticky puddings.

Of course it was not to be so simple.

On Things that Explode

THE VULTURES OF the city peered from the trees, waiting for a corpse. Amidst the darting rickshaws and belching taxis, expensive imported cars cut an arrogant swathe. With their dollar kings safe inside and arrangements of artificial flowers laid out on the rear window shelves, they looked like nothing so much as living hearses carrying the mortal remains of political and industrial deals.

Into this maelstrom stepped a cow, heedless of all around her. The traffic ground to a halt as she made her way gently across the road. A car and a rickshaw shunted in their efforts to miss her. Much shouting ensued.

She made me late. Not much of an excuse in Delhi, a cow in rush hour.

Sourish did not seem to mind. His time was elastic; the morning squeezed between eleven and twelve-thirty, the afternoon yawning from two till eight. His days slipped and slid. Whether I was five minutes late or two hours, I was always greeted with the same smile, the same harassed expression.

'Good story for me?' he asked.

'Yes, I got caught in a *bundh* that was called after a journalist, a known separatist sympathizer, was murdered.'

'Oh, oh, what about the gardens?'

'Well, they're lovely but you have to take a security guard with you everywhere. The army are pouring in. You know, a snake-in-Eden sort of thing.'

Sourish looked blank.

'And you have got some nice pictures for me?'

'Of what?'

'Oh, you know, saris against the tea, baskets of leaves, smiling babies.'

'Sourish . . .'

'Yes?'

Of course I had pictures, endless pictures of saris, flame-bright against the tea, of wicker baskets piled high, of sad-eyed children standing alone, smiling beatifically in front of acres of rolling green. But that wasn't the point.

'What about some pretty pictures of burnt-out villages and dead children?'

'No, no, nice travel ones for a piece about the lovely north-east.' Sourish turned his attention to his computer keyboard.

There was a pause, quite a long pause.

'Sourish, that isn't really why I went to Assam.'

He looked up in surprise.

'But you went to look at the tea gardens.'

'Yes.'

'So that is what is to be written about.' He turned back to his keyboard and picked up the telephone.

I glared at the wall behind his head.

Sourish put down the receiver.

'Okay, okay, a lovely story with a mention of the situation. You know, like just a factual rundown on why and how.'

'Thank you. It will be as lovely as you want and a little sad.'

'No, no, not sad. Say positive things about what is being done to try and solve the situation, how good the output is from the gardens, stuff like that. Sad is not good copy.'

'*Somebody* needs to write about what is really going on up there. Did you know that every garden has to pay protection money, that the separatists get huge sums under the guise of a land tax and a tax on every kilo of tea produced? The money is paid out of state or even offshore. When ULFA goes calling at an estate, the manager knows that he has to pay up. If the company does not pay people go missing. Sourish, we are talking about *crores* and *crores* of rupees. There are over a thousand tea estates in Assam, each one paying a fortune each year to one terrorist organization. What is happening to that money?'

'That is a news story.' He took a slow breath. 'We are writing features, not news stories. That is not the sort of stuff we are putting in the magazine sections. Enough, enough.' He waved away my belligerence.

It was time to retreat.

'News is what I am really interested in. It is where I started and where I would like to be right now,' Sourish added as I was about to leave.

This olive branch stopped me at the door.

'So I understand, you see.'

Sourish had started at *The Indian Express* on the newsdesk. It was where he had learnt about newspapers and met his wife. I was on weak ground, trying to argue with Sourish about news when I had done my learning in the pampered world of glossy magazines. Sourish was a newsman forced into features. For him I would write features.

Yashwant has an expression, 'bitched out'. I was that. Put in place and now without anyone to rage against, I stalked out of the building.

The Indian Express was on strike, though no one seemed quite sure who was striking or even what they were striking about. Whatever the reason a large crowd of journalists and printers were now sitting outside, sunglasses in place. One of the senior editors had settled himself on the marble steps, carefully perched between two popular *paan*-spitting spots.

'So out hop the rabbits,' he said when I smiled at him, trying to remember his name.

There seemed to be no indication of how long the strike would last. There was no rowdiness, nor any sign of union leaders. Someone said his team had walked out because the computers had gone down and the air-conditioning was jammed. The atmosphere was almost festive. Packs of cards appeared, glasses of *chai* steamed, orders were shouted at the stall across the street for chickpeas, popcorn and spicy puffed rice.

The senior editor had thought ahead. He had brought out a pile of English Sunday supplements to leaf through. He offered one to me.

At the *chai* stall the drinkers peered over my shoulder at the pages of the magazine. As they started a conversation about the merits of different foreign cars I found the gossip pages. They were making a film of *The English Patient*. Yashwant would spit. We had argued about the impossibility of ever filming such surreal prose.

A small hand tugged at the hem of my skirt.

'Sister, sister, one rupee.'

I ignored her for a while, but she went on tugging. As I paid for the *chai* I grabbed a biscuit out of one of the large jars and pushed it into the small, persistent hand. There was no smile, no acknowledgement. She had not asked for a biscuit and spat theatrically as she walked away.

By the time Bushan arrived with his rickshaw a storm was about to break. Most of the crowd were still milling about on the street. I could not even muster the good grace to greet him. By the time he delivered me home, vile retribution was about to be wreaked. The weather and my stomach exploded.

The night before flying back from Assam I had been to dinner with some friends of Billy and Alka's in Guwahati. On my left sat the devastating resident commissioner, single, an equestrian champion, the owner of eyes that were like still, brown pools. On my right was a film director with a mind as sharp as the resident commissioner's brown pools were deep. In the midst of the magic I picked up gastroenteritis.

In the lift up to the apartment I was cross-legged. At the entrance Ram Kumar started to give me a message. I fled to my room as fast as crossed legs would permit.

Almost immediately Dhan Singh was standing in the doorway, announcing in grave tones that there had been an accident. He would not be drawn on whom the accident had involved or even whether it was a national, international, local or family accident.

As I lurched for the bathroom again he shuffled off down the corridor muttering to himself.

Yashwant's father was outside the door when I emerged, his moustache bristling. He was ready to tell a tale.

He had been in the accident with Yashwant's mother, the Rani Sahiba. Mrs Prince was now in hospital in Jodhpur nursing a shattered arm. This was going to be a blow-by-blow account.

'Bloody fool driver, do you know if I had been driving this would of course not have happened. But it did. So there we are and my wife is sitting in the middle of the road, very pale and proud. And do you know, a bus driver sees the Rani sitting there in the road. He stops his bus and takes her on board, all the time bowing and scraping and all, and off they toddle to the hospital. It must have been miles off his route but of course no one minded.'

I raised my hand, unable to speak as another spasm wrenched my guts. I rushed back to the bathroom. As I retched, the bus reached the hospital. As I pushed my head against the cistern and groaned, the bus driver addressed the triage nurse at length. When I returned, pale and shaking, my absence had not even been noticed, much less the din of nausea echoing from the bathroom. I was back on cue and just in time for a sympathetic grunt. The storyteller continued until the violence of his audience's sickness made it impossible even for him to go on.

There followed three days of honest-to-God delirium. Giant figures from the *Ramayana* peopled my dreams. Then came Assamese terrorists performing circus tricks in the reception hall of *The Indian Express*, my mother clapping as they juggled rifles and grenades. A friend from London was running the *chai* stall in Hailey Road, giving away copies of *Harper's & Queen* to the rickshaw drivers with every glass of *chai*. This was no novel experience. Kipling had been there long before me.

> I had fever too, regular and persistent, to which I added for a while chronic dysentery. Yet I discovered that a man can work with a temperature of 104, even though next day he has to ask the office who wrote the article.

From a modern point of view I suppose the life was not
fit for a dog, but my world was filled with boys, but a few
years older than I, who lived utterly alone, and died
from typhoid mostly at the regulation age of twenty-
two.

By Kipling's standards I was doing well – I was eight years over the
regulation mark. But if I had written articles during those days of
dementia not even Sourish could have edited them.

On day four I came up to the surface. Dhan Singh was entrusted
with the task of dancing attendance on my needs. He forced me
to drink boiled rice water – disgusting but effective. The following afternoon he propped me up on the balcony with the papers
to take the air. No one else came near, fearful that I might have
something worse than a bad bout of food poisoning. There was
great suspicion of Assam and the general consensus among the
servants was that evil spirits dwelt in Assamese water. Those same
spirits were now malevolently lurking in my gut. I was not prepared to be subjected to an exorcism so I remained quietly on the
balcony in the last of the sun.

Jodhpur Apartments received a daily delivery of *The Times of
India*, *The Indian Express* and *The Pioneer*, the latter the same paper
that Kipling had written for, printed on whiter paper than any of
the others and carrying a distinguished air only slightly marred by
a Bambi character leaping across a full moon between the words of
the masthead. Contributing to its elevated appearance was a cover
price one notch up from that of the other broadsheets. That caught
my attention. Among the papers that Dhan Singh had brought out
was the Sunday supplement from England that I had been given
by the senior editor on the steps of *The Indian Express*. The cover
price was £1, or about Rs. 60. The cover prices of the papers at my
feet were Rs. 1.50 and, in the case of *The Pioneer*, Rs. 2, respec-
tively two and a half pence and three pence. Even the Sunday editions with their four or five weekend sections covering the arts,
food, entertainment, health, travel and *chatteratti* (the gossip
column in *The Indian Express*), cost only Rs. 3, just five pence ster-

ling. This was a staggering discrepancy, notwithstanding the difference in the basic cost of living between London and New Delhi. Both are capital cities. The price of property in each place is almost identical. Yet the newspapers in Delhi cost one-twentieth of the broadsheet Sundays in London *and* they offer the reader page upon page of potential husbands or wives. The enormous price difference reflects one thing. In London the going rate for jobbing writers is about £200 for a thousand words. In Delhi it is about £17.

Working through the English magazine and the Indian papers, another difference became obvious. In contrast to their English counterparts Indian newspapers have very few celebrity columnists. Journalists in India have become familiar because of their writing not because of the measurement of their inside leg or their ability to wear wisps from the hottest designer in town. Reporters report, features writers write features, analysts analyse and columnists write columns. There is a belief among Indian journalists that reporters have no need to model the clothes they are commenting on or play the game of cricket that they have just reviewed. In turn they do not see why a model or a cricketer should write their version of events. At least that was how it was until *The Indian Express* decided to recruit Geoff Boycott to write on cricket. Now the rot has set in. Models are beginning to fill the column inches with air from their lovely heads. The disco-dancing divas of Bollywood will soon follow with their insightful commentaries on life.

At sunset Yashwant finally decided to come within a few feet of me. He was petulant. Mangay, the man of angles and symmetry whom I had met at the rooftop cocktail party, had not been seen for several days. Irritated by anything and everything, Yashwant pounced on the news that *The English Patient* was being filmed.

'It was such a miserable book no one could possibly want to go and see a film of it. Where is that bloody Mangay?' He slapped hard at a mosquito that was not there.

I asked what he thought about newspaper columnists and the idea of people in the public eye being given columns purely on the strength of their notoriety.

'Are you saying that just anyone can get into the national papers because they look good in a dress?'

'That's exactly what I am saying.'

'Oh, good show, I shall write a column. Tell me who I must get in touch with.'

A cockroach scuttled from the corner, antennae twirling. Yashwant pulled himself up to his full height and looked imperiously at the insect. It stopped mid-scurry and reared up on its bristly legs. Yashwant raised an eyebrow.

'You shall die. Come.' The first was for the cockroach, the second I imagined was for me.

The cockroach and I waited.

'Come, come.' The order was definitely for me.

The cockroach bolted. I was not so lucky. I was about to receive my first lesson in cockroach craft. Yashwant feeds them little balls of dough made from flour, boric acid, sugar and milk. They sounded rather good. One bite and the little critters explode or disappear into thin air – no one seems quite sure which. In the kitchen Yashwant was intent on his task. The ingredients were measured out with all the care of a bomb-maker. We made a stately tour of the apartments, depositing tiny balls of dough in corners where cockroaches might roam.

Over tea on the balcony Yashwant announced my full recovery when I had managed to drink three cups without any ill-effect. I told him about the large, glossy cockroaches that stalked the corridors and desks of *The Indian Express*. He told me that it was to be expected in a place staffed by people who knew no better than to throw their food around. He had a vision of the offices as being full of unruly kindergarten characters, with filthy hands and faces, who left trails of uneaten food in their wake as they rushed from one unfinished story to the next. He was not so far off the mark.

Later that week, when I felt well enough to brave the streets, I was dispatched with a large bag of anti-cockroach dough and instructed to scatter it liberally wherever there were journalists with lax eating habits. Yashwant did not think that it would be such a bad thing if a few journalists ate some of the dough balls by mistake.

There seemed to be no harm in trying to take on the cockroach population of Bahadur Shah Zafar Marg. It might provide material for a diary piece for Sourish – 'Cockroaches spontaneously combust at *The Indian Express*'. Even if it never got into print it might make him laugh. Ram Kumar was made to oil his way down the stairs behind me, bearing the bag before him. As soon as Yashwant was out of sight, he began to complain that we had not taken the lift. I took the bag from his hand and ran the rest of the way down. As I fled I heard him clear his throat and spit loudly.

The entrance hall of the *Express* building was both a playpen and a race track for cockroaches, a great feeding ground supplied with gobs of rice and *dhal* that fell from the pressed-leaf plates of whoever was making a protest at the paper that day. Each new party of protesters coming up the steps, their *tiffin* tins stuffed to bursting, was a feast-in-waiting for the cockroaches. This was where I would start.

Without taking the precaution of signing in at the desk I settled myself on one of the reception benches and began to pluck small bits from the great lump of dough and roll them into little balls. Several cockroaches sauntered past, full-bellied and unaware of the terrorist in their midst. I was so absorbed in my task that I failed to notice that I too was being scrutinized.

Just as I laid my first bombs I was seized by a security guard and marched smartly out on to the street, the bag of dough hanging from my wrist. The guard was new to the job and was determined to go by the book. No, I could not try to prove who I was by getting the receptionist to back me up. No, I could not ask Sourish to be called to give a sworn affidavit on my behalf. No, I could not crawl across the hall in supplication. The bag of dough or 'God is knowing what' and I could just get out of there, chip chop, end of story.

I made a bid for freedom and managed to make it back to the top step where I jumped up and down to try and attract the attention of the receptionist. She sipped at her *chai* and waved back with a happy smile. My arresting officer was upon me.

'Stopping this now.' He stamped his foot.

'No, you don't understand what I was doing.' I started to take the bag of dough off my wrist to show him.

'No, no, stopping this.'

'It is for stopping cockroaches.'

'Cocking nothing, stop now.' He was beginning to look desperate.

A dishevelled beetle bomber retreated to the rickshaw and Bushan. It was he who delivered my copy that day while I played with my bag of dynamite in the relative safety of the back of the rickshaw. Yashwant was not informed of my abject failure at pest control.

Out of the false starts, the muddy *masala* of cultural misunderstandings, a routine had evolved at Hailey Road. The kitchen, the sorcerer's den, Dhan Singh's domain of *dhal* wizardry, had been strictly out of bounds in the early days. Guests made requests from the dignified remove of the hall or the sitting-room. Not this guest. Little battles raged. I adopted encircling tactics with packets of cardamom seeds, nonchalantly dropped in as I passed by; two-pronged attacks, fresh ginger root in one hand and a bag of apples in the other; full frontal offensives, diving straight for the kettle, matchbox in hand. Usually I lost these skirmishes but I kept the campaign in sight. Initially I was only allowed to watch from the doorway as the cardamom and ginger were chopped into the bubbling pan of *chai*, or as an apple was washed with painful slowness, placed on a plate, on a white cloth, on a tray with a napkin and knife. Once, when the heat was too much for etiquette, I grabbed the apple off the plate and bit into it. Dhan Singh stood, tray in hand, one eyebrow raised. Such impulsiveness cost me days of coaxed progress. Usually I would just stand a couple of subtle steps in from the doorway and watch Dhan Singh create 'vig cutlit' from fading peas, limp carrots, relatively unscathed potatoes, spices and breadcrumbs, or flip *chapātis* with the deft slap of practice between the bases of his spread thumbs. As the weeks passed he became more expansive, delivering little culinary flourishes and gummy smiles for the benefit of his audience; an extra twirl of the dolly *chapāti* rolling-pin or a risqué flip of the toast on the old Army-issue camp stove.

The sorcerer's apprentice was slowly installed. First I had to master the trick of lighting the gas stove – a torn strip of newspaper screwed into a taper, the small camp stove turned on until the coil glowed, the taper lit from the coil, the gas stove lit by the taper. Matches were too easy, too quick, not at all the right thing. The Frigidaire (a capital letter for the great baby-blue cabinet of ingredients for spells) had a lock and a key. Every time the door was shut the key had to be turned, even if the ingredient that had been taken out was to be replaced immediately. Tea had to be made in a pot and placed under a cosy, regardless of an ambient temperature of 120°F. Fruit was to be peeled and laid out on a plate set on a white cloth. Any transgression meant a restriction of privileges. The eating habits of the sorcerer's apprentice – the desire for fresh fruit, raw vegetables and tea made with strange herbs, no milk or ladles of sugar – were regarded as a sign of insanity.

By succumbing to a filthy disease from the north-east (an area of mad tribals who, in Dhan Singh's opinion, probably ate their own children – raw), I proved beyond reasonable doubt that my eating habits were worse than dubious; they were dangerous. A period of best behaviour had to be observed until I shone with such health that I was, little by little, allowed to resume the strange rituals. Dhan Singh watched and chuckled, bewildered that someone who, in his eyes, must surely have God's own amount of money should seem so proficient in menial domestic tasks. Any attempts to explain that I did not need to be waited on hand and foot were pointless. Still Dhan Singh would nudge a 'vig cutlit' or some *ghee*-drenched *rogan josh* towards my plate on the

Hailey Road in Hindi, in English and in Urdu

off chance that I might pop them in my mouth in a vague moment. I usually did and it made us both very happy.

Further amazement was caused by my passion for yoga, which seemed even harder to grasp than my behaviour in the kitchen. Each session was meant to begin with the sun salutations, supposedly fluid movements, the dance of the body, a flow of limbs. Fat chance. At Jodhpur Apartments there was a great deal of thumping and gasping and a certain lack of seamless fluidity. Then the giggling would start outside the door. Slips of girls in floating saris, ankle-bells tinkling as they skipped up and down the corridors, wanted to see the *farangi* contortions. Any excuse would do. Just a knock at the door, maybe to collect washing or drop it off, a phone call to answer, a request to fill in a cheque deposit form or to write a name in English. Always the tinkling girls were aided and abetted in their distracting tactics by the male servants lurking in the shadows. They never tired of the joke. Each time it made me feel a little less delicate, a little more shackled as they tripped off down the corridors, their bells laughing, their spare bodies genuinely fluid beneath their thin, washworn saris.

Then yoga made a sideways move into *The Indian Express*. I was

having one of those girl-to-girl conversations about yoga outside
Sourish's office, the sort of conversation that men have the unerr-
ing ability to tune into above the din of air-conditioners, printers
and caterwauling *chai* boys.

The story of yoga mornings at Jodhpur Apartments was being
lavishly embellished for the benefit of one of the young journalists. She was the perfect audience, laughing at parts that were not
even very funny. I got carried away. As I finished, the polite journalist laughed once more and took my hand, probably out of relief
and gratitude that the tale was over.

'So you know about yoga,' Sourish called from inside his office.

'That was girls' talk.'

'No such thing in a features department.'

'Yes, I practise yoga.'

'Good, you can write about it.'

'An Indian should write about it. You've been at it for thousands of years. We're recent converts and probably still getting
lots of bits wrong.'

'It would be good from your point of view.'

'I'm not a cheesecloth hippy.'

'A whatie?'

'I mean I'm not a remnant from the Seventies who meditates
on Goan beaches in a crochet bikini.'

'What?' Sourish stopped typing.

'I do it because it means I have a bit of India on hand when
London makes me itchy. It's probably saved me a fortune in
therapy too.'

'And Delhi doesn't?'

'What?'

'Make you itch.'

'No.'

'God, you English really are sadists.'

'Yup.'

'Okay, okay, so where did you learn our ancient yoga?'

'In London.'

Now Sourish laughed. 'So now that you have sorted out our

north-eastern problem what is your next story then, if it is not going to be about yoga?'

Five years before I had climbed into the Spiti valley, a lost place, nudging right up against the Tibetan border in the High Himalayas. The valley had been shut off from the outside world for seventy years: 1992 had marked the first tentative reopening of the area. And in that valley there was a Buddhist monastery that had been there for nearly a thousand years. There a small boy with the eyes of an old man had asked me to come back for the millennium celebrations of the *gompa*.

Now the monastery's big celebration was about to happen and it had turned into a national event. His Holiness the Dalai Lama was to spend three weeks at the festivities giving a *kalachakra*, an initiation to encourage world peace and communication between all warring nations. It was to be the closest the Tibetan monk had come to his homeland since he had escaped into exile in India in 1959.

Stories had been circulating in the press about the thousands of pilgrims who were planning to make the trek to the Spiti valley, many of them hoping to see their leader for the first time. The Dalai Lama had been issuing special passes that would allow people out of Tibet for the duration of the festival. Then they had to return to Tibet. The Chinese had agreed as a token humanitarian gesture. For the first time His Holiness would be in a position to talk freely with his people in a valley that abutted his homeland.

Since relations between India and China were delicate, thousands of police and military were being drafted into the area to control what the government assumed was going to be one long breach of national security.

I waved my arms about in an attempt to convey the enormity of the place to Sourish. He looked indifferent, then faintly interested and finally resigned.

'I take it from all the waving about that you would like to go.'

'Yes please.'

He finally agreed with the proviso that I had to secure my own press pass, pay for my travel and write a story, not a diatribe. There was a further condition. If he was to let me write this story I had to return to the fold afterwards and write about yoga.

'And don't go flying off on any Tibetan refugee causes and telling people that you are with *The Indian Express*.'

I gave him a lightweight sort of promise.

The Dust Monk in God's Library

AFTER A PARTICULARLY bad bout of dysentery Kipling had travelled along the route that leads up to the Spiti valley. He had joined a newly wed couple, the de Braths, and Dorothea Darbishoff, otherwise known as Dolly Bobs, a feisty little mare who snorted and shied at every turn so that poor, bruised Kipling spent more time on the road than astride her. As the third member on a honeymoon trip he was acutely aware of his loneliness, but there was solace among the scented deodars, on the rough scree slopes where great Himalayan eagles drift on thermal cushions, on the jutting rocks above the roaring gorges of the River Sutlej, in the beautiful, pale-featured faces of the mountain women, weighed down with great headdresses of uncut turquoise, coral, pearls and silver. He saw all these things and stored them away for use in the pages of books to come.

My journey to Spiti began at New Delhi railway station. Ram Kumar was with me. That particular morning he was about as popular as Dolly Bobs, in fact less so because I am at least fond of horses. Ram Kumar had cracked his *chappal* against my door an hour earlier than necessary, at about 5 a.m, revenge for a mild altercation the previous evening. Nothing was mild in Ram Kumar's book and he was not one to turn the other cheek, a useful trait for a man considering a future that was not satisfied by the intrigues and double-entry account books of Hailey Road.

My punishment was to sit at New Delhi station before dawn waiting for a train that would not leave for an hour and a half. The shoe-cleaning boys came by, each downcast by the filthy state of my footwear, each flourishing his wooden box of tricks. Finally, worn down by the boredom of the wait, I gave in. The boy crouched at my feet, his backbone arching through his shirt. He only managed to get one shoe at a time: the other I hung on to with tightly scrunched toes. Those shoes may have been filthy but they were precious to me. Two shoes simultaneously surrendered are two shoes lost.

Another half hour dragged by as I waited, clean-shod now and wrapped in a Kashmiri shawl like all the other displaced characters draped over boxes or propped against the station walls.

Will was on time. Of course he was, he used to be in the army. Now here he was, still the same punctilious, punctual Will, a gangly English photographer striding up the platform in the same way that he strides up mountains or into cocktail parties – shoulders slightly bent from carrying cameras, eyes always scanning the crowd for a good face to photograph. We had worked together in India before. He and three others had climbed into the Spiti valley with me in 1992.

A *chai-wallah*, moving at speed to keep up with the loping giant, bumped into me as Will stopped to field a selection of station porters carrying his bags. Hot tea flew through the air and glasses rolled.

'A bit early for tea.' Will stooped down to kiss me. 'So what time is our train?' He ran his hand over freshly shorn hair. 'Like the hair?'

'It's a bit severe perhaps. The train goes in about twenty minutes. Maybe we should wait until we find our seats before the next round of *chai*.'

'Well, if you don't like the hair I think the Dalai Lama might. Very monkish – I thought it would be good to blend in.' He patted his dark red shirt, the same shade as the robes of Tibetan monks.

'Will, you're six foot two. You'd have to chop your legs off to blend in.'

He shrugged and began to herd his collection of porters towards the platform for Chandigarh, our first stop.

The Shatabdi Express, the bullet-train of North India, whipped us from New Delhi to Chandigarh, capital of the Punjab, in three hours. It would have been even quicker but for the first consti-pated push out of town past the rat-pocked banks where bloated rodents scurried in and out of the rubbish that forms the shifting foundations of the railside shanty towns. Their male inhabitants crouched beside the track, faeces al fresco, staring intently at the train with no hint of embarrassment, warming their balls in the first sun while emptying their bowels. There were no women to be seen. A peacock in a leafless tree looked on. On board, hermeti-cally sealed in an air-conditioned coach, Will was making the best of the metallic tea and chilli omelette. He produced a clever little gadget to snip the corner off the sachet of tomato sauce. The small child next to him was not so careful, squirting his face and Jurassic Park T-shirt with the entire contents of first his and then his sister's sachets. He started to cry and was immediately joined by his sachet-deprived sister.

Chandigarh is a shoe-box city, purpose-built by a Frenchman with a dream. Some see the city as Le Corbusier's great joke played upon the Punjab. As you try and wander the streets you realize why. Chandigarh has no soul, no pulse, in fact not much sign of life at all. In trying to create a spacious capital the architect came up with a series of military-style cantonment areas just in case the Punjab should ever try and forget that it was once a part of the barrack-spined British Empire.

In search of transport for the next leg of the journey Will and I arrived at the taxi services of one more Mr Singh. This Sikh gen-tleman wished us to bounce on the back seat of every Ambassador taxi in his impressive stable to check for 'most comfortable seating as imagination can bring'. Once our selection had been made he was keen that we should join him in his office while several of his staff were ordered to polish the chosen vehicle. They set about their task using spit and small handkerchiefs.

'You see, dear friends, I only wish that you are being seen on the road in the utmost of style and comfort,' said Mr Singh, waving towards his polishing minions. 'Now you will take tea as a sign of our business doings.'

Tea and business doings done we set off in the freshly shined car. Our driver liked to go gently along the straight lines of Le Corbusier's roads, but he felt it important to accelerate into all junctions and roundabouts. In fits and starts we left Chandigarh behind and headed out along the road that passes the wedding-cake *gurudwaras*, the temples of the Sikh heartland where one of their greatest gurus, Guru Gobind Singh, the warrior saint, called his men to arms in the fifteenth century with the five Ks. *Kesh*, uncut hair. No self-respecting fighting man can go into battle with a short back and sides and a baby-smooth face. Flying hair and a beard are much more alarming for the enemy. *Kang*, the comb. The flying hair and beard have to be kept in order. When a Sikh unties his turban and combs out the fall of hair, it is a heroic and beautiful thing. *Kara*, the steel band on the wrist, to protect the raised fist in the face of attack. *Kirpan*, the dagger, always to be worn. *Kach*, underpants, never to be caught down. The plains of the Punjab are dusty and men of war cannot march with sand-chapped buttocks.

As the *gurudwaras* and the turbans fell away, the road cut in from the plains towards the hills and there was a new smell – of cool clouds, leaf mould, resin, the green fingers of deodars – and a whiff of unfamiliar wool from the coats, shawls and blankets of higher altitudes.

We paused in the Kangra valley. This was only a fraction of the way to Spiti but we were tired, for once into the hills the roads had erupted in monsoon blisters and trenches. Progress slowed to ten miles an hour, every crow mile becoming a series of switch-backs chipped out of the sides of the mountains. Will has a tall man's back. Every bounce and bump in the road hurt. So we side-tracked to Kangra, to the village of Pragpur, a place where old men with inside-out faces wear even older regulation British army jerseys over *dhal*-spotted *kurta* pyjamas. They gather under the *peepul* tree, the broad-branched heart of the village, crouching down, sucking on *biris* through curled hands. They watch the young men in jeans and T-shirts who drink Coca Cola and check out the passing girls from behind cheap sunglasses. The old men stare as long and as hard as they want at the pretty young figures swinging by. Age allows that.

The houses are mud-plastered, a mixture of cow dung, pine needles, chopped straw and chaff. Donkeys polish the cobbled streets with hooves hot-shod from the farrier's fire at 35p a set. The going rate in England is about £60. Aubergines piled high in the vegetable stores are polished with rough linen cloths until the shine is so bright that passing dogs shy away from the gruesome fish-eyed reflections of their own snouts. There are not many Pragpurs left.

When Simla was the summer capital of the British government in India the sassy young men of Pragpur left home and headed there to make their names as lawyers and bankers and friends of the *sahibs*. They came back to their village and built Italianate mansions as a mark of their success. The British left and the lawyers and bankers of Pragpur joined those who hammered the new India from the anvil of Delhi. As they shaped the future in the big city their grand houses in Pragpur emptied and the monsoons sucked away the plaster and crumbled the bricks. These great houses then began to fill up with new tenants, many families dividing the houses between them, unconcerned when lumps of ceiling or wall fell away. They were happy to pay their pre-Independence fixed rents of just a few rupees each month for properties that had once been the pride of the new men of India.

And when sometimes the owners retired and felt the pull of the old place they could not return. The tenant families sat merrily amidst the falling mortar and refused to budge. 'No can do, Raja-Babu, we're here to stay,' they said, pulling their nice bright nylon cardigans around their *salwar kameez* and throwing another chair leg on the fire that blackened the marble surround, carved for another man in another time.

One grandson of an Indian judge knighted by the Empire was

not to be deterred. The gardener, a certain Milki Ram, who had styled himself the new lord of the manor, was forcibly evicted using the brawn of some local likely lads, egged on by bellies full of booze, and 'The Judge's Court', a manor-house in a small place of tall tales, was nursed back to life.

We came to Pragpur and sank into this house surrounded by its orchard. Fruit fell everywhere: oranges, lemons, limes, pomelos, mangoes, grapes, peaches, plums, apricots and lychees. High-hipped bullocks pulled a wooden plough so that wheat could be planted, wheat that went into the *chapātis* made on an open fire under an old grape vine.

And then Spiti began to call. We climbed back into the Ambassador and headed for Simla, still accelerating around each hell-bend of the Himalayan corniche.

Simla is a rambling place that freefalls from the spine of a mountain. Down narrow alleys and up steep ones, through stair-ways and corridors, directed and redirected, we sought the Assistant Deputy Director Tourism in a town of assistant deputy deputies all twice removed from anyone at all – a wedding cake of bureaucracy as towering as the altitude. His desk appeared out of nowhere just as we were giving up: his desk and a long queue of razor-tempered Israelis and *wunderkinder* Swiss flashing passports like loaded weapons. We were all there to get visas into Spiti. Just as the Tibetans had to be granted permission so too did the raggy-taggy foreigners in their cobbled-together clothes, with their cow-byre hair and thousand-dollar cameras. Quite right too. An expensive camera is no meal ticket to compassion.

Fill in this, that and that. Yes, five of them and five passport photos. The Israelis shouted. They had already got two passport pictures. The Swiss looked glum and stamped out to the smiling photo- and copier-*wallahs* along the corridors, fingering their bank rolls under their *kurtas*.

Tomorrow, *yaar*, *yaar*, come back tomorrow, visas will be all tip-top ready by then.

The Israelis wanted them on the spot. The Swiss should have had them the day before. Will and I wiggled our way back through the alleys to drink coffee at the United Indian Coffee House.

Here fresh-faced lieutenants had once brushed the ankles of the major's lovely young wife, sipped coffee, talked, stroked and schemed for a tumble while the major took parade. Still the clipped tones of the sepia *sahibs* fill the cloudy air of the coffee house. The steam is just from the coffee now, though who is to know? The brown *sahibs* have taken the place of the frisky lieutenants who were packed up, shipped out, sent home. These are old boys who were taught the manners and moods of the ruling order when they were just slips of lads. Clinging to that way of life and carrying a strange smell of desertion about their well-pressed clothes, they sit over their coffee cups with eyes turned out by time. A hint of it comes from the brasso polish on their blazer buttons, from the glassy finish on the tips of their brown brogues. 'Taught us all this and then buggered off, not *pukkah* at all, Johnny, not *pukkah* at all.' And the policemen in starched-fan turbans outside at Scandal Point still direct the traffic wearing white gloves.

Just a few hundred years from East India Company touchdown to Johnny-go-home. Only a pebble in the vast pond. The last of the ripples are fading into the stillness of the water. The white gloves, the memsahibs, Victoria Regina, Kaiser-i-Hind have been sucked away like all the empires before them, and the old boys with polished buttons are left to watch the structure crumble, to become the mothballs in the mould.

'What's the matter with you?' asked Will.

I could not seem to get out of bed. I too was stuck in the time-warp, seduced by the corseted ectoplasms foxtrotting on dear departed parquet floors, pinned to my pillow by the past.

'Can you get up?'

'Not up as in the vertical sense, but I can crawl.'

'I'm going to get you some Flagyll.' Urgh, Flagyll, the most fearsome antibiotic of them all, no longer sold in virtually any other country.

'I can't take it, I'm allergic to it.'

'So are you going to crawl to Spiti then?'

'I suppose I could.' I was too weak to think beyond crawling to the bathroom and back.

'We're leaving the day after tomorrow. I am going to have some lunch. Do you want some?' Will had his hands on his hips.

'I don't think so.'

Will looked worried.

I had acquired another companion in Assam. Now it had an official name – giardia, a stinking disease and a gobbler of energy. When Will returned with the Flagyll, I took it, desperate to get to Spiti and aware that Will was being forced to travel with a vomiting, flatulent sulphur cloud.

At some point on the road to Spiti it began to rain. It could have been the first night or maybe the second. The passing of time had become somewhat casual. Bumper to bumper the pilgrim buses ploughed along the mountain road, hundreds of exhausted windscreen wipers sweeping drunkenly across smeared windscreens, thousands of bodies pressed together, doubling the official capacity of every bus in the winding convoy.

At the front of local buses there is a little back-to-front dicky seat for the driver's pal, the small-bottomed provider of cigarettes, sweets and gossip to entertain the man at the wheel. For the journey to Spiti the seat was ours, Will's and mine, six foot two Will and pear-hipped me, cheek to cheek, shoulder to chest. We were going to drive through the night. Day or night it made no difference. The antibiotics were making me sick and I seemed to be developing flu. Half-way through a spell of darkness the driver decided to stop on a bleak stretch of road lined on either side with a few blank-eyed houses.

Two hours on, two hours off, that was the deal made by military man Will. I had the first two hours in the little seat while Will roamed the streets. Bang on time he returned to find me crunched in sick sleep.

'My go.'

'So I'm going outside?' Compassion, please, compassion.

'Yup.' A deal is a deal.

It was raining. I lay down on a concrete slab and waited in the wet.

And after the rain and the interminable delay came a landslide. The busloads of pilgrims backed up, mile after mile, as the men from the Border Force Security – Roads went to work with a dumper truck and explosives.

Now we were quite high into the mountains and in the morning the icy cold of the night gave way to ferocious sun. As we waited, lorries jammed with fruit and vegetables for the festival began to compost. Tarpaulin covers were removed and apples, oranges, bananas, grapes and carrots changed hands for a few rupees. The travel-weary pilgrims did not bother to go more than a few paces from the road to empty bladders and bowels. Diarrhoea was rife, playing merry havoc with stomachs chilled by night, boiled by day, quenched with questionable water and fed on raw vegetables. Still there was optimism in the air. We were all pilgrims, off to see the leader, the little man in robes the red of drying blood, Buddha's direct phone link.

A day later and the landslide was mined. Relief was marred by the filth the makeshift camp had left behind. The convoy stopped at a housing settlement for hydro-electric power workers. There was an immediate queue at the tap, the foreign tourists clutching sponge bags, the native pilgrims scrubbing at their teeth with *neem* tree twigs.

The last stretch. Kipling's Kim had ridden through this same landscape with his travelling companion, the old lama:

> Glancing back in the twilight at the huge ridges behind him and the faint, thin line of the road whereby they had come, he would lay out, with a hillman's generous

> breadth of vision, fresh marches for the morrow; or, halting in the neck of some uplifted pass that gave on Spiti and Kulu, would stretch out his hands yearningly towards the high snows of the horizon . . . All day long they lay like molten silver under the sun, and at evening put on their jewels again.

The Border Patrol post that marked the entrance to the valley consisted of just two small huts manned by tired men with thick stubble and thin patience. Each pilgrim had to pass through the huts, every passport and visa had to be checked and stamped. We were nearly there but not quite. There was a security alert. Some of the special compassionate passes granted to Tibetans by the Dalai Lama were just not quite special enough for the Border Police that day. Drilled and drilled again into believing that every wide-browed Tibetan was probably a Chinese spy, they were in a take-no-chances kind of mood. Now there were thousands of the smiling spies lined up on the edge of their valley of dreams. The police said no, the sacred permissions were not worth the paper they had been written on. Signed by the Dalai who? Worth thousands at a Buddhist fund-raiser on Long Island but no good, no way, not today. Back you go, you slant-eyed spies, you. We have Mr President coming for this jollification, we're not taking any risks with you lot. V.V.V.V.I.P coming this way. Back to your yaks and your rosaries. A foreign tourist, yes sir, how green is your dollar? Green enough for me. *Yaar*, sir, through you go.

The Tibetans lined up across the road and sat down in protest. Some were monks, some nuns, some just ordinary people on the pilgrimage of a lifetime. They sat in prayer. An hour of ineffectual bargaining passed. The police shouted and the Tibetans sat in silence, except for one young monk with jug ears. He spoke quietly to the police and they ranted back at him. He spoke Tibetan, they Hindi. Nothing was achieved. Those in the silent protest bowed their heads and the dollar tourists looked on, uncomfortable voyeurs.

Then the buses started up in unison and began to move towards the sit-in. As peacefully as they had sat down, the Tibetans parted to let the buses through. The shouting drivers shut their mouths and, for the first time, their rude horns were still.

Three Tibetans had buried themselves under rugs at the back of our bus. The other passengers pressed around them, unsure how to behave, secretly terrified of being pulled into someone else's fight. We were so nearly there.

A border guard whacked the side of the bus. The brakes engaged. The three Tibetans were dragged off and no one made a move to intercede; too foreign and too afraid.

Tabo is a small village on the flood plain of the Spiti river. If you climb the valley on the other side of the river and throw a stone it might land in Tibet. It is a place perpetually blasted by the swirling *wullie-was* of the high plateau, tarantella winds that spin dust into every pore and line the lungs with the sediment of the old river bed. There used to be just two streets in the village – one leading to the monastery, the other leading away. Flat-roofed houses lined the two streets. One of them was the post office where I had played five-card stud with under-employed postal workers four years before. Another was the village shop where the novice monks bought stick jaw, Indian toffee, that yanked out their milk teeth. The *gompa* was the heart of the village but it was unlike other Buddhist monasteries. Its smooth-shouldered walls of sand plaster looked more Aztec than Tibetan. The pulse of the *gompa* was the flying footfall of the young monks, boys running to and from classes and meals. Wind and dust play tag at Tabo. If you want to know which way they blow, take a look at the prayer flags in the central courtyard or at the monks' airborne robes. They only ever blow one way, always into your face.

Four years was not so long, but everything had changed except the wind. Welcome to the Tabo Millennium. Now the village was surrounded by acre upon acre of tented camps. There were great aeroplane hangars full of beds stacked a family high, flanked by bath huts, all mod. cons. they said. Middle-echelon pilgrims got middle-ranking tents with a lower head count per square foot. 'Delux' camping entitled the richer pilgrims to a shorter walk to the loos. Five-star 'Supadelux' offered yet more space and as much chat as you fancied from the fast-talking, leather-jacketed Kashmiris running the show. Whatever the choice, the pervasive dust came as standard.

Will rebelled. He was not going to listen to the gibberish designed to flatter pretty Israeli tourists into parting company with their dollars and their underwear. He was not going to submit his lenses to gritty hell. He struck out on his own and found a Tibetan home in the village with a grain store to spare.

'We can clean it. It doesn't look great at the moment but it'll scrub up. Come on, it's quite a long walk.' Will collected his bags and picked up one of mine as well. Gratitude made me retch. After fifty-two hours in transit we had arrived.

The outskirts of the village had become a makeshift bazaar. There was a shop selling nothing but blankets, another piled high with Tibetan relics. Yet another sold all the things you might have left behind – stoves, soap, pans, pots, pillows and bedrolls. A bunker building was draped with the interstate and international telephone signs. Drifting groups of Indians, Tibetans and white trash in too-short shorts circled hastily erected cafés. One thing was clear in my nauseated haze; there were large crowds of policemen everywhere.

At last down a narrow passage and round a corner, we found the grain store – four mud walls, a mud floor liberally scattered with insect corpses, live relatives munching on the dead, two windows without glass, two *charpais*, strangely stained. Too tired to care we lay down on the dirty string beds and fell asleep.

During the first few days of the festival we set up house with new mattresses and pillows, carriers to collect water from the communal pump, a bucket for washing and a broom. There was nothing we could do to improve on the long-drop loo that was shared by our landlord and the other four surrounding houses. The makeshift arrangement was fine when it was only being used by the five families. But now there were pilgrims packed into every inch of floor space. Fifteen monks had set up home on the roof. There was an extended Tibetan family on the top floor, the owners were in the middle, some Indians were camping in the stable and Will and I had the grain store – a few too many for the long drop, especially with a roof full of monks with a casual attitude and aim when it came to lavatorial hygiene. Will and the other men had it easy. The girls tied handkerchiefs around their faces and tried not to breathe in.

Will had two missions in Tabo: the taking of great photographs and the search for the company of Buddhists with a sense of fun, preferably blonde ones. I had three: washing, writing and a third that turned up unannounced.

There was a queue at the vegetable store just a little way down the road from the house, though everyone seemed to queue out of habit now rather than for any particular reason. A couple of Tibetan women near the front were losing patience. They had queued enough. We had only recently parted company at the line-up for water, and that was at the end of a day spent queuing for food, benediction, ablution and now vegetables. Someone inside was taking up too much time and making people laugh.

'What I am saying, guys, is that it was the talk of the valley because of your mangoes. Not just pancakes and special sauce but special, special sauce. Everyone had two loads. So I need mangoes and bananas and mangoes and more mangoes. Let me out there piled with mangoes. I'm cooking with love,' came the voice that was taking up too much time.

Johnny Whitright was perched on a jute sack. His long blond hair was tucked under a pirate-tied bandana. His glasses were smudged, bones jutted through his clothes, and his hands waved, flipping and flapping to demonstrate his pancake skill.

Johnny had followed the first of the pilgrims to set off from Dharamsala for the festival. When he arrived in Tabo he met a Tibetan-Spiti man called Peme-La, a sharp man who knew a money-spinner when he saw one. Peme-La had planned to open a Tibetan café in the side of his home that just happened to be on the main route from the village to the *gompa*. His menu was limited: *thukpa*, Tibetan broth with vegetables and noodles, *momos*, vegetables, mutton or yak meat in steamed dumplings, and vegetable chowmein – just the same as the countless other Tibetan cafés opening from doorways and courtyards all over Tabo. With Johnny's arrival the café's horizons broadened – French toast, pancakes, cakes and porridge, fare that would bring in the raggy-taggy foreigners who were ready to pay huge premiums for a small reminder of home amid the dust and the dumplings. Peme-La had made rapid mental calculations and had worked out that the emaciated Johnny was definitely worth more than his fading weight in gold. And all this crazy, gaunt hippy wanted was bed and board. He was going to be cooking for love. He just wanted the pilgrims to go to their leader with their bellies filled with good *karma* from Johnny's kitchen. Beneath his yak-trimmed coat and tall astrakhan hat Peme-La was a burgeoning entrepreneur. Peme-La could translate Johnny's cooking into a Rolex and Ray-Bans.

Peme-La's Café opened before most of the others. News of the gangly cook spread fast. Johnny's pancakes with special sauce became a mealtime mantra for the hollow-cheeked hippies stripped to the bone by too many months on rice and *dhal*. They jammed themselves on to the scrubbed wooden benches of the café, thigh bone to thigh bone, eating banana cake with butter frosting washed down with Johnny's Himalayan *caffè latte*, a double shot of precious Nescafé and bubbled yak milk, thick and rich. The raggy-taggys opened their eyes wide and begged for more.

Johnny had too much to do – cakes to bake, batter to beat, frosting to invent, charm to scatter. Peme-La's wife was glad to have Johnny sleeping on her floor and laying the golden egg but she was not going to help him whip up his fiddly *farangi* fare. If Tibetan food was good enough for her it was certainly good enough for the rest of the world.

Then Evya came down from the hills, striding out of an illustrated children's bible with curling beard, spirals of disciple hair, leather sandals, olive skin, olive eyes, strong, lean legs girded in rainbow cottons. Here was a sous-chef of startling proportions with a sense of humour as wild as his curls. But still Johnny needed more help.

Biblical Evya, Johnny Whitright and cake

I joined the staff of Peme-La's Café the following morning.
Here was a microcosm of the festival, where Tibetans, Indians,
foreigners, monks and laymen met to break bread and eat cake.
They were not all so easy to love. Some intransigent Swiss and
fanatical French insisted on St Germain standards. Israelis

97

ordered things that were just not on the menu – boiled egg and raw vegetable salad is just a pain at fifteen thousand feet with thirty orders pinned to the wall. The eggs take twenty minutes to boil and the raw vegetables are too fiddly to wash and shred.

Johnny cooked with tenderness. After all, he was feeding the people who were going to pray for world peace. Better to feed people with a clean heart than pray with a clouded one, said Robert, a Buddhist monk from Holland, as he tucked into his second slice of coffee cake. Would he notice the tears I had cried into the cake mix or Evya's laughter in the coffee cup?

At least Will had free food. For those in the kitchen it was impossible to sit down at one of the scrubbed tables in the café and eat the food that had been under our fingernails all day. We foraged elsewhere. The rooftop monks of our house often ate at another Tibetan café, just down the road. When in Tabo, follow the monks. There is no stinting on ingredients where the robes feed. The kitchen was filled by a great bear of a Tibetan, his hair tucked away under a Rastafarian woolly bonnet. He chopped vegetables with a big, square blade, wound noodles from hand to hand like flying yarn and made fresh *momos* for each order. This was his art, the food of his culture. This really was cooking with love.

His Holiness the Dalai Lama came in a helicopter. Saucepans and plates clattered to the floor when we heard the thuk, thuk, thuk of the chopper blades. His route to the *gompa* was lined twenty deep. Johnny and I found an empty corner. For some reason no one seemed to think that he would pass the spot. He had to, it was right beside the door of No. 1, Nirvana, His Holiness's board and lodging for the festival. As he moved through the crowd he was hidden from most by the density of the throng, his head and shoulders not high enough to swim above the sea of faces. His arm was raised in front of his face, a corner of his robe protecting him from the dust. As he reached the door he turned and his hand came down. Johnny and I were right beside him.

That afternoon a Tibetan who had rented the cow byre in the house next door to us was arrested by the police as a Chinese spy, last heard screaming for a rebate on his rent as he was dragged away. Across town an oracle went into a powerful trance and foresaw a catastrophe. The Border Police and the Office of His Holiness started to argue about who was allowed press passes to sit up front for the teachings in the *gompa*.

Peme-La's Café became a melting-pot of gossip. Some said Richard Gere had flown in. Others said it was Harrison Ford. If they had, they were camping in the helicopter because no one had seen hide or hair of the Tinsel Town Buddhists. Some said that the dust had been so thick in the afternoon that they could easily have slipped by without anyone noticing. As pancakes and *caffè latte* poured from the kitchen the chatter rose but there was not a word about global peace or Tibet in pain, just 'More carrot cake' and 'Have you heard . . . ?'

The Dalai Lama surveyed the tented acreage and went quietly to his meditation.

Now Tabo was ready to burst. The supply lorries could not come in fast enough to refuel the hungry hordes in the cafés. A black market of stashed food supplies flourished. The hillside that overlooked the village bristled with people squatting among the rocks. The local authorities threw barrels of chlorine into the mountain streams in an attempt to protect those collecting water at the bottom from the dangers of Ablution Hill.

There were some caves half-way up the hill, old cells where the earliest monks of Tabo had made their homes. Families from surrounding villages and a few committed back-packers had moved in when they found that there was no more room in the local houses and that the tent prices were too high. Making their way back to their troglodyte homesteads in the dark they ran the stinking gauntlet of mounting piles of shit and crouched toileters straining under cover of night.

The old telegraph office on the outskirts of the village had become the communication centre. Nobody could play the smart card with a mobile phone or a modem link because there were no signals, no mains supplies. We were finally off the technological superhighway. All links with the world beyond the peaks had to be conducted via one of two telephones. The foreign journalists, each believing that their story or their publication was more important than anyone else's, jostled and shouted. The Indian reporters seemed happy enough to chat and wait and drink more *chai*. They had their revenge. The two telephones were next door to each other, barely a foot apart. If an Indian was on one line and a foreign journalist on the other, the Indian would shout so loud that conversation on the neighbouring phone was impossible.

Sourish could not hear a word that I was saying and all I could hear was the bubbling and gurgling of the interstate line.

The second arena for the press pack was outside the Dalai Lama's residence. His Holiness's right-hand man, The Translator, was the giver of press passes. Each request had to come with a convincing story, a compassionate angle, the backing of a respected publication and several passport photographs.

The Translator was the man to watch. Will and I learnt his daily routine, his favoured time for breakfast, lunch and tea. The poor man was stalked as his stomach growled from prayer hall to bathhouse and back. We had no omnipotent international publication deal to brandish. All we had was a book that I had written after that first climb into the valley in 1992. The cover photograph had been taken by Will. It showed the great door of the *gompa* being closed at sunset by one of the youngest monks, a boy in ochre robes. The young monk was still at the monastery, taller and pubescent now. Sweat broke out on his downy lip when he saw his picture. He became the novice supermodel when a couple of copies of the book made their way round from hand to hand. The words meant nothing, the pictures everything as the boys of the monastery identified themselves in Will's photographs. It was those powerful pictures that won us our press passes.

The Dalai Lama started to teach. He drew the lines of the *mandala*, a representation of the circular flow of the cosmos, the skeleton to be filled in with hair-fine lines of coloured sand. As the *mandala* grew so the teachings filled out the flesh on the bright bones. Steady hands bent over the Buddhist heart, steady words from a steady head.

At noon each day the teachings began. The café emptied as the brunch crowd took their alternative theories and bothersome bowels to the monastery courtyard. We kitchen staff would go to wash away our bad, sad thoughts of kerosene burns and fried-rice fingers, to be clean for the great teacher.

Like the fairytale world of Indian novelists or the chitter-chatter language of a child, the teachings had a vocabulary and rhythm of their own. Words familiar to the Buddhist ear but strange to a foreigner fell in waterfalls – Sharnam, Siddharta, Shanti, Shanti – sibillant sounds that sat in the particle cloud over our hot heads, caught in the shafts of sunlight that cut through the thin cotton awnings above the crowd.

The Dalai Lama sat as portrayed in red robes, with sloping shoulders, thick glasses pushed up against his nose, the corners of his eyes crinkling to match the ellipse of his smile. His speech soared and dropped, rolled up in a crescendo, then leapt off, swooping down to the pit of his stomach – Lhasa Tibetan, a gunfire language from the people of peace. The temporary refugees from the closed land understood his words. The rest of us relied on translations. In the case of the English speakers it was the voice of The Translator, the giver of passes, that guided us. His voice spread, butter in the sun, over the staccato chirping of the Tibetan tongue.

These were the *mandala* teachings, the highways and byways of the universe, the song of the stars. His Holiness looked out over the sea of people and said that we all talked too much, that the buzz from the cafés was inappropriate to meditation on the state of mankind. To prepare for the *kalachakra*, the initiation for peace, we should withdraw from the social world and centre ourselves. Tabo was not a bad place to do it, he said, as all the chatter just filled our lungs with dust. He called for a break and suggested that those who wanted to go to the loo should do so. His nose wrinkled and he chortled into his microphone. The Translator looked ruffled and hesitated. His Holiness slapped his thighs and popped back inside. The crowd looked on, too serious to laugh.

The café was temporarily in a subdued state, not because of the words from the Dalai Lama but because Johnny was sick, his body finally rebelling against his lifestyle of continual deprivation.

I found him lying on the floor. He was catatonic or comatose – it was hard to tell which. His ribs jutted under his skin, barely a layer between bone and air, the pale surface bluish grey, the same colour as the walls of his room or of his eyes.

'Johnny, you are really sick,' I said from the door.

'Hey, who says?' The eyes snapped open, still blue though redrimmed. 'I'm just dealing with my bad *karma*.' The eyes shut down.

'Come on, Johnny, this is serious. I think you should take a proper break. Evya can cover for you and I can do a bit.'

'What, no cakes, are you kidding?'

'Here.' I handed over my precious stash of vitamin pills, hoarded for the lean times. For Johnny this was a very lean stretch. 'Please take one of these a day and one of the arnica tablets to try and get your suppurating sores under control.'

'Hey, sweet thing, you know you can be really soft, you know? It's that voice, you gotta do something about it.'

'Thanks, Johnny. A voice is just a voice.'

'Go tell that to the babes on the sex phone lines.' He opened his eyes again.

'I don't think you are dying.'

'Come on, how can I die when His Holiness is about to start spinning for world peace?'

On a wall beside the café sat an old man with flying ears and a village drum. In those great ears were large silver loops weighted down with turquoise and coral, great chunks of it like so much ballast. His glasses were crooked and held together on one side with sticking plaster just as they had been four years before. The old man was called Tashi Zangpo and he came from the village of Mudh. He lived in the Blue House, the largest house in the village and the first place that we had reached on climbing into the valley in 1992. Tashi and his family had treated us as if we were the best toys they had ever been given. They never got tired of playing.

Bemused in a gentle mountain way by my enthusiasm at seeing him again he sat on the wall with a cup of tea from the café, slurping and nodding as he leafed through the book about that earlier trip. He stopped on each page as if he understood the English, almost as if the pattern of the words on the page was enough to satisfy his curiosity. His youngest son, Phunchok, the gap-toothed eleven-year-old of last meeting, was now a young man wearing a shiny bomber jacket and an almost ready-to-shave upper lip. He took a more worldly attitude and flipped past the text to the photographs. The old man beside him put his hands to his face and laughed. There was his kitchen in the Blue House, there was his family and, better than any of these, there he was standing in his fields with his younger brother, straight-backed in the ripe barley. His expression changed at the sight of this picture. He studied it close up then held the book away to get a full view. He patted the page in approval. Will had caught the gravitas that Tashi had been looking for, an image of a big man from a small village where the barley that he stood in was his own. Both men, tall Will, small Tashi, smiled at each other with that manly look of a deal well done.

Tashi and Phunchok were going back to the Blue House. They had come to the festival so that the old man could play his drum for His Holiness. Now that was done he had barley and wives and yaks to get back to. Mudh village was a two-day walk from Tabo. Tashi asked if we would like to return with them.

Johnny was sick and the kitchen was in uproar, but Evya shook his curls and said that it was all under control. A few days away,

Long, tall Will

no problem. The Johnny sympathy vote had inspired a few more smiling girls with curious tattoos to come forward as galley slaves. Peme-La's Café would not be short of staff or body art.

We walked out of the dense cloud of dust that cloaked Tabo. The quality of light changed and the river ran clean. On the valley sides were wild roses, their carmine colour faded to a dusty pink. There were no lorries, no queues for telephones, no shouting, no thick, stinking air.

We spent that night in a room above cows and donkeys. The house belonged to Tashi's cousin. As the neck of the valley narrowed and the villages got smaller, everyone was everyone else's cousin. We arrived in the dark and climbed the ladder to the room. The floor was covered in vegetables laid out to dry in bright battalions. Two half-strung badminton racquets hung on one wall, a Tibetan mandolin on another. There was a cupboard full of printed mantras bound in red silk, a drum hanging from the ceiling, some of the goat's hair still clinging to the stretched skin, a poster of two chubby Bollywood stars next to the mantras. A butter lamp burned dimly in front of a small Buddhist shrine. The smell of the animals came up through the floor, warm and grassy. We went to sleep in all our clothes listening to Tashi and Phunchok telling festival tales to the family in the kitchen across the mud corridor.

In the cold, aching morning I climbed down from the room through wedges of sun in which dust from the stable hung. Outside the house was grass and dew, and above rose the valley walls.

The bridge across the angry river had been washed away. Just one wire remained. Tashi and Phunchok lashed us to it with a rope and we pulled ourselves across, painfully, hand over hand. Momentum was lost in the middle at the lowest point of the wire. Bouncing there, just above the shouting brown water, drowning seemed easier than the drag up the other side.

Will's voice strained above the crashing and churning.

'Go on.'

Okay, Will, if you say so.

Old man Tashi, heavy blankets lashed to his back, scurried along the wire like a monkey, his weathered face tilted back to see where he was going. Perhaps he wasn't so old.

At the end of a day on the mountain, a long day on threading paths that only just stitch their way across rock slides from melting glaciers, we reached Mudh village. In the kitchen at the Blue House the cast was almost unchanged. Grandma was still bent over the same earthen pot, crooning into her hairy chin. Drunken Uncle Djorje was still swigging on hooch. But Tashi's elder son and his wife had brought a new jewel into the Blue House, Tashi's first grandson, a boy, Lobsang, a bright light.

As twilight came, the kitchen filled with girls from the fields, all long plaits and moon faces, come to hear the news of the festival. Mrs Tashi made *momos* over the fire that tasted of soot and the fields, and poured evil-tasting salt tea into dainty flowered cups. The baby Lobsang sat silent on my lap, staring with wide eyes.

Will and I were given the room on the roof, a new room built

THE DUST MONK IN GOD'S LIBRARY

since we were last there, with windows that looked up the valley to where we had first walked in over the high pass. Will woke early the next morning, his photographer's brain engaged, to catch the village as it yawned. I sat on a day bed outside the room in the first warmth of the sun and wrote. Phunchok came up the ladder and sat down beside me to watch. I smiled a tourist kind of smile. He reached bravely into his vocabulary.

'Are you married for Mr Will?'

'No, we are not married. We are friends and we work together.'

'My father is saying for you and Mr Will it would be a good thing.'

'He is more important to me as my friend.'

'You are good for to sit on my bed.'

'Thank you, Phunchok. I am sorry. I did not know it was your bed.'

'I think to make you happy.'

'Thank you, Phunchok, I am very happy.'

'I think to make you happy now.'

'Ah, Phunchok, I am happy as I am.'

There was a look of bemusement but he dug deep again.

'I think for you I am good and make big smile.'

Make big smile, what a pass. Remember that one, Phunchok.

'I am your friend,' I replied.

'I am thinking to make you very big friend.'

'I think friend is enough for me.'

'I and Mr Will same then.'

Smart kid.

I got up from the bed and took a long look out over the edge of the roof at the bright barley below. Phunchok sat on the bed alone.

'Today is my gainful day to college,' he announced.

'That is wonderful news, Phunchok. You must be so proud. Is it published in the newspaper?' There were no telephones in Mudh, the nearest line was in Tabo, if you felt inclined to fight it out with the journalists. College entry announcements seemed to be obvious fodder for a local paper.

Mudh village, hanging between the river and the peaks of the Pin valley

'No newspaper. One man from village council has the news to give.'

The valley drums had spread the word that Phunchok of Mudh had a place at college in Kaza, the area capital. There were no newspapers in Mudh. There were no newspapers in Tabo. The people of the valley had no interest in what the politicians were doing in Delhi. They were a mountain range away. The soaring financial houses of Bombay were half a subcontinent away. Tales from Communist Kerala in the toe of India meant nothing to a mountain man. There was no room for the puff of a newspaper in this rare air. In addition to this there was the problem of censorship. The Chinese had insisted that the printing presses of the border area be closely monitored. Any publication printed in

Tibetan or a similar dialect would be censored, suppressed or 're-edited', as the Chinese explained it so artfully.

At the mention of newspapers Phunchok roused himself from his semi-sexual reverie and disappeared down the ladder. He returned with a neat package covered in yellow silk and tied with green tassles, and unwrapped it. Inside were three newspapers – a copy of *The Times of India* and two of *The Indian Express*, all nicotine-stained with age. The date of the first was 31 January 1948, the day after Mohandas Karamchand Gandhi, the Mahatma, was assassinated, the news broken in stark words, black-and-white brutality. One issue of *The Indian Express* was dated 22 May 1991, the day after Rajiv Gandhi was killed on the threshold of what might have been his return to power. In contrast to the older paper, *The Express* had a huge canonizing photograph of Rajiv with a picture below of the carnage at the scene of his assassination: 'Rajiv killed in bomb blast. Blast rips off part of ex-PM's head.' There was the body of Rajiv Gandhi, contorted on the ground, part of his head blown away, the mangled leg of one of his security guards by his side and, most poignant of all, his gym shoes blown a few feet from his body, empty but neatly lined up side by side. The weather forecast at the bottom of the page was for 'a generally cloudy day with recurrence of rain possibly leading to thundershowers'.

The third paper was not from 1 November 1984, as I had assumed it would be, the day after Rajiv's mother, Mrs Indira Gandhi, the Prime Minister, had been gunned down by her own Sikh bodyguard. Perhaps Tashi, the paper collector of history, had felt that having the nation run by a woman was a step too far and not an example to be held up in the village as a rallying cry to the matriarchs of Mudh. Instead the third paper was from the day after Rajiv Gandhi's funeral. On the front page was the haunting image that has lingered in the Indian mind in the same way that pictures of Jackie Kennedy and her children at that other funeral have become part of American mythology. Rajiv's Italian wife Sonia, in a white sari, stands at one end of the pyre while her son Rahul bends down to light it. On that day Sonia Gandhi, the butcher's daughter from Turin, became the sphinx of Indian politics, inscrutable, isolated, the carrier of the dynastic mantle that obsessed the nation. That is, until it suited her to change her mind.

These papers, preserved like butterfly wings, were fragments from the outside, interlopers from beyond the high hills that seemed to have no relevance here in a place where the roll of time is governed by the green shoots in the fields and the birth cycle of the yak, the cow and the goat. But change creeps in.

Four years before there had been no electricity in the village. The days ran with the sun. Now there are quivering bulbs, the filaments flickering in the dusk. Television has not arrived but it is on the way. On the walk from Tabo we had seen satellite dishes on some of the rooftops of the villages.

Before the amorous interlude on the roof I had been writing copy to send back to distant Delhi. Cutting through the dust of the festival, the Dalai Lama's constant theme was that all sentient beings should use the wisdom of careful dialogue to create harmony. Patiently he delivered his message to the hot pilgrims sitting in the midday sun at Tabo; to the policemen with their tapping *lathis*, waiting for the next call to go and beat up another potential Chinese spy; to the politicians, blowing hot air and making empty promises; to the Chinese as they snip-snipped away at the heart of his home. This was a man in exile now so close to home and surrounded by the village faces of Tibet that he had grown up with in a different time.

The journalists listened and nodded and lined up at the telephone booths to pass on the news. We seemed to be missing the point. Here was a monk giving a message in a valley that did not move with the outside world. He had talked about impermanence, how we too become like the dust we breathe. He had said that nothing mattered, all was as nought. Did this mean that the gentle war he waged to set his country free was as nothing in the turn of time, that all his work, his travel, his pain would amount to nothing? No one could pose the question. We were there just to listen, something most journalists failed to do. Now from a rooftop in Mudh, the festival no longer seemed to be news. It was the same cycle of history that the Dalai Lama lived over and over.

The morning we left Mudh we lined up on the kitchen bench in the Blue House for a self-timed picture with rictus grins and crinkled eyes. Lobsang, the precious grandson, wailed as I kissed his damp forehead. They all said that it was a sign of good luck. From the temperature of his forehead it felt like the start of a cold.

Across the valley in Tabo the monks had gone into overdrive, robes flying, mantras filling the air as thickly as the dust. The *kalachakra* teachings had begun but the pilgrims were losing strength. Tabo, an isolated, high-altitude village, average population 1,700, now had 32,000 mouths to feed and bowels to relieve. Even the great message of spiritual peace was not enough to overcome this health-trap.

Bucking the trend, Johnny had recovered – a bit. He now moved around the kitchen with a little less love and alacrity. More time was spent out in front, propped up at a table, chatting to the punters. The celebrity chef had come of age. His sous-chefs were entrusted with the cake-making, though Johnny still frosted them in his blue-grey room, away from the prying eyes and thieving fingers of the punters and the *plongeurs*. His moments of culinary creation needed peace.

The beautiful blonde Buddhists of Will's dreams had materialized as part of café life, but not at Peme-La's. They were doing it their own way. Here was tough competition for Johnny. Not only were they much prettier but they were serving Mexican burritos to a host of jaded palates. Immediately Will switched his allegiance from Peme-La's with hardly so much as a goodbye and thanks for all the cake.

The web of the coloured sands of the *mandala* was in place. His Holiness pointed out the path through the *mandala*, through the cosmos, through the inner eye.

'Enter the eastern gate of the soul,' he said.

Everyone was supposed to close their eyes in order to follow the path. Some of us were too engrossed in watching the show even to try and participate. I was out there in the viewing gallery. All around the participants took step one. The Dalai Lama told them to tie a red cloth across their eyes to cut out the world. Then he told them to take the flowers that had been handed out with the red cloth, give them a bit of a lick to make them stick, and place them on the forehead just above the red blindfold. Drop the head back a little to keep the flower in place. This would open the inner eye, for the petals of the flower were the petals of the mind.

There was total silence across the sea of flowered, tilted foreheads. And all I wanted to do was laugh. All those days dishing out mango and banana sauce and now I had missed the big moment. I was tired of listening to travellers' tales. I had heard too many complaints about pancakes, ginger tea and chowmein. Now all I could do was laugh, the bubbles bouncing over the thousands of blindfolded faces. I was told to leave, sent out through the *gompa* gate to stand like a naughty schoolgirl, still gasping and gurgling as the pilgrims inside received their blessing.

As the teaching was still in full flow there was no queue at the telephones. For the second day running there was no answer on Sourish's line. Something had happened in Delhi.

The party was breaking up. Evya was about to stride back up into the hills. Robert, the Dutch monk, had a fever brought on by his initiation experience, a burning-out of the soul. He sat groaning over lemon tea, telling terrible tales of the black-market racketeering of Peme-La. Johnny was singing in the kitchen, baking a spiritual cake. His baking song sounded sad, the words tear-drops in the mix. Not love cake but goodbye cake.

There was one last thing to do, to see the *mandala* in all its intricacy. Will and I lined up by the gate to the *gompa*. A small group of us were let in and His Holiness, the Dust Monk, appeared, his expression grave, his thoughts making patterns in coloured sand somewhere else. He sat down with The Translator at his feet.

There was silence, then the Monk blew his nose. An earnest

The Dust Monk

man with a neat beard put up his hand first. He was from shoe-box Chandigarh.

'Your Holiness, why do you give more *kalachakra* initiations than any other Dalai Lama before?'

'Because we have aeroplanes now,' smiled the big man.

I laughed, the second naughty laugh on the big red carpet. The Dust Monk looked at me and laughed too.

'I am a refugee, you see. I do not have a country so it is easier for me to travel around.'

Now the rest of the pack laughed, polite, correct laughter.

He answered some questions directly, some through The Translator. Sometimes he would interrupt the middle man and tell him that his translation was not right, then he would proceed in slow English, each word paused upon and played with, just to check that it was going to mean the right thing when it came out.

Everyone was trying to find a clever question but there were none. The Dust Monk sat for a while with his head to one side, then he waved to one of the journalists wearing a *kata*, a prayer scarf, to come forward and be blessed. Most of them had *katas*. Will and I did not. We hung our heads.

His Holiness got up from his chair, stood for a moment and then walked back into the *gompa*. He waved as he went.

But it was not quite over. We had a secret from the Blue House.

He was riding shot-gun when he came round the mountain, not like other people, safe in the back, shrouded by bullet-proof glass, but up there on high in his Range Rover, the smile riding in the front seat for all to see. The big car moved slowly so that the dust did not obscure the view. The Translator ran at the back, a handkerchief across his mouth, a curious kind of guard – not the slick, gun-hipped man in black of the presidential motorcades, but a stocky monk in flapping robes hopping over pot-holes on a village track.

Behind The Translator galloped a herd of centurions, local warriors, wrapped in thick bright coats that caparisoned their tiny ponies. The yelps of choking heroes rose with the sound of neatly drumming hooves.

Each side of the road was lined with the people of the village. The women wore their best velvet dresses, turquoise, coral, pearls and silver at their necks, on their wrists, in their ears, crusted on great wings of lambskin on their heads. Monks hastily replaced their yellow croissant hats and put the great conch-shell horns to their lips. Older women came out of the shade of the trees where they had been sheltering their ancient velvet frocks and dried-petal skin from the blast of the sun. At the entrance to the village were two whitewashed domes, perfect milky breasts fed with wild thyme by old men in faded robes. They burn thyme to purify the air on great days of faith. This was one.

The village of Kungri, a hamlet high up in the valley away from Tabo, is a quiet place surrounded by a chequerboard of barley and grass. This was the secret from the kitchen of the Blue House, passed on in stilted English so that only the *momos* and the flowered cups of filthy tea could hear. His Holiness was to give a private blessing at a new *gompa* in Kungri. No tourists, no cameras. We went as the guests of Tashi Zangpo, of the Blue House, Mudh, guests of honour, wrapped in layers of billowing local cloth to merge our faces and forms with the crowd.

In a big chair on the fresh cement steps of the new *gompa* His Holiness spoke to the packed courtyard of the village in a dialect that they did not understand. Their satellite Tibetan is not the language of Lhasa and the *mantras* but a blend of the border and Pahari, the mountain tongue. The greeting was understood. The Dust Monk told them in their dialect that he felt honoured to be with them and that it was so much like the home that he had left so long ago. They smiled, clapped, waved and settled down to listen. What followed came in the rattling rhythm of unfamiliar Lhasa Tibetan. There were no translations to pass on the message of moderation, compassion and gentleness. There were no awnings to protect the people from the drilling sun, trussed up in their bright thick coats and heavy, high-day silks. Slumped on each other's shoulders they dozed and fidgeted. Some talked with their backs half-turned from the plush chair on the new cement. Picnics were unrolled from inside silken sleeves, food was shared out as the teaching ambled on.

When it ended they rose in a wave, roaring their approval, chanting and cheering, wild enthusiasm for an unheard speech. His Holiness planted a tree beside the *gompa* steps and blessed it. He hoped that it would grow tall and strong, nourished by the people of Kungri as the new *gompa* would nourish their hearts and minds. The people looked on and smiled blankly at his moving mouth. He giggled and they did too, merry fellow Buddhists. At last he was free to giggle and the eyes disappeared into a sea of wrinkles, just a Tibetan monk for a moment, laughing in a crowd of familiar features, removed from the world stage, happy to be in a place that felt like home. And all around, the great tiers and stacks of rock that seemed to form God's library looked down on the laughing Dust Monk in his moment of grace.

Two hours later the village was still. A row of unsaddled ponies stood against a wall, tiny hooves lashing at fat, late-afternoon flies. The yelping warriors dozed under trees, alcoholic fumes riding their snores. The women packed away their velvet dresses and settled around the kitchen fires to bitch about their drunken men.

On the fresh cement of the new *gompa* a large television had been set up. The village children sat in rigid attention before the wriggling dance sequences of a Hindi movie. Away down the valley the fawn Range Rover drove to set the Dust Monk on his way to London, to arrive in another capital and sing his song of compassion to gym-slim women and mobile men with voids as big as a valley to fill.

We followed him down the valley on foot and then by jeep, lorry, bus and train to New Delhi station. This time it was goodbye to Will and his camera bags, now stuffed full of photographs of monks, *mandalas*, fading ancients in the smoke of burning thyme, proud Tashi with his golden grandson, and the Dust Monk's laughter caught beside a newly planted sapling in Kungri.

Body in Mind

BACK IN FAST, fiery Delhi the pavements were so hot they were dotted with bright patches where the bottoms of plastic shoes had melted on to the stones. All was quiet at Hailey Road. The Rani was still in Jodhpur nursing her broken wing, the Maharaj Sahib at her side puffing on his collection of pipes. Yashwant was in Dehra Dun, in the foothills of the Himalayas, staying at his old school, the place that strayed so often into our conversations. He came back on a night when the bullfrogs puffed and the air was too bored to move.

'Ah, you've returned.' He extended an elegant hand and touched my cheek.

Cousin Gita and the servants had each come to greet him by touching his feet. I was exempt, wrong colour, wrong family.

'Orff, you are so burnt. Wrinkles, wrinkles, you are going to shrivel up and wither away. You must have an egg-white face-pack. They feel terrible but they pull all those nasty lines tight, tight. Where have you been? You are burnt to a crisp. Look at your nose.' He pointed an accusing finger.

I gave him a brief account of the festival.

'Why do you want to spend all your time with these peasants? I thought that you wanted to understand this country. You will never learn from peasants. What can they talk about?'

'How was the old school?' I asked in an attempt to avoid the inevitable argument.

'Ahh, so beautiful. Not like your ugly peasants at all. Now that is where you find really beautiful people.'

'Were you happy there?' I asked.

'Of course I was happy. I have never been happier in my life.'

Back he went, back to Woodstock School thirty years ago, a school run by missionaries in the hills of Mussourie, full of sporty Americans whose fathers were touring the diplomatic circles of New Delhi. He told tales washed by time of his lack of success on the hockey field and of his prowess at verbal fencing. None of his classmates had come close to the stiletto tongue of Yashwant, his speciality, practised from the pram and honed to battlefield skill.

'It was a mixed school, you know. That was very far ahead of the times. Looking back at it now we had a very good childhood. Very open and honest, no question was unanswered.' He paused to make sure that he had my full attention.

'Are you listening? *Acchhā*, we were off to see your lovely Dalai Lama in Happy Valley at the other end of Mussourie, and on the way back what should we find but a stall in the bazaar stacked high with cheap pornographic magazines. Of course we bought the lot.' He threw back his head and laughed.

'Well, then I had them at the back of my cupboard at home and for some unearthly reason the Mother decides to get her hands dirty and sort out my cupboard. Naturally she found all the mags but she was not even cross. Very healthy attitude in my family, you see.' He paused and narrowed his eyes.

'Why are you writing this down?'

'So that I get it right,' I replied.

'I will sue if you print a word of this. In fact I am going to start proceedings right now.' He seemed almost serious.

'Don't interrupt again. Where was I? Oh yes, you see no one went to mixed schools, far too risky to release their precious children to run with the opposite sex. But the Mother and the Father thought it would be a good idea for us. I think it all made me sort of freaky.'

'Did you have fun?'

'*Acchhā*, fun? Of course we had fun, the very best kind. Look, look, you have to look at me for this story.'

He paused to check.

'So we have the dormitory. Just all those terrible beds and pillows that crick the neck. Well, in the corner there was a huge cupboard, tall as you can imagine. Now all the junior boys are asleep, all sweet and asleep. The seniors, that is me of course and my circle, decide to play our game. This was the greatest game – the Maharaja Game. The trouble is none of them had the imagination to play it. Of course I had to show them all.'

'What was the game?'

'Hush, I am telling you. The bit I hated was having to get up on top of the cupboard. It was hideous. I had to climb up on a bedhead and then jump up on to the cupboard. It would wobble around. Terribly, terribly dangerous, you understand. So I am up there being the maharaja. That is absolutely right, of course, as they are all foreigners and have no idea how to be maharajas at all. The most ridiculous thing is that I had to be all dressed up before doing the pole-vault up on to the cupboard. You know those dreadful bedcovers with all the fluffy bits on them? Four of them, they would wrap me up in four of them, round and round we go, like great long togas.' His arms whirled around, toga-tying twirls.

'Then three more, all different colours, rolled around my head in the most enormous turban you have ever seen. Just imagine how big that was. Then I have to jump up on to the cupboard with all this rubbish on, tied up like a great big present. They had awful taste, always putting orange and pink bedcovers together, too terrible, so ugly you would not believe.'

Yashwant was striding around the room, his arms still swirling the folds and rolls of the dormitory toga and turban, his face alive and mobile.

'Sometimes they would want to play the maharaja which was ridiculous. But of course I would pander to them. They would get up on to the cupboard and then just fall apart. Oh, all glossy and American, no idea about how to pretend to be a maharaja, no idea. So they would climb down and beg me to go back up and take over again.

'That is when the fun would start. They would ask me to give them orders. They were my courtiers, you see, so I could tell them to do whatever I wanted.'

He sat down for a moment, waiting.

'And?' I asked obediently.

He crossed his legs and paused for effect.

'It was usually rather dull. Just do this, do that, run here, jump there. But sometimes they would push me, demand something more.'

Another pause.

'So I would tell one of them to lie down on the floor and then another one on top and another and another. Piled high they were. Oh my turban would fall off because I was laughing so much. I am sure I must have fallen off the cupboard though I don't remember, black and blue, black and blue, wrapped in orange and pink.'

'I'm sure it was all very innocent,' I said, sounding prim.

'Good God, whatever are you thinking? Of course it was. We were children. It was nothing. We were terribly young, you see. It did make me laugh so much.' His hands fluttered up and down, still keeping his balance on the tottering cupboard, held up by the bright wings of memory. Then they fell to his sides.

'It was all such a long time ago.' He stopped, deflated now, party over, time to go home.

Where were they now, the boys who had played the maharaja game? He did not know. Bloated, balding players in corporate middle America perhaps, full of dead and dying dreams of India.

Some voice from down a long corridor of a past palace pulled Yashwant's shoulders back.

'Carry on regardless. Never say die.' He slapped his legs and got up, back straight, chin held high, heart in transit from another time. He put his head around the door and shouted for Ram Kumar to bring him another packet of *biris*.

'You should write about my school, much more interesting than all those bloody peasants. Oh, the curse of the British peasant lovers.'

'Buddhists.'

'Whatever.'

Ram Kumar appeared with the *biris* on a tray. Yashwant scowled at him.

'Matches?'

Ram Kumar scowled back and slunk away.

'I will write about your school.'

'Of course you shall.'

Carry on regardless.

I still could not get an answer on Sourish's line. The lack of any response had a familiar flavour. Kipling had written of the difficulties of working in the hot season.

> The native staff of the offices are not much use in the morning. All native offices aestivate from May at least till September. Files and correspondence are then as a matter of course pitched unopened into corners, to be written or faked when the weather gets cooler.

Perhaps Sourish was suffering and following their example. No, that was not his style. As with cows in traffic jams, heat was no excuse, a paper still had to come out whether or not the staff were answering the telephones. Bushan drove me down to Bahadur Shah Zafar Marg. The building still stood and blue-jeaned journalists continued to move up and down the marble stairs, slower now, weighed down by the hot denim of their media uniform.

All seemed calm in the hall. The receptionist was in her usual place, her mouth full of stuffed *paratha*, a lump of potato on her lip, fingers dripping mango pickle. She smudged a chit for me. Shri Ram Nath Goenka (18 April 1904 – 5 October 1991) smiled down on the children of his empire from his great portrait as he always did, black, white and benign. The noticeboard with the signs of the companies on each floor still had *The Indian Express* on the ground floor.

I approached a security guard with my chit.

'Sourish Bhattacharyya?'

'*Kya?*' He rattled his gun.

This was the ground floor, but the corridor that had once been the ringroad of the paper was now empty. A national newspaper can't just disappear, can it? Besides I had seen it on the newsstands and in the bus queues.

A post-prandial, snack-in-hand herd of journalists crossed the hall and disappeared down some stairs. Chit-waving, I pursued.

The paper had gone underground to join the printing presses, banished to the mechanical thunder in the bowels of the build-ing. The route to Sourish's new office wound deep down, right past the great Harris Graphic printers, past tightly packed rows of reporters at their desks, putty-skinned in the subterranean light.

The new office was bigger, with chairs to spare and a sense of order. Sourish smiled happily, the green print of his screen reflected on one shiny cheek. He seemed bigger than before.

'Oh, oh. See, we are mushrooms now, no light, no air, but still we produce.'

'Hello. I've heard a different version.'

'Fed on shit, I know, I know. How was the Dalai Lama?'

'Very well. How are you?'

'Like the Dalai Lama. You will write about it for me?'

A curious question.

'What happened here?' I asked.

'A fight, you see, Goenka politics.'

'So the flagship goes underground?'

'Journalism of courage.' He offered me a chocolate, and his stomach rolled with laughter.

The chocolate immediately melted in my hand. Sourish told the tale while I licked chocolate off my fingers.

Though two Goenka brothers controlled the newspaper empire, an estranged aunt held sway over the *Express* Building. She had been totting up the lost rent on the ground floor of the building. She had waited for five years out of respect after the death of Ram Nath, but now she had come to collect. The rent the paper was paying her on the ground floor was less than a tenth of the market rate. So down to the bowels the paper went. No one complained, there was no Wapping-style rebellion, just acceptance of the neon life and the black belching roar of the printing-machines.

'So what are you going to write for me?' Sourish was tentative.

'Oh, bits and bobs, gorgeous village dancing, wise teachings, international bonding, a secret day with the Dalai Lama, beautiful places, arrested Tibetans, bad preparations, the effect of the sewage of 32,000 people on a fragile environment, the ecocatastrophe.' More of the usual thing.

'Sewerage?'

'There was none.'

Sourish raised his eyebrows.

'If there had been sewerage it would have been okay but there was nowhere for the sewage to go. Think how much shit 32,000 people produce per day in a village with a normal population of about 1,700. That is too much poop.'

'Oh, oh, here goes Annie Besant again.' It was high praise, but Sourish did not say it to flatter.

Annie Besant had worked on the staff of the *National Reformer* in England. In 1914 she set sail for Delhi and there bought two Indian papers. She used her publications to advocate a political line even bolder than the Nationalist murmurings of the young Congress Party. In 1917, as Indian troops poured into the theatres of the First World War, battling Annie had written:

> Young men cannot be expected to make the sacrifice asked for unless they are inspired by a passionate love for their motherland such as emptied the universities of Great Britain. Love for a foreign dependency cannot do it. Love for an empire in which they are a partner will do it. The prospect of prolongation of inferiority will not inspire; the love of liberty and the hope of winning it and of becoming citizens of an empire of free nations will inspire.

No wonder a cynical rhyme had come into being about Annie, friend of India:

> Annie Besant, Annie Besant
> Filling our ears with all her cant . . .

'Didn't Annie Besant own the papers she wrote in?'

'*Acchhā*, she did and I don't think *The Indian Express* is for sale. So can I have an interesting piece about the festival such as you were telling me you would write before you went off up into the hills? Just fifteen hundred words and some nice pictures as soon as you can. Then you can go on to do the pieces about yoga that I think I remember you said you would write next.'

There was nothing more to say. The meeting was over. I bet Annie Besant never wrote articles about yoga.

I sat in a medium-sized cloud of bad temper on the steps outside *The Indian Express*, brooding on a nice story about Buddhism with nice pictures. For the bank-account Buddhists of the First World the refugees streaming into the once-Indian hill station of Dharamsala represent another twentieth-century diaspora in need of succour, comfort, dollars, pounds and francs. Yet on the streets of the town the Tibetans and the local people are caught in a struggle far removed from the image of a cloud people on the roof of the world, the image that fills the dreams of Betty, the bouffant Buddhist from Buffalo, Texas, and her crowd of donation darlings. While Betty and her friends meditate on good deeds their dollars take strange sidetracks into black-market feuds. The Tibetans and local Himachalis clash on the damp and dirty streets of Dharamsala. There is cross-cultural confusion. There is rape and murder in the town where compassion is pictured as being so thick on the streets that you can cut it up and take it home. All is not well in the House of Buddha.

Just below the steps where I sat there was a peanut-seller. Beside him was a trestle, piled high with nuts and resting on elegant, old-fashioned bicycle wheels. Balanced on top was a smoking earthenware pot where, handful by handful, the seller roasted the nuts.

Smoke from the pot climbed around his head, uncoiling in the afternoon heat. He was making neat cones from newspaper, popping in three or four unshelled nuts, then carefully folding the top of each one before adding it to a perfectly proportioned stack on a round tray. At rush hour he would take his peanut pile and hawk it through windows in the heavy traffic to bored commuters with idle hands. Just fifty *paise* a cone, less than a penny for each careful little parcel. He went about his labour meticulously, watching me sitting in my dark cloud. I looked up. There was no frustration in his eyes. Was he happy in his work? How could you tell? There was no bitter smell of injustice rising with the smoke from his barrow. But he could smell it on me. He smiled, a neat peanut smile; fold and smile, and carry on regardless – a nice story, nice pictures, yoga to suit every need, just do your job said the peanut-seller's smile.

Nice was not the word for the pictures that Will had left behind. In a photographic studio in Connaught Place I stood and cried while the slide cutter shoed the tears away from the light box. There were hundreds of transparencies, roll after roll, laid out in the light: the broad smooth brows of Tibetans, a sea of red robes at the teachings; His Holiness's face filling the frame; small boys with great aluminium kettles pouring tea into the proffered cups of dust-dry pilgrims; Johnny and Evya outside Peme-La's café, self-conscious and gaunt, tea and plum cake in hand; Tashi of the Blue House wading across a river to Mudh, the force of the water throwing up a silver arc, caught in the moment before it drenched the little man; the empty ponies in Kungri, lined up while the warriors went to booze. But they were not the ones that made me cry.

One series, separate from the rest, had been taken at Tabo inside the *gompa* during one of the afternoon teachings. In the shade of a doorway, away from the crowd, sat an old monk, ninety-seven he had said. He bent his head around the door, staring with

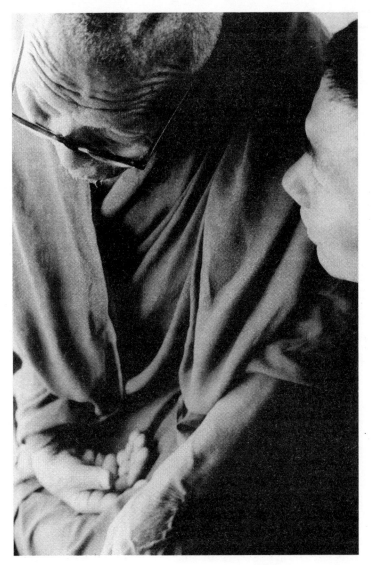

Tired Tibet in exile

almost blind eyes towards the voice that he could not hear. Beside him was a young man who shouted the Dalai Lama's words into his ancient ear. Tears of age and exhaustion ran down the monk's time-tunnelled face. In one frame his hand was raised to his ear, the lips of the young man passing on the words; in another his body leant round the door as he tried to see beyond his cataracts, his clawed hands twisting worn prayer beads. This was tired Tibet in exile.

The slide cutter pulled the reels towards him and examined them through a magnifying loop. He looked up from the ones of the monk.

'Too old for living,' he said and turned his attention back to the smooth-skinned girls in their dancing finery with sweet, shy smiles.

The dancing girls were colourful but the old man represented all the turbulent twentieth-century history of Tibet. I put a note on the series for Will to find. 'Thank you, these made me cry.'

Back at Jodhpur Apartments I sat down to write a nice story. There was the look in the peanut-seller's eyes and the history hands on the worn-out prayer beads to draw on. The time had come to mend my ways and become a more proficient member of the Indian press, time to surprise Sourish by giving him exactly what he had asked for without a wrangle.

Kipling had tried to break the bounds dictated by paper and empire. One of the unsolved mysteries of the man is the lost manuscript of a novel that he started called *Mother Maturin*. In a letter to his aunt, Edith Macdonald, he described the book:

> It's not a bit nice or proper but it carries a grim sort of moral with it and tries to deal with the unutterable horrors of lower class Eurasian and native life as they exist outside reports and reports and reports . . . I know it to be in large measure true.

After three fever-ridden hot seasons champing within the parameters of the *Civil and Military Gazette* in Lahore he had taken his annual leave in the summer of 1885 in the cool comfort of Simla. There he created an Irish-Indian brothel madame, Mother Maturin, living in the social underbelly of Indian life, and in doing so he exposed the ugly side of the Anglo-Indian sex industry that served the empire.

It was an industry that had been accepted as part of the colonial structure until rumours reached London that the boys of the Empire were being amused by official ladies of the night. There was uproar and the order went out from Whitehall to Calcutta that the brothels should be closed down. With the camp supply of prostitutes removed the soldiers went out into the narrow alleys and stinking, sensual streets to buy their sex. The consequent epidemic of sexually transmitted diseases amidst the soldiery so alarmed Whitehall that the official prostitutes were quietly reinstated.

In his first draft of the novel Kipling probed this world, prowling the alleys and bazaars, catching the scents and scenes of the night. *Mother Maturin* was never published and with it disappeared the passion on paper to which Kipling had given free rein. Yet though the darkness of that novel was lost, some of the shadows of an Anglo-Indian existence later found their way into the pages of *Kim*.

Here I was, playing the same game, translating shadows, mixing truth and tat, Buddhism and balance, yoga and science – not quite the same underbelly, though each had its own twist.

The tat came first. The initial yoga piece was accepted not only with alacrity but with an enthusiasm that I had not expected. Sourish beamed from behind his desk. He had a plan.

'You see we are having this new look. Every day we will be having a magazine section. Habitat one day and that will be all design and interior thingy for the home. Gourmet, all the food stuff, and Body and Mind for health and fitness. Now this will be very popular. You know it is what everyone is getting into now.' His fingers drummed on the swell of his belly.

'I was lunching with a group just a few days back, all of them intelligent people with all sorts of things to talk about. One of our top designers was there, a beautiful woman, what is her name, *acchā*, whatever. And what are we all talking about? Treadmills, how long they all spend on the step machine, which gym they go to, how much they pay. And look at me, I am the unfittest man in Delhi. Not very much I could say.' He hugged his stomach, loving its circumference, his mark in life.

His deputy walked in, dishevelled and petulant in a suit, shirt-tails hanging out and hands thrust deep into the pockets. Sourish laughed.

'Karan, what the hell are you doing in a suit?'

Karan mumbled something about a fashion show and pushed his hands still further into the brown pockets of his very brown suit.

'God, I've never worn a jacket in my life,' said Sourish.

'You mean you have never worn a jacket, ever?' I was incredulous.

'Well, you know at school you have to wear a blazer and tie and stuff. Oh, oh, but I was always pulling them off at the first chance. Never since then.' He stopped and thought for a moment.

'Oh, oh, almost a lie. I did have to put on a tie when I went to *The Wall Street Journal*.'

'What were you doing there?'

'Oh, just a social sort of thing. *The Express* has a business news tie-up with them. I was just putting in a courtesy call. Such a hullabaloo. There I am, being forced into a tie, to meet the editor that we link up with. My God, the stress that man was having. I have never seen anybody so tied up in my life. No time for anything or anyone. Always pushing his hand through his hair, pulling the damn stuff out. And all for one page. I told him I was bringing out eight pages a day and without anyone getting in a pizzle at all. I don't think he liked that very much. There was so much pizzling going on in that place. All so damn tense. They should wear a few less ties.' He laughed again.

'But really, Karan, this is not you at all. You will not fool anyone, I am telling you, *yaar*. They are going to be seeing the real you sneaking out of your pockets.' More raucous laughter.

Tired of being the butt of sartorial comment Karan dumped some copy in front of Sourish. 'So what did you wear when you got married?' he countered, his free hand still deep in his pocket.

'Oh, oh, you were there, don't you remember? *Dhoti* and *salwar*, like all good Bengalis,' Sourish replied.

'But you're not Bengali,' Karan retorted.

Sourish waved his hand dismissively. Karan prodded his belly and they giggled. I sat and enjoyed the show. It finished with another round of chocolates from one of Sourish's boxes. Karan stuffed his sticky fingers back into his pocket and shuffled out, shambling, chocolatey, contrived shirt-tails hanging.

'Eight pages a day?' I asked.

'*Yaar*, and more now with the new sections. Oh, oh, that is where we were before this whole jacket thingy. Yes, Body and Mind. What about a weekly piece on a health or fitness issue?'

Oh God.

'I was thinking that you do all this climbing about in the mountains and yoga and stuff.' He stopped for a moment.

'Great.'

Sourish's head popped out from his shoulders rather like a bird's.

'Perhaps it could be a series rather than just sort of disjointed pieces,' I added. The battle was lost: the rest of the war could wait.

Sourish was still popping his head.

'Yes, yes, you could come up with some ideas. We could kick off with another yoga piece. We have the introduction now, so perhaps a more general piece, maybe on how it is good for stress and things like that.'

He pulled out the spreads for one of the early editions of Body and Mind. Page one: 'The Bitter Prick – Diabetes is not a leading killer but it is up there when it comes to myths. Body and Mind have consulted not one, not two but three experts – If soccer legend Bobby Moore can cope with insulin jabs so can you.' Page two: 'Two Snips and You're Out – You Think – Horror stories of post-vasectomy pregnancy abound. Body and Mind dig underneath some of the myths of the big male snip.' Page three: 'Tract trauma – Flushing out infection of the urinary tract.' No myths here, though some very helpful advice: 'Prevention – Clean your private parts at least three to four times daily with soap and water.' Page four contained a tiring interview with some taut-torsoed tennis pro from a five-star hotel about his daily exercise regime. The exercise boom has finally hit India, borne aloft by the have-to-have advertising campaigns of the mighty shoe manufacturers. Middle-class India just loves sportswear with a logo.

Yet while the India of one-too-many *gulab jamuns* takes to the gym, 70 per cent of the population are still out in the villages, fighting to keep cerebral malaria at bay and drying cow dung as fuel for fires to cook *chapātis*, rice and *dhal*. There is no variation to the menu.

'Can I do a bit of myth exploration?' I asked.

'How?' Sourish was suspicious.

'Say the series started with Fit for Life, looking at the gym obsession and how people become addicted to the exercise cult. Diet for Life would deal with the diet industry and how it feeds itself by creating a diet–binge cycle. Fast for Life would look at the value of some of the old forms of medicine and the re-emergence of alternative treatments. Lust for Life could examine the new wave of promiscuity spreading with the nightclub scene.'

Sourish bird-necked again. This was it, at last a role defined, health correspondent with forays into more serious matters for good behaviour.

'When do you want the general yoga piece?'

'Whenever, as soon as you can and with a picture of you doing yoga or something, to give the readers a look at you.'

'Check the merchandise?'

'Oh, oh, something like that.' He gave a slightly embarrassed laugh.

There had been a long conversation with cousin Gita at Jodhpur Apartments about yoga. I had been ashram-hunting and she had told me about the one she had been to. Gita also talked of gurus and meditation, of auras and mental powers. Gita was the guru guide.

She was not at home. Yashwant was.

'Have you seen Gita?' Yashwant had his back to me, his face pressed against his beloved fish tank.

'I cannot see a thing, I am virtually blind. Look, see how I have to be almost in the tank to see my lovely fish and still I cannot see the expression in their eyes. Blind, blind, I am going blind.'

'Do fish have different expressions?'

'Of course they do! They all smile at me.' He stroked the glass as one passed close by.

'Come here, sweet child, there is a miracle to behold. See how crystal clear the water is?'

'Lucky fish, have you cleaned them out?'

'No, no, look! You see the great ugly black thing? It is a sucker cat. It eats all the filth.'

'Is that why its eyes bulge so?'

'Don't be so base. You're looking at the wrong one, and you are not to be so rude about my angel fish. Look at this one. It is a picture of ugliness. Just look at it.' Yashwant's tone was imperative.

In contrast to the somewhat cultivated ugliness of the angel fish, with its chiffon black tail and glossy hammer head, the sucker cat was truly hideous. Side by side in the sick green light of the aquarium we studied its fleshy orifice sucking at the side of the tank, the body mottled black and brown.

'Shit, shit, let it eat all the shit, say I.' Yashwant stroked his finger affectionately against the glass where the awful orifice pulsated.

'Gita?'

He snorted.

'Where is she?'

'With her wizard.' He threw his hands up in the air and rolled his eyes.

Just where Gita, the guru guide, was supposed to be.

The wizard was a man with the face of a saint and the body of a sinner. He was Gurujee to his followers and he liked to laugh about his huge stomach. He said it was because he ate too many *laddus*, the heavy yellow sweets made of semolina and chickpea flour and slicked with a thick gloss of sugar and *ghee*. He also had a penchant for *barfi*, another sweet of alarming sugariness that made him go weak at the knees. What can you do when you are a guru and your followers know you love *barfi*?

Gurujee claimed to be a direct telephone link with 'the god on top'. He had been an engineer. It seemed an interesting job change and certainly a remarkable feat of engineering, well worth pursuing for spiritual enlightenment and some research.

Gita took command and an elegant invitation arrived requesting that I attend an important day in Gurujee's celestial diary. He was holding a *pooja*, a prayer ritual, to celebrate Shivratri, the birthday of Shiv, the destroyer.

Sindoor and Sex

IN THE FERMENT of Friday morning traffic, shawls and shirt-sleeves protected our mouths from the fumes as Bushan's vulnerable rickshaw bumped and ground around the spewing columns of cars.

Two little girls came to hang off the side, one pretty and pale-skinned, the other stocky, dark and not much of a marriage prospect, if you were looking at it from her father's point of view. The prettier girl started to stroke our feet, laying her open palm on my lap with a beatific smile. The other had a different tactic, jumping up and down and yelling 'One rupee, choclit! Two rupee, choclit!' Pretty ran round the back of the rickshaw and belted Stocky on the head. A chase ensued with a great deal of screeching and pulling of hair. I dug around in my bag. Gita put out her hand.

'Don't give them money.' She waved them away.

They both snarled, the whole charade a waste of time. Winsome children, marriageable or otherwise, should be in school: Gita was firm. And able-bodied men and women should get jobs – middle-class Delhi was crying out for domestic staff. Lazy, that was her opinion, too lazy to do a day's work. Lepers and amputees were the ones for alms.

On cue a leper, half life, half decay, dragged himself through the snarl. Rags for hands pulled him on his wooden tray, his withered back bent into an S bend by his contortions across the road. As he reached us he tilted his sorry head and held out two stumps.

Mute we sat there clutching our bags. The lights changed, the traffic moved. We left the leper behind on his tray, an island in the flow until the traffic halted again and the rags reached out.

We stopped at Aggarwals Sweets to gaze at shelf upon sugared shelf of sweet fat food: pyramids of *laddus*, *gulab jamuns* floating in syrup slicks, *barfi* stacked in pale rainbow shades, *jalebi* curls dripping high on the counter. The glass cabinet reflected the smudging of hundreds of finger prints. Two fat women pressed up against the cool of the display, their loose stomachs spreading across the glass. They shouted their orders and picked at the piles of *mithai* with thick, manicured fingers rippled with gold rings. Gita ordered two boxes of *laddus*, one for her and one for me. She did not even have to speak. The *mithai* man knew her order – five *laddus* in each box, it was always the same. They were offerings for Gurujee and a bit of cupboard love for the deities. I held out some money to pay. Gita snatched it out of my hand.

'No, no, you cannot pay for both of us. We have to pay for our own otherwise it is not a proper offering.'

The *mithai* man smiled. Gurujee was good for business.

In a residential street in a good neighbourhood, sticky *laddus* clutched in our hands, we climbed the stairs to a courtyard where shoes lay in conversational groups in a shaded corner. Gita ushered me before her across white sheets into the prayer room. There they were on the walls, the usual coterie of flushed, acrylic gods and goddesses, plump, pink-cheeked and funfair bright. Garlands of marigolds and palm leaves strung in lines hung from the windows and shelves. At one end of the room was an altar piled with flowers, goodies and bank rolls for the delectation of the god on top.

The *poojari*, the Brahmin *pooja* practitioner, was a man with busy hands. Neat, quick fingers made small bundles – a pinch of rice, a touch of red *sindoor* powder, a coconut chunk, all folded into a shredded palm leaf and tied up with string. Favourite things to throw into a fire to celebrate Shiv's birthday.

Smiling upon his dais was Gurujee, involved in his own pre-*pooja* prayers, drifting around in the divine telephone exchange

Gurujee's poojari

waiting for his connection. His glasses reflected the bright gods and goddesses on the walls, the sides of them tucked away into a dark red cloth wrapped around his head. His eyes were still in the exquisite mobility of his face, his grey beard streaked with gun-metal shades set against the patina of teak. Beneath the cabaret of his face his stomach swelled magnificently through his white *kurta*. He gurgled and shuddered, high theatre, but no one moved. Gita leant forward to say that he was going into a trance and not to be put off. Both his hands flew up to his face as if trying to deflect some great force. He cried out, sucking at the air. His eyes rolled, his arms flailed. We sat around as if we were just having an average coffee morning while Gurujee writhed up on his dais.

Others arrived, touching the feet of the vibrating Gurujee. We sat and fidgeted, waiting for something to happen, shifting from cheek to cheek on the hard floor. The *poojari* fell asleep, quietly nodding off after his final preparations: a fire laid in the centre of a small brazier with symmetrical logs of mango wood into which the parcels were to be thrown, a metal *thali* tray from Mrs Gurujee's kitchen marked up with the swastika for *pooja* day, further little piles of rose petals and scattered rice to feed to the fire. A line of dribble glinted on the *poojari's* chin.

A widow in white flicked the end of her sari at the sleeping Brahmin. He nodded and yawned. Gurujee gave a particularly loud shriek and the proceedings began. He hopped off his dais and picked a cassette tape from a pile in the corner, stacked under the fax machine. As the *poojari* began to chant so too did another sing-song voice from another *pooja* locked somewhere inside the tape machine, a cacophony of ritual in two different keys, an air on 'D' and a mildly off-key 'C'.

Smoke swirled. Rose petals passed in and out of hands, into dishes, on to the fire. From a bag of Hindu-ritual ready-mades came more piles for the pyre – sandalwood chips, *khus* shavings, lotus seeds, sugar candy, dried coconut and betel nut mulched together with *ghee*. Back and forth went the crowd of hands, over the fire, into the smoke. Then there were pink paper napkins to wipe the ritual fingers clean. Thick yellow smoke poured from the burning offerings. Regulars turned away, wise after too many years of carrying the thick fog of prayer in their lungs on *pooja* days, but not me, the initiate. Blinking and snuffling I faced up to my responsibility as ambassador for an England where spiritually anything goes.

The *poojari* clapped his hands. Now was the time for the tying of the sacred string, on the left hand for those married, on the right hand for those of us who were single. Gurujee joined us from his dais on high where he had watched and nodded as we sweated around the fire. He had a wristful of sacred strings.

We were nearing the end. The *poojari* picked up a tray with a butter lamp for the final *aarti*, the blessing. Round the tray went, from hand to hand, each one circling the flame in a slow movement, the cycle of life, the great O of the universe. Each caught the heat of the flame in cupped hands and passed the blessing over their head, the solemn widow, the boy in a brown waistcoat, the pale young man with a patrician profile, partly here, mostly still asleep. We had been in the small room for over two hours.

Gurujee was now cross-legged on the floor, blessed offerings piled on either side of him – bananas, apples and divine nibbles care of Aggarwals Sweets, going-home presents for the *pooja* attendees. When most had eaten and left, Gita ushered me forward again.

'Go on, Gurujee is going to bless you.'

As I knelt in front of the dais, my nose buried in its red satin covering, there was a great shuddering sigh and a hefty bang on my back, a blessing from the god via the strong hand of Gurujee.

'What do you want to ask?'

Gita leant over to whisper. 'Don't jump from one question to another. Finish one thing and make a stop before asking something new.'

'Will you stay?' I whispered back in a nervous voice.

'No, this is your private time with Gurujee.' And she was gone.

A panic-stricken moment. There had been no preparation for this, no ordering of questions. I kept my eyes closed. It seemed safest.

Gurujee asked again. Thinking fast, I opened my eyes to meet his.

'My father is ill. Will he recover?' I gave his name and where he lived, nothing else.

Gurujee replied with an accurate description of my father and a thumb-nail sketch of his personality. He shook his head in his hands. This was not good. Then he looked up and threw one hand in the air with a flick of the wrist.

'He will be up and about soon. Have no more worry, he will be wholly well. Another chance. What is it you say? Yes, another leaf.'

'Thank you, Gurujee.'

'Do not thank me, thank the god.'

Hands in prayer, I turned to the picture of the god with rose-bud lips and enviable hair.

'You will be married soon.'

'What!' Not me, Gurujee, wrong girl. Women born in the year of the horse are indomitable, not good as little wives. Those born in a combination of the horse with fire (only once every sixty years, mercifully) are wild and dangerous to marry, or so the theory goes: 1966 was one of those years. While England wallowed in World Cup victory, Beatlemania and the first stirrings of free love, a great number of Asian women who found themselves pregnant resorted to abortion to avoid the chance of giving birth to daughters with no marital prospects.

'Gita.' He called her back into the room. 'Tell her she must be married soon.' So he was checking my sell-by-date and deciding that it was running out, chop, chop, quick, get hitched or get shelved.

He spoke to Gita in Punjabi.

'Gita?' I appealed to the guru guide.

'He is not saying that you have to get married now. He is saying that you must be open to the idea of marriage because it is coming to you and you must not have a closed heart.' Where was Gita, the feminist in the sari, the champion of single status?

'Anyone I know, Gurujee?'

His head was in his hands again. There followed one of his

groans and a flurry of arms, waving me away. My hands were on his dais, creating interference with his reception. He was getting a crossed line.

We waited for a reconnection. Gita asked something else. He answered in Punjabi with another flick of the wrist and turned to me. 'Off, off, fly away.'

'He says that you will not find your marriage here but somewhere else, that you must go away from this place.' Gita looked very serious.

'What, I have to go right now?' This was absurd, I had come to see yoga of the mind in practice and now I was being told to leave the country to get spliced, pronto, quick, quick.

'No, no, all in your own good time. But it is out there, it will happen. You have to start to focus on it.'

Gurujee settled back into the cushions of his dais, worn out by the telephone call, and waved Gita to our two boxes of *laddus*. He blessed them and sent us out into the courtyard, a *laddu* for each of us, four for the birds to wing our prayers to the gods, and the rest to give out to the poor and needy to improve our *karma*. Fat sleek crows hopped up and down the wall where the *laddus* were scattered, the fattest, sleekest crows I have ever seen in Delhi – fit prayer carriers of the house of Gurujee.

'If my father had not been going to recover, would he have told me?' I asked Gita as we bounced through the fumes on the way back to Jodhpur Apartments.

'Oh yes, he misses out nothing, that is why you have to be careful what you ask because he will tell you as it is.'

'And the shuddering, the waving, the whole showtime bit?'

'I know, I have told him so many times that it looks a bit cheap, like in all the Hindi movies where you have some fat old actor jiggling about pretending to be a guru with beard and scarf and all. He says to me that he knows that but that he cannot help it, that the god controls him when he is in the trance.'

139

'So the fat old actors are getting it just about right?'

She laughed but did not answer.

My cynicism was obvious in the fingers that worked the edge of my shawl, tugging at stray threads, tearing them away from the weave.

'You have to believe him. He is not a fraud. I would not go to a fraud.' She addressed my shredding fingers.

'I know that but I am just not sure that I want to believe. Why did he tell me that I should be getting ready to marry when I'd asked him a question about my father?'

'The two things are linked, you see.' Clever Gita, a convenient answer.

'Why, because a father has to cough up for a wedding?'

'No, no, because Gurujee was seeing the important men in your life and he must have seen a very important one on the way. He was saying that you must be open to that and not push it away.'

'In case it is my last chance?' I stopped fiddling with my shawl and pulled it around my face. We spoke with our mouths covered, filtering the filthy air, guarding our women's talk.

'You must not judge but do as he says. We cannot understand so we have to accept.'

There was no room for cynicism here in a place where spirituality and religious superstition hang about on every street corner – in the light of a butter lamp in a hole in the wall; in the sacred *sindoor* between the eyebrows of the freshly blessed; on the head of every turban-bound Sikh. If the loosely stitched quilt of the early national press had united India in her bid for freedom then spirituality has bound her more profoundly still, spilling trainloads of blood on the surface but creating an aura of belief that hangs over the whole country as surely as the thermals riding the hot-season dust or the black thunderheads of the monsoon.

To be cynical about the importance of spirituality in India is to meet a luminous stranger and not bother to ask his name. An introduction to the mystery lifts the veil and, as the light of familiarity pours in, so the edge comes off the beauty. There is no

Gurujee, direct telephone link with 'the god on top'

magic. The heaving spirituality of India comes with all the usual human flaws.

If I was to look at the role of yoga of the mind then cynicism had to be packed away with prejudices and millennium woman rap. Those who pursue yoga are in essence ascetics, shipwreck-ribbed characters reminiscent of the withered Siddhartha Gautama before he became the enlightened Buddha and understood the value of a good square meal. They live in ashrams in the hills, beside still lakes or down quiet alleyways in the less fevered quarters of the cities. They sit with faraway eyes and their legs in their laps among students who could never imagine being so old, so thin or so flexible. They are called *swami* or *guru* and seem to speak with a common singsong voice.

There have been exceptions. Swami Mahadevananda, a monk at an ashram in the Cardamom Hills of Kerala, had been there for eighteen years teaching the five yoga disciplines of the Sivananda school: correct exercise, breathing, relaxation, meditation and philosophy, and diet. Despite this stringent code the *swami* was a great butterball in orange robes, a smiling misplaced Roman sent to eat rice and forget the days of pasta and *gelati* as he spread the word of headstand power.

Then there was Dr K.N. Panda, author and yoga teacher. His publicity declared that his 'books on Naturopathy and Yoga, Nature Cure of Diabetes, Miraculous Sprouts and Yogasanas etc are highly appreciated by the intellectuals. His advice/treatment is most available to seekers of help. He has been working as Chief Officer of Health Consultation in some most reputed 5 star hotels in Delhi for long.'

The great man himself was there in person each day around the corner from Jodhpur Apartments, ready and waiting to teach me beside the pool in our class of two, just Dr Panda and me. He came to teach in a tight shirt and a tie, and would line up the pens from his pocket, his change, his watch and his notebook in a tidy row before the class began. It was rarely a flowing class. There were slightly frantic groups of postures punctuated with strident arguments about the differing methods of yoga. His twiglet legs waving in the air in a headstand, he would answer every question with the precursor that he had been lecturing and demonstrating on Delhi's local television station since 1982, as if the roll of the camera set his teaching methods in stone. When I queried some of his methods, also upside down, he would look into my red, inverted face, narrow his eyes and wave his legs a little threateningly at mine. When Delhi flu struck, Dr Panda insisted that I drink two litres of water first thing every morning and then make myself 'do violent vomiting for clearing of all pipes and tubes'. He talked incessantly through every class and posture, the same lesson every time, until it became the mantra of the poolside hour: 'Now we are pulling tight our rectal muscles for benefits of fistula, veins of the anus, stools of loose and hard. Now we are staring at the eyebrow centre until we are getting pain and the tears are rolling down, good for concentration and control of cataracts and of all seeing-eye problems.'

Not a great deal of yoga was learned but the medical terms alone were an education. The arguments over teaching became a petty ritual that we both seemed to enjoy. Sometimes Dr Panda would look at his audience of one and sigh deeply: 'Madam, we are coming here for the spirit and peace. So let us proceed.' Then he would immediately start to niggle for another argument.

It was hard to find the stillness we sought with his babbling commentary and the five-star package tourists popping in just to see what was going on.

Sourish seemed happy with the outcome of the yoga research and the series was set in motion. The government fell. There were fist fights during an afternoon session in the Lok Sabha and I went out to interview the young clubbers of Delhi about whether they had sex in mind when they went out on a Friday night.

The Joint United Nations Programme, looking at the global increase in AIDS, estimated that in 1996 India had somewhere

143

between four and five million HIV positive cases, one-fifth of the world's infected population.

'But', came the cry of Ph.D India, 'it won't happen to us. We are middle-class, we are safe.'

One-third of HIV cases occur among teenagers and young men in that air-conditioned comfort zone. Over a ten-year period HIV cases have increased by 100 per cent. By the turn of the millennium, if the statistics are correct, one in every five Indian families will be infected and affected by HIV.

Yuppie sex has become the latest commodity of upwardly mobile modern urban India. Premarital sex used to be an unspoken thing that happened in the cheap bazaars, a thrust up against a wall or on a *charpai* in an anonymous room. For a large number of the middle class their first sexual relationship came with marriage. Whether or not the chance for premarital sex is taken up in the bazaar or on the university campus there is now the increasing lure of extramarital sex that comes with the supposed sexual freedom of the travelling businessman. Now suburban housewives are getting HIV positive results, passed on from husbands who have been celebrating business deals with sexual transactions on the road, either with prostitutes or in the newer shape of more sexually casual female business colleagues.

Prostitutes, by the nature of their profession, continue to be the main source of HIV infection. Their commodity, sex, is dictated by the price that is paid. A little bit extra and the barrier comes down, maybe just fifty rupees more for unprotected sex, not much, two *masala dosas* and a couple of glasses of *chai*. It is a cheap ticket for a disease that now has free passage from brothels to boardrooms via some teenage dreams.

But this is a country associated with virgin brides and chaste women of the veil, where even in movieland there is rarely more than a kiss, a heaving breast and a slightly lingering touch; a land reluctant to make a public admission that lust is out there and equally reluctant to educate its young about the dangers that await them. And yet at the same time its historical and religious culture moves erotically behind a chiffon veil.

The same refusal to face reality was apparent to Kipling a century before AIDS became part of the sex trade:

> I came to realize the bare horrors of the private's life, and the unnecessary torments he endured on account of the Christian doctrine which lays down that 'the wages of sin is death'. It was counted impious that bazaar prostitutes should be inspected; or that the men should be taught elementary precautions in their dealings with them. This official virtue cost our army nine thousand expensive white men a year always laid up from venereal disease.

AIDS is moving through the population of late twentieth-century India at about the same pace as back-street syphilis and gonorrhoea afflicted the red-blooded boys of Victorian England, lads let loose in a country of overwhelming sensuality.

Every night pumped-up young Delhi fills the nightclubs of the city, the hip-hop spots, set in the lush grazing grounds of the five-star hotels. Among swaying hips in sprayed-on jeans, sidelong glances in the strobe lighting dish out temptation, and testosterone and oestrogen rage.

The mothers and fathers of upholstered Delhi look at the late-night faces of their children over the breakfast table. Amidst the puffed *puris* with their fresh doughnut smell, the loud linen, the bright white milk, there is the scent of suspicion.

'Pass the *puris* and orange juice, sweetheart. Who is it that you are meeting this afternoon?'

'Oh, just some guy I met last night.'

'Anyone we know, sweetheart?'

Pause.

'I'm sorry, I did not quite catch the name.'

There is no name to give because there were no names. He did not know her name, she did not know his. Last night when the hormones strutted there was no polite conversation or discovery of common interests. Last night was about trading the new commodity. Sexual innuendo was the deal.

'I don't buy that,' said a female journalist on the prowl, quizzing me on my research, her smooth face pulled tight.

'I'm just working with statistics and the evidence I see.'

'Which statistics?' she enquired.

She did not seemed moved by India's world-dominating HIV figures. She wanted proof of the theory that AIDS was pouncing on the middle class.

'Private HIV clinics in India's major cities are treating an average of 30 per cent more patients year on year. One of the doctors running an AIDS awareness campaign in Delhi has made the point that the middle class seems to have a curious belief that education and a good salary buy immunity from AIDS and other sexually transmitted diseases. He has pointed out that it is just this kind of attitude that is helping to spread the disease.'

She took a deep breath in order to interrupt my ramble but I ploughed on.

'These were not off-the-record comments and statistics given over a cosy lunch to make me feel better about picking up the bill. He said all this at the Fourth International Congress on AIDS in Asia and the Pacific.'

'So what did you talk about at your cosy little lunch when you picked up the bill then?' Sharp, very sharp.

'Liposuction and child pornography.' Ha.

'And what is it that makes you such an authority on teenage Indian sexuality?' It was a good question.

'I am not presenting myself as any kind of authority, I am just observing.'

'So you are making assumptions about our culture.'

'As I said, I am just an observer.'

'So you are not passing judgements on how poor Third World Indians are being so ignorant about AIDS.' Now she could smell blood. 'Are you pretending that you are one of us?'

'No, I am making it very clear that I am an outsider.'

'But you want to be an insider, *yaar*? Why else would you want to work for an Indian newspaper? It can hardly be for the salary, or do you have some big dark secret back at home?'

'I am just trying to learn.'

'And who are your teachers?'

'Everyman, the *chai*-stall pundit, the politician, the *ghazal* singer, you.'

'How many parties and nightclubs have you been to in India?' she asked.

'The usual round.'

'Is that enough?'

'Obviously not.'

'Obviously not,' she echoed.

'When did you last go nightclubbing?' I asked, a whisper of confidence now returning.

'Last night.'

'Ah.' She smiled. I smiled back in defeat.

'It was the first time for three years.' A laying down of arms. And then a gauntlet. 'We will go nightclubbing.' It was a command, not an invitation. 'Come on, it will be fun, you will see.' She took my number. *Chup*, case closed.

It was not fun. High-earning, cash-casual, exhausted Delhi man does not like to dance. He likes to drink and watch. At parties, a man who dances, who can twirl a girl, is begged, cajoled and bribed back on to the dance floor again and again until he can do no more. By the time he and his rare breed have flagged, the girls have the bit between their teeth. They dance together, in sinuous groups, *dupattas* and shawls flying, arms out, flailing free in the spirit of just enough whisky and soda.

The men stand in groups, talking money and man matters, eyeing suspiciously their fancy footworking peers and their adoring female fans lining up to be spun and schmoozed. As the midnight hour arrives, and all is looking set for a late assault on the dance floor, dinner finally appears, lined up under serried ranks of silver domes kept warm by spirit lamps. Once piled plates have been finished, everyone leaves, usually with indigestion. That is the party scene. There is little variation.

Discothèques are different, subterranean lairs of busy floral carpets, chandeliers and dimly lit tables with hovering waiters bearing bowls of cashew nuts to accompany each rent-cheque drink. The dance floor is a tribute to the danceramas of the '80s, inlaid, sprung, five-star naturally, with dry ice, strobes and a heavy boogie beat.

There is a lot of body talk and peacock strutting but that seems about all. Girls and boys sway at each other and their reflections in the mirrors but usually leave with the same gang of friends. The predators of the night are the older men. They do not erupt on to the floor. They camp at corner tables or by the bar in studied relaxation. They are of middling years, some married, some still single, but all beginning to get the whiff of old age in their early-morning breath. They are regulars at the clubs, known and welcomed for their spending power. They wait and they watch and then they quietly buy drinks and send them to tables where the merchandise has caught their eye.

On my research disco-date with the female journalist I skulked behind a pillar and listened to a variation on a familiar theme, a routine I heard in nightclubs across the capital – different faces, different names but always the same motivation.

'Hello, Jaya.'

'Hello, Uncleji.'

'How is your father?'

'Good, thank you, Uncleji.'

'Come, come, sit down, have a drink.'

'I am here with friends, Uncleji.'

'Jaya, I have known you all your life, you make me feel very old calling me Uncleji. Please, I am Hari to you and your friends. Why don't you bring them over?'

Jaya looked in pain. There was a question mark in her heavily made-up eyes. Why was Uncleji Hari apparently alone in a night-club? Partly out of family duty, partly intrigued, she wiggled off on her platform trainers. Hari waited, his fingers in the cashew bowl.

Loitering behind my pillar, trying to blend in, I stood within earshot of Hari's game, up close to catch the conversation over the wall of sound. When Jaya had gone to find her friends Hari noticed me watching him. He beckoned me over in the way some people call a waiter. I raised my eyebrows and made a pretence of not understanding. A wink from Hari and that was me marked out as white and wanton, easy come, easy go, a little bit older, a little bit more desperate and apparently alone as well.

I was rescued by the sharp-tongued journalist.

'Come on, let's dance. You won't get any of the flavour just standing there.'

Oh but I had.

Among the strobes I tried to watch Hari and Jaya but there was too much dry ice to keep pace with what was happening in the darkened corner. At last a track came on of such a tortured and hopeless beat that we were able to walk from the floor, damp, panting and desperate for cool air and peace.

'Can we go?' I asked.

'If that is what you want.'

Once again I'd been defeated. I was not a competitive night-clubber.

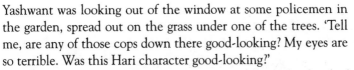

Yashwant was looking out of the window at some policemen in the garden, spread out on the grass under one of the trees. 'Tell me, are any of those cops down there good-looking? My eyes are so terrible. Was this Hari character good-looking?'

'That is not quite the point. In a society where this kind of thing is so hush, hush, how is an eighteen-year-old girl going to know how to protect herself when she is picked up by some much older man? I just don't believe that she is going to give Hari a little speech about using a condom, and no, none of them are good-looking. They are just a bunch of very ordinary cops with little moustaches minding their own business under a tree.'

Yashwant continued to peer at the group, narrowing his eyes to try and focus.

'Of course, she should insist on a condom. I think the one on the left is nice. What do you think?'

'Of course she should but she won't necessarily because she is afraid and believes that HIV is just for queers, prostitutes and street junkies. No, he is not remotely cute, just thin.'

'Homosexual or gay, not queer. I think you are underestimating how pushy Indian women are. Yes, he is definitely cute. I am beginning to focus now.'

Sourish was less distracted than Yashwant when his turn came for comment.

'Are there any rules and regulations about what I can and cannot say when it comes to writing about sex?'

'No, no, as long as it is not puerile or gratuitous.'

'And what does *The Indian Express* regard as puerile or gratuitous?'

'Indian politics.' Sourish broke into his great belly of a laugh. 'No, no, really, you know the sort of thing. As long as it does not come across as being pornographic, unless you are quoting someone in context, then we can just star anything too bad to give a general thingy.'

There was very little gratuitous 'thingy' when the article was printed. It came out under the headline 'Safe is Sexy' and seemed innocuous. Uncleji Hari did not get a mention. The facts, figures and comments were alarming but they were twinned with two big colour pictures of laughing crowds dancing in holiday-camp settings, the text's impact lost amidst what looked like good clean fun. I had not said anything but I had assumed that the picture desk would go for a contrast – an image of an HIV clinic or one of the AIDS awareness campaign posters that were on the hoardings, something to act as a visual jolt.

Even with this soft approach readers were disgusted by my insinuation that their dewy offspring could be dabbling with a disease associated with what one commentator described as 'tarts, tramps, drug addicts and the sexually perverse'. The AIDS awareness bandwagon was rolling but it was not necessarily giving the right message.

The director of a sexual health helpline in Delhi had read the article. She was concerned and depressed that some of the advertisements that were ostensibly promoting AIDS awareness were actually adding to the confusion and she rang me.

'You know there is one advertisement, just your typical kind of ad painted up on hoardings in the standard way. It shows two men leering at a woman in a skimpy skirt, smoking a cigarette. To your average man a girl in a short skirt with a cigarette means one thing, fast, flash, easy and Westernized. Some callers responding to that ad have told us that they are safe because they do not sleep with such types of women. But the fact is that "such" types of women are not available to "such" types of men and neither are "such" types of women the only ones who could give them the virus. One of our great problems is that apart from prostitutes and gays, who are beginning to realize the impact, every other sector of society seems to feel that it is immune because they are too poor to go to prostitutes, too clean to get infected or too rich to be touched by the virus. Every day we feel that we are at war, not against HIV and AIDS but against the prejudice and ignorance.' She took a deep breath.

'You know we had a case recently where a young woman was in a government hospital suffering from AIDS and they put a placard at the end of her bed saying "Bio-hazard". You know the ward boys, the *ayahs* and the nurses were treating this woman as if she was an untouchable. Families with AIDS sufferers are experiencing rampant ostracism. They are boycotted, thrown out of their jobs – the sort of treatment meted out to criminals. What does that say about this country? All we hear the whole time is how modern we are becoming, joining the computer age, the space age, whatever. But look at this, we are creating a horrific new kind of caste system because of our basic ignorance.'

Her use of 'untouchable' was a surprise. Here was a woman fighting the prejudices of society, yet she still deferred to the order of the caste system when it came to finding a simile for what the public viewed as the detritus of humanity.

'People I have spoken to were shocked by what you wrote, you know, and all you were doing was giving them the official figures and some of the hazards of having a blinkered attitude towards the virus. I wish you had been much more aggressive. You see it is easier for you because you are a Westerner, it does not leave such a bitter taste for people. They can still take it in but keep it at one step removed. Can you imagine the panic if we released the unofficial figures on the virus, if we told some of the real stories and exposed some of the VIPs and Bollywood people who are HIV positive? I am glad that you wrote the piece but we need that kind of stuff in every paper, every day, until people just cannot ignore it.

'This is one of the times when I really wish we could take the example of the West, you know, give the whole thing a profile led by stars and politicians to show that nobody is immune. You see no one is really brave enough to be the first one to admit that they have AIDS because that means all the dirt in their past will come out at the same time.'

Two days later there was a report in *The Indian Express* about a young man called Tarun (not his real name, you understand). He had been admitted to hospital.

> He was suffering from jaundice among other infections. He was admitted to the casualty ward, where he had to share a bed with another patient for a day. Scared that Tarun might be deprived of the little attention that he was getting, the family did not inform the doctors of the infection. But on the advice of an AIDS counsellor, the family told the doctors of the situation. Shockingly Tarun was immediately taken off the bed and put on the floor, where he lay for a week without any appropriate medical care.
>
> 'The attitude changed so drastically, that is what was so humiliating,' said a member of Tarun's family. 'They wrote the words HIV positive on the case chart in big bold letters. But more painful was the contempt in their eyes, it was just too painful.'

After a week, the next Saturday, the doctors said that Tarun would have to be shifted to AIIMS (All India Institute of Medical Science).

'There the staff simply told us to come in on Monday. He died on Sunday, at home,' said a member of Tarun's family.

On World AIDS Day in December 1997, while Tarun's family grieved, the Minister of Health gave the massaged figure for HIV cases in India – 70,000 as against five million. Nowhere in the announcement was there any mention of AIDS being spread by homosexual contact.

While the AIDS workers raged at the veil of silence, residents of the archetypal stomping grounds of the great emergent Indian middle class frowned and moved on, popping down the road to catch the latest Hollywood offering, *MIB – Men in Black*, at war with a huge man-eating cockroach from outer space. It seemed a good enough distraction from the fear and ignorance hovering just outside their homes.

At Jodhpur Apartments, Ram Kumar was itching for a fight. I was his victim. He complained loudly to Yashwant. I was accused of ordering tea whensoever I pleased. Even Dhan Singh, who had burnt his hand making *rotis* and so was not in the best of moods, decided to have a gripe. Tea once a day did not seem so demanding. Ram Kumar was shouting. Yashwant stood, one eyebrow raised.

'Has she mistreated you?' Yashwant asked.

Ram Kumar was silent.

'I wish she would. When will she learn to take my advice? I may have to buy her a whip to beat you.'

Ram Kumar smiled. I fled from the room.

Depressed by AIDS and tea I went to join the crowd at *Men in Black*.

The gentleman who sat next to me in the rustling, nattering gloom of the cinema first ploughed his way through popcorn, patties and cola. Then he looked bored. The show had only just begun. He squirmed in his seat before lifting one side of his ample posterior. I held my breath. What emerged was a cellular phone. The gentleman was 'becoming bore' as he informed his friend on the phone. Anyway, the great big bug on the screen had reminded him to call about getting the number for pest control that they had talked about over *pakoras* and whisky just the night before.

MIB, *Men in Black*, and vast exploding cockroaches, for the MIB – the Moderately Incomed Blasé. AIDS day was just another day for Delhiites, not just another day for Tarun's family. The AIDS workers banged their drum and people walked on by, pressing their cellular phones to their ears. But there was also something else in the air, something much more palatable.

Mrs Krishna and Mrs Windsor

AS WINTER APPROACHES, the city breathes again. Sweeter air moves down from the Himalayas. The evening breeze brings the exquisite novelty of goosepimples on bare arms, the first caress of the cool season. Around the *chai* stalls recumbent figures start to move. Their *kurtas* no longer clinging to their damp bodies, they stretch, pull out their shawls from the back of their rickshaws and crank up the old jalopies for the busy time. The running-track around Lodi Gardens fills again with morning and evening joggers, out and about in expensive trainers that leave their logos imprinted in the dust beside the decaying arches and domes of Sikander Shah's sixteenth-century tomb. The shakers and movers make their garden rounds at a rolling mid-pace, not quite an out-and-out jog. Delhiites don't run but they need to speed-shuffle to get in shape for the autumn. They have to keep their eye on the ball – the party season is about to open.

The marigold farmers of Haryana look at their fields of flowers and clap their hands. The lorries begin to roll in to take away the bright blooms to make garlands for thousands of *poojas* and parties. This year there was another excuse for celebration, a visit that was to set chattering Delhi alight.

Back from the hills came the city matriarchs, buzzing with carefully laid plans for the festive season. They rushed to their wardrobes and threw up their hands in horror. What to do? So many parties, so many festivals, and nothing to wear. Shawls and wraps were hastily dispatched to the tailors for dyeing, retrimming and reinventing. And then the ladies set sail for the sari showrooms. Last year's 'Garden Green' had to be replaced with this season's 'Setting Sun', a blood-orange shot with puce to the untutored eye.

Setting Sun was perhaps an appropriate colour. The visit was that of Her Majesty Queen Elizabeth II, and as the returned-from-the-hills luggage was still being unpacked a nasty little jibe made the rounds of the sari and jewellery stores where the matriarchs gathered, trailing their fingers through trays of gold bijouterie. Blousey Brenda was coming to town, her first trip overseas since the death of dear Diana.

'And what does Her Majesty think she is going to find? A sympathetic ex-colony dishing out the TLC, *na*?' Their cheeks wobbled merrily at the thought of the Queen of England, daughter of the last Emperor of India, having to scuttle half-way across the world to seek solace in cool-season Delhi.

'Come here, Priyanka. Look at this lovely necklace, beautiful, *na*? I would say so. So perfect for your pretty face, sweetheart.' The Miss Priyankas of Delhi stood by, pouting in skin-tight jeans, gossiping with similarly denim-sprayed Miss Smeethas about the boys they liked, as against the men that they had been prescribed. They still had a few weeks in which to play before being packaged, painted and primped into their wedding clothes.

Even Sourish was mulling over the wedding season.

'How about a piece on the fall-out of the whole death cult of Diana and how it might affect the royal visit?' Neither he nor I were paying much attention. We were leafing through a new magazine, the first bridal publication to hit the newsstands of India. In a country where the rituals and trappings of a wedding are a matter of rigid tradition, this was a gamble. Indian mothers-in-law-in-waiting, be they from Bangalore or Delhi, are not ones to bow to the whims of magazine editors.

Sourish shook his head at each page: the pre-wedding hip-busting package, the make-over, the make-up, the dress-up, the up-town reception, the cool-down honeymoon with the hot-to-trot lingerie.

'Oh, oh.' Sourish was laughing now. 'This will never work.'

'I don't know. It has a captive audience.'

'Captured, shackled and caged. Oh, the poor brides of India.' He wrinkled his nose.

'I don't mean that. At home one of the first things a girl does when she gets engaged is to go out and buy all the bridal and setting-up home magazines.'

'Well, here the market is just looking down a tunnel of tradition. There is no deviation. No one wants to do anything different. There are only two things that are predestined in an Indian woman's life, the arrangements for her wedding and the fact that her first child should be a son.' He lingered over an exquisite blonde strolling along a honeymoon beach, alone and tempting.

'Rubbish. Every girl wants to make a slightly different impact at her wedding.'

'No, no, you are wrong. Believe me, the bride has nothing to do with it and no mother is going to buy this magazine.'

'Why not?'

'It's not in their nature. Their mothers arranged their weddings for them and they will do the same for their daughters. Anyway, look at all this flesh. They will think it most unsuitable. I am being general of course.' He was still lingering over the beach blonde.

'What about women who are getting married in their late twenties when their parents may have died?'

Sourish laughed. 'So you are thinking that this is a magazine targeted at orphaned women in their late twenties who are getting married, a sort of mother-replacement venture? I am telling you it won't work. Have a chocolate.' He pushed a box of After Eights at me. 'See, they are English. Please have some. I have them coming out of all corners.'

It was the festival of Dussehra in a few days' time, celebrating the victory of Rama over the wicked Ravana, the demon king of Lanka, part of the *Ramayana*, one of the great epics of Hinduism, mounted as a series of public plays (called the *Ramlila*) for the ten days of the festival. This was also the first party-season excuse for the giving and consumption of huge quantities of sweets, corporate India's chance for a show of excessive generosity to most favoured clients. As a features editor with the power to write all sorts of promotional pieces, Sourish was on the receiving end of a constant flow of tinsel-tied boxes full of every variety of sticky sweet.

I took an envelope from the After Eights box, found it was empty and screwed it up.

'I think everyone has had that one,' said Sourish.

'Really?'

'No, no, I mean the Diana story thingy. We did so much stuff at the time and I think people have had enough.'

'But there was a picture of her today in the foreign news section, a great big picture with just a caption about some New York charity queen selling one of the Princess's dresses for some obscene amount of money.'

'Oh, oh, pictures are different.'

The wedding glossy had been abandoned and he was flipping through some of the weekend supplements of the imported English newspapers. Gaunt, heroin-chic models jutted from the pictures in surreal haute couture. It was London fashion week.

'London, that would be good.' He popped his hand into the chocolate box again.

'You want me to write about London?' Another empty envelope was snatched from the box.

'We can run it the weekend that your Queen is here. Everyone is going to be doing stuff about England – Yorkshire pudding, steak and kidney pie, jam roly-poly, all that sort of thing.'

'Is that really how you think we all still eat?'

'Well, it is what they are having at all the five-star hotels for their celebrations of English cooking.'

That was that. England was still the land of batter pudding and jammy roll.

'So you want something a bit different about London, white-hot London, most happening city, blah, blah, that sort of thing?'

'Whatever.'

We both dived for the chocolates at the same time.

'Oh, oh, and you are doing the piece on fasting for next week, no?'
'Of course.' I popped a chocolate into my mouth.

The painters were out on the streets, painting Delhi clean with pots of whitewash and coconut-husk brushes, a white town for a white queen. On the outer circle of Connaught Place, a small boy with a dried-date face squatted beside the kerb, watching his own bottom with fascination. A thin man in a dirty municipal uniform nudged him to one side, quite carefully, without upsetting the boy's balance, so that he could paint over the splashes of urine.

The Queen was due in Delhi between the festivals of Dussehra and Diwali, the latter honouring Lakshmi, the goddess of good fortune, and providing another *mithai*fest opportunity. In the bazaar, a few minutes' walk from Hailey Road, were two of the most famous *mithai* shops in Delhi. Every few days I would go in on my way back from the fruit and vegetable market to buy just one piece of some gooey confection. At first it amused them, then it became an irritation. I was buying one sweet at a time for a few rupees when Delhi dames were elbowing to the front to buy kilos of the stuff. Eventually they got used to my inane requests. It became a game, trying to second-guess what I was going to choose, or to tempt me with the latest concoction. That week my favourite shop had made a special kind of *mithai* for the visit of Her Majesty. It was the colour of last year's 'Garden Green' with patches of regal silver *varq* on top. The *mithai* man offered me a piece to try. It was disgusting. He offered me another piece, unusual behaviour for a *mithai* man. He shrugged. It was not selling very well, he said. There would be a very good discount if I bought a kilo. With patriotic zeal I ferreted in my bag but found only enough for five hundred grams. There was no discount for that, but by now I had been given three pieces to try and was too embarrassed to refuse. It was called 'Royal Surpriz'. It was aptly named.

The Rani Sahiba sat, as a queen should, in elegant, regal isolation, Dhan Singh a couple of paces to her left, Ram Kumar obse-

The mithai *man*

quiously bent over the accounts book at her feet. She smiled her
serene smile and enquired about my day. Satisfied that it had not
been spent hanging around unsuitable *chai* stalls she handed me
an invitation. In a curlicued script it read:

You are most cordially and honourably invited to
The prestigious enactment of the Ramlila
for Dussehra
at the Ramlila Ground, Old Delhi.

'Yashwant tells me that you would like perhaps to go to one of these evenings. Have you been to a *Ramlila* before?'

'No.'

'Then you must go,' she proclaimed.

Cousin Gita, Yashwant's beautiful young friend Mangay, and I squashed into the back seat of an old taxi. Yashwant took the front seat, conducting the driver through the traffic, arms and orders flying. The driver was resigned to the performance, the price of driving royalty. Mangay, all angles and symmetry, giggled and kept saying that he was going to be so bored. Gita was not enthused. Yashwant was enjoying his own performance. I felt carsick.

The showground was a rolling, seething thing, a human jungle, full of food hawkers and festival devotees, children in tears (not the right coloured balloon, not enough tinsel on Rama's memento bow), gaggles of teenagers drawing hard on cigarettes, hands running through ever-flicking hair, and a curious group of nuns buying balloons and eating sweets, the Sisters of the Convent of Mary and Jesus, Baba Kharak Singh Marg, New Delhi, ever open to alternative spiritual development, especially if there was a show thrown in.

The taxi drove right into the thick of it, the driver urged on by Yashwant in defiance of the policemen's waving *lathis*. When our passage was finally blocked by the sea of humanity, Yashwant stepped from the car and surveyed the scene.

The driver reversed gratefully into the crowd, nodding at Yashwant's shouted instruction on where to wait. Beyond the main crowd was a red carpet. Waving the curlicued invitation at whoever barred his way, Yashwant led us through the fray. We marched on to the carpet between lines of Black Cats, Delhi's security élite. As we were led to the seats at the front of the great dust-bowl Yashwant turned. 'Do we really have to sit through the whole of this?'

'No, we shall go as soon as we get bored.' Gita stepped prettily over a fat child who was beating his fists on the red carpet and screaming.

Towards the back of the arena stood a gargantuan effigy of the demon king Ravana, his leering expression set off by a drooping moustache and crimson lips, fashionably matching the reds of his eyes. This was the personification of evil. It would be burnt on the climactic day of the festival when Ravanas all over India, from playgrounds to capital stadia, would rise up in flames and be cast into rivers and open sewers, to clog the waterways with their singed sneers and bloated bodies.

The stage was a great pantomime setting. Rama and his monkey helpers were stage right, among banana trees and tissue flowers of sky blue and baby pink. Ravana lurked in glorious, flaming evil stage left. On to the scene came actors in singing-telegram monkey costumes twinned with spangly shorts and a series of frightful wigs.

The performances were constipated. Rama, with his flowing mane and eyeshadow to match his tissue flowers, lolled about the stage. The podgy bouncing monkeys, their masks reminiscent of the squashed testicles of sleeping dogs, were similarly lacking in thespian zeal. Just as there was a chance of the tension mounting with the imminent appearance of the leering Ravana and the simpering, whimpering, captive Sita (Rama's bride and the cause of all the trouble), there was a kerfuffle in the crowd. Surrounded by Black Cats waving their guns and nonentities brandishing mobile phones, a politician, a member of the Cabinet, an oleaginous individual in the national political uniform of the white *kurta pyjama*, was ushered forward. The lethargic actors were finally roused by this sideshow into a brief display of lively acrobatics before a man in a grey suit stepped on to the stage. The gods were forced to stop to make way for politics.

Gita was incensed. 'How dare they? This is a religious festival for the people. What do they think they are doing turning it into a political rally? Look at that disgusting little man. Imagine, we have people like him running the country. It is like a bad dream.'

Up on stage the politician listened to a series of sycophantic speeches, while the monkeys in their spangly shorts and itchy masks fidgeted in the background.

'See him standing in the middle of all those silly monkeys. Which are the animals and which are the humans, I ask you? Come, we have to boo.' She began.

It was hard not to follow suit, her indignation at the interruption was palpable. Mangay sank down in his seat, humiliated by such wanton behaviour. Yashwant clapped and urged us on (princes do not boo). Around us people lost interest in the speeches and embarked on picnics. The politician was presented with a garland and a gift as a mark of esteem from the most honoured organizers of the *Ramlila* and then he retreated behind the guns and the mobile phones. The gods returned. There was a particularly loud cheer from our group when the gorgeously evil Ravana and his crew burst through the flames.

'Ravana for PM,' hollered Gita and I.

Now that he had seen the demon king, Yashwant was ready to leave. He gathered his courtiers round him and off we went into the night, falling into pot-holes and dodging hawkers as we tried to find the taxi. Mangay was dispatched to scout. Yashwant had better things to do. He had found a pet bazaar and was trawling the cages in search of a brilliant bird, a companion for his ring-necked parakeet that was going bald with boredom.

Captives behind chicken wire looked out, their coats and plumage ragged and dulled by fear, malnutrition and diarrhoea. The newest arrivals were the most likely to sell, for they still had their dazzling colours and shining coats.

Yashwant called from somewhere in the stinking gloom. 'Good show, see what I have found, the most beautiful thing you have ever seen. *Jaldi kāro*, hurry up. Come, come.'

It was a perfect parakeet, a Greater Alexandrine, its plumage a bright shade of green, a much more attractive shade than 'Royal Surpriz' and perhaps the grateful future recipient of my half kilo that still languished uneaten.

'Gita Singh, stop sulking. Come, admire this beautiful thing.'

Gita was standing outside, away from the cages, her *dupatta* pulled across her face. She picked her way through the piles of droppings.

'Come, Yashwant, it smells disgusting here. You can catch the most terrible diseases from some of these birds. You cannot buy that. What will Rani Sahiba say? Anyway you have no money. Come.'

Yashwant waved his hand. He did have money. He had just arranged a loan from me.

There was little traffic on the way back but the road was still smudged by the pollution of the rush hour. We were squashed in the back in the same order as we had come, shoulder to chest, elbow to ear. In a fluster of embarrassment, Mangay had put his arm behind me on the back of the seat to make more room. He sat rigidly, willing the arm not to belong to him. Yashwant was up front with the miserable bird on his knee, its head popping just as Sourish's did. Gita was pretending to be cross with Yashwant for buying the bird. We sat in silence watching the rear lights of other cars swaying around the road, the weaving pot-hole dance of night-time Delhi roads. There was no lighting.

Out of the blackness a figure lurched. It was pitched up into the air and fell under the back tyres of the car in front. The car drove on.

Gita screamed out to stop and Yashwant shouted to carry on. The driver shrank down in his seat. He slowed but did not stop.

Yashwant silenced Gita. 'We cannot stop, it is not safe.'

'We must report it immediately,' Gita cried.

Through the back window the body receded into the gloom, other cars and rickshaws swerving around it. No one else was stopping.

'He might still be alive,' Gita shouted.

'If we go to the cops it makes things very convenient for them. They just pin it on us. The Father says we must never stop. You never know who is out there. We will ring a hospital as soon as we get back. Someone will stop.'

We hadn't. Why should they? The traffic would dance around the body as it did around the pot-holes.

Dussehra passed and children went back to school after the ten-day holiday, a brief dip into academia before the wild Diwali weekend. The Queen flew in from Pakistan. She wore a big yellow hat and white gloves, the fairly new Foreign Secretary by her side in a panama hat and with his foot in his mouth.

It was dubbed Snafu Week, an appropriate use of a crude English acronym beloved of Battle of Britain pilots in the seemingly hopeless numbers game against the Luftwaffe. Very English, very Indian. 'Situation normal: all fucked up', or fouled up, as the more delicate Delhi velvet-sofa set preferred to say. The Foreign Secretary represented a new British government, a New Britain, reinvented for fear that the old one was falling apart. The Queen was now portrayed as open in all things, a richly exportable Royal set against a fading Union Jack, diluted in a sea of spinning, smiling political puff. The grin of the Top of the Pops British Prime Minister threatened to become the logo of a country that Indians felt was beginning to suffer from a personality disorder.

The enduring image of the tour was a photograph of an ageing lady in a yellow frock wearing a pair of fluffy socks as she was led through the Golden Temple at Amritsar. The Delhi dames hooted – fluffy socks and teapot hats, too, too much. Naturally someone was to blame. Did British officials think that they could rely on a gush of sepia-tinted fervour to sweep their monarch across an ever-grateful subcontinent?

The kerbstones of Delhi were white but the pens of the press were dipped in deep, dark vitriol. They licked their lips as the catalogue of gaffs grew. First came the suggestion from the man in the panama hat that really it was about time Pakistan and India sorted out their differences over Kashmir and that he would willingly help to broker peace. The Indian press puffed up its chest. 'Did he really stoop so low as to use Her Majesty's visit as a chance to garner the Pakistani Labour vote back home?' they asked.

The Indian Prime Minister held his head high at the Kashmir bodyline bowl. 'What did the honourable Foreign Secretary of a third-rate country think he was playing at?'

Then came the fated visit to the garden in Amritsar,

Jallianwala Bagh, the scene of a black day in Imperial history where in 1919 General Dyer ordered Indian troops under his command to open fire on a peaceful crowd, gathered to protest against a British order that outlawed meetings and demonstrations.

Seventy-eight years later the Prime Minister of India felt that if Her Majesty was to visit Jallianwala Bagh then she should make an official apology to the people of the erstwhile empire for the massacre. She took the course of compromise and referred to the 'unfortunate' incident in British Indian history. The press pack howled and republican sympathizers rubbed their hands in glee.

Lest the Foreign Secretary felt alone in being unloved the Duke of Edinburgh reliably popped his foot in his mouth on a visit to the Cochin Club in the spice city of the south. The four remaining British residents of the town were lined up on parade. The Duke peered at the secretary of the club, one of the final four.

'Couldn't you afford the ticket home at Independence?' asked the Duke.

'Sir,' said the secretary, 'I could afford the fare. I also met your uncle, the Viceroy, around that time. Had much better manners than you.'

There was no reply.

It had all been so very different in 1963 when a pretty young woman and her elegant husband had toured a country that in so many places still wore its coat of British India with pride. Thirty-four years on and the coat had worn thin, too moth-eaten to survive the sartorial rigours of another royal tour.

Back in Britain the comments in the dailies were as barbed as those in the Indian papers. One gentleman of the press alighted on a question that particularly titillated the republican element of the Delhi drawing-room scene.

'How', he enquired, 'could any tour of India by a British head of state be successful until the head of state was elected by the people?' No one seemed to be able even to understand the thought process behind the comment but it appealed to some as being the sort of feeling that had set neat white hats upon the heads of the early members of Congress in the Quit India days. Yet even as the whetstones ground on in the news rooms there was a hum of discontent at the lack of courtesy towards a royal guest in a foreign land.

The Delhi dames muttered and the papers poured forth their outrage but the show went on, alighting in Delhi. The Queen surveyed the streets and remarked that it was rather a dirty city. It was a valid point and no one could really disagree. The Prime Minister blamed the city council, the city council blamed the workers, and the workers blamed the baldness of their coconut-husk brushes.

The moment had come for the cream of Delhi to greet the Queen. Those who had fought their way on to the invitation lists by dint of achievement or birth scurried to their tailors and designers to pick up trappings suitable for a royal occasion. They stood in line to bob and bow, sweaty-palmed as Her Majesty approached. Did you wait until spoken to or pop in a breezy remark? Was it Ma'am to rhyme with jam or Ma'arm to rhyme with arm? She walked, she shook hands, she charmed and she passed on, briefed to the hilt on who was who and how they had got that way.

Some went away nodding in agreement with the sentiments in the press. Others left in awe. A few were quite unmoved. Nevertheless, the fact remained that they had all bobbed and bowed and caught a whiff of an elusive but vaguely familiar scent, one that lingered for a while even after the gangplank of HMY *Britannia* was hauled up for the last time. They caught the ephemeral scent of mystery that hung in the empty marquees among the floral glut of frangipani and tuberose when royalty had passed by, the potent aura of something from a different place, something a bit better than the cheap digs in the press, the political manoeuvring, the petty fights over etiquette and who sat where or stood in which queue. They would have liked to identify it but it was gone in the puffs of dust made by the sweepers after the party was over.

Once back in London the Foreign Secretary went so far as to say that he thought it had all gone rather well. Not even Her

Majesty bought that. In Delhi the feathers began to settle. People shrugged and said that she had looked rather old, but then so did they. Others said that it was just not the same as when Lovely, Living Diana had sat alone in front of the great white tomb in Agra. Where had that sort of glamour gone, they wondered, as they sent their party best off to the dry cleaners again for Diwali and the great wedding rush.

'I have to write about weddings,' I told Yashwant.

He was at his fish tank, mourning the death of his silver-scaled tin foil bard, one of his most favoured aquarium exotics. He was trying to maintain a low profile, a contradiction in terms. He had been keeping the new Greater Alexandrine parakeet secreted in his bathroom. Now he was worried that it was suffering so out it went, on to the balcony, swapped with the other slightly balding bird. He had his door ajar to hear any outbursts.

'Oh God, what a boring subject, awful parties, arranged by fearful women to destroy their daughters' lives. Thank God I never submitted a girl to that kind of torture.'

'That would hardly have been appropriate.'

'What do you mean? It would have been the most appropriate thing that I could do. The elder son is required to produce an heir regardless. He marries some poor, beautiful young girl, impregnates her somehow and then ignores her. That was not for me. I could not allow some girl to spoil her life just so we had the charade of looking right.'

'And is this really still happening, girls agreeing to settle for that kind of lop-sided arrangement?'

'Of course. There may be many royal families but there are never enough to satisfy everyone. You really do not understand what it means to marry into a royal family here. Some girl with ambitious parents is always going to get herself bullied into it.'

'There can be friendship in that kind of marriage.'

'Ha, how can there be friendship if everyone is laughing at the poor girl behind her back, even sniggering in her face? Oh, it would have been a great big joke. They may laugh at me now but at least I am living by a code of honesty.' He rested his head on the cool green glass of the aquarium.

'I think I might just skip the controversy of heterosexual pressure on the homosexual Indian aristocracy.'

He gave me a cold look, pulled from amongst the weed where the fishes swam.

There was a sound of surprise from outside. Yashwant waved for silence. It was his mother calling from the balcony.

'Dhan Singh, come here at once.'

There was a pause as Dhan Singh slowly shuffled from the kitchen.

'Dhan Singh, what have you been feeding this bird? It has changed colour.'

Dhan Singh told her that the food had come from the Raj Kumar himself. I could almost see one of her fine eyebrows arching in disbelief.

'Yashwant, Yashwant Singh, what is this bird?' she called out.

'Tell her it's my parakeet. You bought it with my money so it's almost mine anyway,' I whispered.

We strolled out on to the balcony and Yashwant explained that the bird belonged to me.

'And are you going to be taking it back to London with you or will my son be adopting it from you? What have you done with the other one, Yashwant Singh, or has this thing eaten it?'

The topic of weddings was raised as a counter-offensive. The Rani sat down with a flutter of her chiffon *pullāv*.

'What would you like to know?'

'Everything, please.'

'May I suggest that you go out to some of the gold shops and wedding designers and listen to the chatter that goes on. That may give you some idea of how the whole great edifice is built. Tribhovandas, the gold merchant at the top of Janpath, is perhaps a good place to start.'

And so it was, especially on a Sunday afternoon when the

affluent of Delhi, the families of brides-to-be, converged on the jewellers in order to part company with fat rolls of rupees.

As I made my way up the red carpet to the great glass door, a plump woman pushed out past the doorman, her hand to her chest, gasping for air. 'Ahh, too much of people,' she groaned, leaning against the wall and fanning herself with the other chubby hand, knuckle-dustered in jewels. She was right. The place was heaving.

I sat on a rather small velvet mushroom of a stool and introduced myself to Mrs Krishna and Mrs Gupta, each there with a pouting prenuptial. Mrs Krishna held the floor, her voice the loudest in the scrum bent over the twinkling trays. Her dimpled arms flew as she issued orders at break-neck speed to a young man who ran from case to case.

Gold is a national necessity. Every woman from the village fields to the grandstand at a royal polo game wears it as a mark of the worth that she has brought to the house of her husband. It is the first thing that welcomes a woman into her married life and the last thing that she has to sell to buy rice if her family is starving. It is the currency of the dowry negotiations that fill the months leading up to the wedding season and it is hiked to ridiculous prices, way beyond the market rate.

This was not what was on Mrs Krishna's mind. She was busy keeping a weather eye on Mrs Gupta. Mrs Krishna was going to buy better wedding jewellery than Mrs Gupta. The reason emerged as Mrs Krishna consumed a glass of alarmingly orange juice. Her daughter Poonam and Mrs Gupta's daughter were perched side by side, admiring each other's nail polish.

'You see these two girls are like sisters. We live so close and they were going to school together all their lives. If ever any of Poonam's things went missing I could always be sure to find them lying with the Guptas. Our home was her home and the other way round, you understand.'

A home from home it may have been but there was a distinct lack of female intimacy between the mothers.

'Now Poonam is getting married in just one month to such a

charming young man, you know. You would like him, I can tell you, and he is doing such a good job with an American company.'

Mrs Krishna reached out towards Poonam to give a confirming pat to her maternal dreams. Poonam looked sour. Her mother reapplied herself to the matter in hand.

'It is to be a November Sunday night. It is going to be so beautiful. She is going to be so beautiful. Yes, sweetheart, you are.' She patted Poonam again. Poonam looked as if she was going to be sick.

Mrs Gupta's daughter was to be married the weekend before Poonam, also on a beautiful November Sunday night. Mrs Gupta's daughter was prettier than Poonam, she had a degree in English that Poonam did not have, and she had a lovely smile that Poonam did not have. So Mrs Krishna had to find a set of wedding jewellery to make up for these shortcomings, to go one better than Mrs Gupta.

Poonam was not interested in the gold but she was very interested in my gym shoes, the have-to-have accessory of upward, urban life.

'Are those Nikes?' she asked.

I looked down. I had no idea.

'I've just got some of the new Nikes. Fantastic, the best, I am telling you.' Poonam's face came alive.

'Do you wear them clubbing?' How old did I sound?

'*Yaar*, sure, and I have this great new dress. You must have seen them, everyone on MTV is wearing them. A little kind of clingy thingy, you know.'

'Mrs Krishna, may I borrow Poonam for a moment to show me some of the other wedding sets upstairs?'

Mrs Krishna looked surprised.

'You will not find any better there. These are the best here. Come, sit down and see.' She patted the vacant mushroom beside her and beckoned for more of the alarmingly orange drink.

'I know these are the most beautiful but I really would like to see the range, to see what is on offer to people who are perhaps not able to buy the most exquisite sets.'

Mrs Krishna purred. 'Go, Poonam, go with Auntie and show her the upstairs things.' She gave a flick of the wrist, permission granted, a regal gesture in recognition of her recognized buying power.

Mrs Krishna thought that I was safe. She had referred to me as Auntie. It was not a tag I relished but it meant acceptance.

Away from her mother's dimpled command Poonam became confident. Even before we had reached the top of the stairs she was issuing commands to another nervous young man. She wanted this and this and that, and she waved for two of the stools to be put by a particular showcase so that we could sit down and look. In time, once the Nikes had strutted their stuff, she would become just like her mother. She alighted on a set and, in unconscious imitation of her mother's gestures and tone, she demanded that they be produced upon a velvet tray for her to try. Mrs Krishna may have been concerned about getting value for money, but she had better taste than her daughter – just. Poonam had selected a piece of such tinselled vulgarity as to come straight from scene five, wedding dance number, Hindi movie spangle-land.

Perhaps on account of her extreme youth or the fact that Mama's buying power was safely being exercised downstairs, the young man did not seem to be particularly interested in Poonam. He was, however, very keen to sell to me. He kept pressing until I chose a very simple piece. As with most things simple, particularly in jewellery shops, it turned out to be not only the most expensive piece but also an antique.

'Here, Poonam, you try. It is such a lovely necklace and it will look so perfect on you. I am all the wrong colouring.'

She tried it on. For a moment there was a glimpse of the elegant, sensual woman she might become.

'Are you looking forward to your wedding?' I asked.

The moment of poise passed and Poonam was again the pouting little girl teetering on the edge of a grown-up world.

'Of course.'

Of course.

'How long have you known your fiancé?' The big question.

'Some months.' She paused, nervous fingers fiddling at her throat. 'He's a good man and he has a very good job and future prospects.'

'So your mother said. Do you have things in common? Does he like the nightclub scene?'

'I am not sure. I think he likes to read and he is very interested in computers.'

The silence was broken by a call from below.

'Come to me, sweetheart. I am really not going to come up all those stairs.'

Arranged marriages are a subject of such delicacy, such controversy, that they must be danced around on tiptoes. With Nikes and nightclubbing have come the love marriages of the West, sweeping before them the concept of the dowry, subservient loyalty and dynastic alliances. Yet still each week the matrimonial columns are full of matches to be made. Still I had to queue for hours on Sunday evenings at the local international call booth, because mothers were lining up with scrolls of their sons' and daughters' astrology charts to be faxed to that day's advertised brides and grooms-to-be.

Soon after the shopping spree with Poonam and Mrs Krishna I had supper with friends who had just celebrated their thirty-fifth wedding anniversary. He was a successful industrialist, she a former Sanskrit scholar, a mother and now a grandmother. Their marriage had been arranged.

'Our fathers were great friends, you see. There was no pressure. My father made it most clear to me that if I did not wish to go ahead with the marriage then he would back me up. That was not a usual attitude to have at that time. He was an enlightened man.' She waved to the houseboy to fill up my plate again. 'I liked him from our very first meeting and I think he liked me.'

We had been talking earlier of the Queen's visit and the conversation now turned to the subject of dynastic arranged marriages and to one in particular, the obvious one.

'Diana Spencer was only nineteen when she was engaged to the Prince of Wales. How on earth can anyone know how their life is going to turn out when they are that age, or even how they intend to run it?' I asked.

'I got married when I was sixteen and I knew perfectly well that I was marrying a man who had to be allowed to be king in his own home. If he was not a king there then how would he be able to hold up his head as a man?' Her husband had left the room.

'Of course, not all of my friends agreed with me. Some of them said that if you allow a man to rule supreme in his own home then you are putting yourself into an inferior position, into a pattern that can never be changed once it is established. But a husband is a man above all else and he must be made to feel that way.' As her husband came back into the room she returned to the subject of the royal marriage.

'If you marry a king you are not marrying a commoner and you can never forget that. She decided for whatever reason that she could have her cake and eat it and then throw it up as well. That is not a marriage, that is the act of a selfish woman who can only focus on herself in the end.' Her elbows were on the table, firmly planted as she made her point.

Her husband shifted in his chair and cleared his throat.

'But we are talking about a different culture. You are applying your rules to the marriage system of another country. We are talking about two different games.' I wanted her to go on.

'There is no game, there is just one rule. You must do your duty. Your wants and needs are secondary. They must be satisfied by the role that you have agreed to take on. If you marry a man who is going to be king that is enough.' She picked up her fork again and focused on her food.

There was silence around the table for a while.

'Have I said too much?' she asked.

'No, baby, you said just enough,' her husband replied.

The wedding season took off. It was just after eight one evening. I was in Bushan's rickshaw crossing Delhi. The long red lines and swell of Lutyens' parliament buildings rose out of the gloom. It could have been a night fog, drifting up and down the roads, that gave the cars cartoon cones of light, but it was not. Pollution had settled its great suffocating buttocks over Delhi. What had been an irritant in the hot weather was now dangerous and debilitating. The recently busy jogging track in Lodi Gardens was empty again, the flab-fighters of Delhi too nervous to venture out into the carbon monoxide soup. The city moved with a handkerchief or a shawl end across its mouth.

Bushan kept leaning out of the side of his machine to peer through the haze. We moved out on to Shanti Path, Peace Road, long and straight, lined by the tall gates of the great embassies and high commissions set in their huge gardens. Here was a slightly rarer air for the diplomatic folk to breathe. Off the wide boulevard we plunged into the higgledy-piggledy of a residential area where the air sat down again with a thud. The roads were edged with carpets, an endless roll of red. It had been raining and they had all been soaked at various washed-out weddings around the city. Now they were set out to dry, watched over by small boys. The carpets were someone's livelihood.

Out of the metallic fog appeared a band, men in Walt Disney white uniforms with epaulettes making star-burst shelves across narrow shoulders, their caps shiny-peaked, white and gold, bearing flute and horn, trumpet, tambourine and *tabla*, marching out of time and out of synch. Some stepped high, as if they could be seen in the grey light, others just shuffled along, thin bodies in over-sized costumes, grubby spats covering even grubbier shoes. Behind them came a white horse, pink-eyed and rose-nostrilled. On it rode a young man in a white high-collared wedding tunic, lit by hundreds of candelabra bulbs carried head high around the horse, their glass pieces jangling to accompany the band, gold on tinsel, tinsel on gold. The young man was not happy on the horse. His fingers were curled tight under the pommel of the saddle, his stare fixed through thick glasses on the animal's glitter-woven mane. A turban of pantomime vulgarity perched lop-sidedly on his head, pulling one side of his glasses down and adrift across his nervous face.

Meeting wedding parties was part of daily cool-season life. There had been an almost enchanting meeting the night before, on the way back from the bazaar. The service lane behind Hailey Road had been filled with the members of a large band. This had been a rich wedding – a landau made nuptial with marigolds and glittering cloth, the two horses waiting with their muzzles buried in piles of hay. I had crouched down for one of those sentimental horse chats. The keeper of the groom's horse pulled me over to see his mount, a great sleek, well-fed thing. He offered me a ride. Thrilled by the idea of an evening backstreet trot, I reached for the reins. He grabbed my bosom and gave it a fulsome tweak. It is called Eve-teasing. I had felt neither Eve-like nor teased and had scurried home sweating with embarrassment. Now, with Bushan to watch over me, it would be safe to approach the new evening's wedding party.

'Can we stop, Bushan?'

He ignored me above the whine of the engine. It was Hindustani-speaking time. I tapped his shoulder.

'*Ruko!*' I shouted.

Bushan turned round in disgust, without stopping.

'*Yahā rukiye?* Please will you stop?' he corrected. He was

Bushan, my king of the road

adamant that I speak graceful Hindustani rather than the imperative bark that was so common. He turned his attention back to the road.

'*Bushanji, māf kijiye, yahā rukiye?* Esteemed Bushan, please to be excused, but please will you stop now?' There was a heavy emphasis on the *now* – we were well beyond the marching band.

Placated he stopped and the wedding party caught us up and passed on, heading for the bridal home, decked in garlands of orange and red marigolds. There would be his bride, ear to nose to throat in gold, hair piled high, hands and feet henna-patterned, her eyes black with kohl, butterfly fingers at her hair, ready to set off and make a man in a twinkling turban a king in his own home. It was hard to tell, looking at the young man in his thick glasses clinging to the saddle in the polluted fog, whether he would be a good, kind monarch or one who would abuse the privileges of his position.

Bushan collected me later in the evening, his face wrapped up in a tartan scarf. He was waiting outside in the dark as I walked out of the warm glow of the house. I was not sure whether he had been home in the intervening hours. He was jumping up and down in the cold air, his arms wrapped around his thin chest, his breath leaving little puffs as he bounced in and out of the circle of a street light. It was just after midnight. I had been lolling variously on silk carpets and an overstuffed *chaise longue*, eating fresh, hot *pakoras*, *petha*, a rich yellow pumpkin curry, and *ras malāi*, dollops of cream cheese, flavoured with rosewater and doused in cream.

As the whisky count went up the discussions on government corruption became more verbose. I retreated to a silk carpet where I talked to a man with grey-green eyes about the cruelty of owning dogs in towns and the sexual proclivities of the late Maharaja of Patiala. The man with the grey-green eyes told me that I was like a *djinn* of the night, a spirit of Delhi, one rank down from an angel. I tried to rise above the waft of whisky as he fed me cardamom balls flecked with silver paper. It seemed a good time to leave in case I fell in love with a man who made me laugh and popped sweets into my mouth.

I was warm and fed. Bushan looked cold and thin. I did not ask whether he had been waiting outside for four hours. Still thinking of grey-green eyes I did not want to know.

As we whined through the mist to Shanti Path, figures appeared out of the gloom, white figures in ill-fitting costumes with oversized epaulettes. It was the band from the wedding we had passed earlier in the evening – not a complete band now but a few stragglers, their shoulders hunched up, their peaked caps pulled down, their pipes and horns slung over their shoulders, a dishevelled bunch. They were not marching now.

Bushan was in high dudgeon, waving one hand in the air as he raged about how little these talented musicians were paid and how the fat Delhi matriarchs could not even arrange for the players to be transported home.

I called above the whine, in the polite form, for Bushan to stop.

There were four of the band just beside the rickshaw when it came to a halt. They all managed to cram themselves in, bending double into tight balls, nothing of them beneath the oversized uniforms. The instruments were more of a problem. Bushan sat on a drum, with a trombone and a trumpet at his feet. We tied the second, bigger drum on to the roof with Bushan's belt and the end of my shawl, and then we made our way very slowly towards the area of Old Delhi, just beyond the Red Fort, where they lived. They managed to light *biris* from their crunched positions and Bushan immediately stopped and made them put them out, muttering furiously about it being an insult to me. I melted for the second time that night and we headed on for the Old City, the boys singing a Hindi movie favourite to make up for the smoking ban.

High Teas and Aquarium Blues

'THERE IS a slight problem.'

This was an unusual opening shot for Sourish.

'You see you are doing too much storytelling.'

'Oh?' I had been lolling across his desk, comfortable and tired. I woke up and sat up.

'That is fine in your English papers and thingy. You know how sometimes you have up to five thousand words and then you have so much time to build a story. There is not time for that here. I need reportage. You know, more quotes, more comments from the people themselves and pictures of them too.'

I thought I had been behaving so well but now we had come to another point of conflict. While I was not allowed to approach stories that touched news issues, the pieces of no great consequence that had become my territory were to be approached as if *they* were hard news, to be served with quotes that punched and pictures that pulled. Sourish wanted the names of people, places and designer labels in every line, bang, bang, bang, with no comment, hard-hitting stories about nothing particularly important.

'But reportage is for news.'

Both Sourish's eyebrows shot up.

'Reportage is for anything you like, news, weather, features, sport. Oh, oh, yes, sport.' He stretched his arms out wide and laced his hands behind his head as he pushed himself back from his desk, all bad signs. Sourish was about to speechify.

'Oh, oh, you know at the polo last Sunday, when I bumped into you with the polo crowd. Let's do a piece on that. You know, the whole scene, who's in, who's out, what clothes they're wearing, what shoes, which brand of designer sunglasses.'

On the day in question Sourish had caught me socially red-handed, slipping into the post-match tea tent with an elegant polo patron. He had taken in the people, nodded at me and filed away the information.

'Hasn't it been a bit overdone recently?'

'Oh yes, there's been lots of coverage but I think it has all been a bit *chamchā*, you know, sycophantic. We should do a piece that really gets into it with a bit of an edge. *Yaar*, you mix with all the right sort of crowd. It will be no problem, polo reportage.' He bounced his hands on the top of his head.

Thank you, Sourish, just what I need, to turn the pen on my few friends in town.

'Instead of taking a dig at the game and the people right in the thick of it, what about the clash of the old guard and new money in the grandstand? I haven't seen anything written about that.'

He was back at his computer again.

'Okay, by Monday, seventeen hundred words and I'll go to the sponsored match on Sunday with this piece in mind. Then I can pop in any names and quotes and all that you might miss. You'll probably be there with your pals, won't you?'

I rolled my eyes and Sourish waggled his head – end of discussion.

'Oh, oh, don't forget to do the stuff about the high teas that they do afterwards where all the hob-nobbing goes on, the cucumber sandwiches and all.' He laughed. 'Bet the thingy on Sunday will have a good tea.'

Ah-ha, now we had got to the point. Sourish was not a horse-lover but a finger-tea fan.

'So what did you like best at the tea last Sunday?' I asked.

'Those little chocolatey thingies and the baby meringues with strawberries. Did you try the éclairs? I can't remember when I last had ones with real cream.' His eyes were alight.

Sourish, the girls and a chocolatey thingy

'I didn't have any tea.'

'Why not?' He popped his head at me.

'I couldn't get anywhere near the serving tables in the feeding frenzy.'

'Such a waste.' Sourish rose above my comment. 'Oh, one more thing, don't forget to have a go at the whole sponsorship thingy.'

Oh good, biting the hand that feeds the cucumber sandwiches as well as betraying my intimates.

Corporate sponsorship is a recent addition to the sport of polo in India. The game of the rajas is being taken over by the new rajas of industry, the men who pay PR agencies to make sure that the matches they sponsor get lots of flattering exposure – pictures of sponsors' hoardings behind flying ponies and glossy-maned girls. Where once the kings of the Indian turf rode under royal banners and regimental colours, players now go forth under the brand-names of widget-makers and elevator manufacturers. Oh for Jodhpur, Jaipur and the captains of the 61st Cavalry.

With the arrival of the logos has come another innovation –

cheerleaders. This has the old Army boys, the guardians of the sport since Independence, choking on their *chai* as leggy lovelies with twirling pompoms jig about on the sidelines shouting and pouting the sponsors' names every time there is any chance of a goal.

Sunday afternoons at the Jaipur Polo Ground, the most glamorous of the playing venues, in the heart of New Delhi, have become quite a regular item in the diaries of the upwardly mobile. The Anjulis and Aartis, the professional aspirants of the social scene, roll through the dust in their gleaming Mercedes, as polished and preened as any show pony. I had gone by rickshaw.

On the left was the polo field, on the right the race-course, acre upon acre of green in the middle of the city. The pollution cloud hovered around the edges but it had not managed to seep across into this great stretch of greenness. The race track was deserted except for a few children throwing handfuls of dust at each other, rolling around in a confusion of arms and legs just beside the finishing post. An older boy was raking along the edge for cigarette stubs. Beyond him were the cars of the polo crowd, big expensive machines watched over by drivers who were busy with their dusting cloths. And beyond the polished cars was the constant movement of the pony lines. Ponies slicked with sweat were led around, their flanks pumping after a game. Those about to be played spun in tight circles as grooms warmed them up. People shouted and ran, bringing ponies in, taking ponies away, washing down, tacking up, the ponies kicking and squealing. And beyond the pony lines was the field where ten players did battle at the gallop beneath a large hoarding singing the praises of the latest, smallest mobile telephone – a smiling Westernized businessman telling a colleague that the deal was done as he punched the air with the fist that was not clutching the very small, very brilliant portable phone. The ponies shot back and forth in front of the successful transaction. I cannot remember the name of the telephone company, but Dolly was voted the best pony of the day.

I walked along the line of the field towards the grandstand as both teams roared past, the player in front arched out over his pony's neck as he tried to hook the ball out from under churning hooves. The teams shouted and ponies crashed against each other to the sound of bits on teeth, leather on leather. The ball was hit away and mouths gagged open as the players wheeled their ponies round, forcing their hocks right down in the dust as they braced and turned. An Argentinian player swung through, and out of the frenzy came a goal. Play stopped and the referee cantered grace-fully across the field.

There was muted clapping from the grandstand as the Anjulis and Aartis tried to establish which side had scored the goal while they pitched orange-glossed kisses into the air, roughly in the vicinity of corporate likely lads with gel-stiff hair and very small mobile phones. Aarti cooed over the Argentine goal-scorer and the way he turned his horse, so fluid, so whatever. But the action on the field wasn't really enough to hold their atten-tion. Here they could actually brush past the exquisite Gayatri Devi, Rajmata of Jaipur, wife of the Sawai Man Singh, the last ruling Maharaja of Jaipur. The late Maharaja had died in a blaze of glory on a polo field in England, a top-quality nine-goaler and one of the greatest players of his time. That was of less interest to Anjuli and Aarti than the fact that the Rajmata of Jaipur was wearing a Cartier watch and that she kept her fingernails short and unpainted unlike Anjuli who sported talons painted in this year's 'Tangerine Blush' to match the belt wrapped around her just too-new blue Versace jeans. Or look over there, isn't that Scindia's daughter, or is it her cousin, the princess? Too good, too much to see, so much to remember to tell everyone tomorrow.

Then the commentator announced the start of the 'breath-taking hanky-picking event: not a new thing. Even a hundred years ago, princesses used to throw their hankies out of windows hoping that some young prince might chance upon them.'

Aarti tried not to scrabble in her St Laurent clutch too obvi-ously in search of one to cast among the heads of former royalty. An American corporate man smiled at her and she smiled right back. New royalty, old royalty, who cares?

That was when Sourish had found me and caught my arm, casting his eye to where I had been sitting, unsuitably among the heady ranks of the great and the getting there.

'What are you doing here?' He was as surprised to see me as I was to find him out at a social function, just a couple of days after becoming a father for the first time.

'How is the baby?' I asked.

'Oh, oh, it's a baby.' His face lit up in spite of the nonchalance.

I congratulated him and made an excuse to go. My host was following me and I knew Sourish would sink his teeth right into him. I stumbled off down the red-carpeted stairs from the grandstand as my host floated out in a sea of flunkies and satellites.

'See you maybe later or at the office,' Sourish called after me.

The tea tent bubbled with the social cohorts gleaming in purple, gold, 'Setting Sun' and 'Tangerine Blush' as they elbowed their way towards the silver trays of nibble-sized samosas, little chocolatey thingies, baby meringues and éclairs with real cream.

A woman layered in peach and cream was talking to an acquaintance in a superior tone.

'It was a terribly good party, you know. You really should have come. What could you have been doing? Anyway, I was saying how much fun it was. Mark Tully was there, you know. He really is terribly serious and clever. I am not so sure that I would want to sit next to him for too long, you know these BBC types. Oh look, there's my Birla cousin, come, come, meet her, she has the best parties.'

Anjuli and Aarti were juggling plates of chocolatey thingy. Anjuli was beside herself with excitement. A sort of friend from her old school had been espied in the company of an almost famous actor. The sort of friend did not seem quite so enthusiastic about the encounter. She stood aloof in the corner with a nippy smile beside her almost famous companion. Anjuli dumped her plate on Aarti and ran to make contact.

The woman in peach and cream was holding forth again.

'You have to remember, darling, they are gods out there on the field. The trouble starts when they get out of the saddle – nothing doing.' Her new audience, a Miss Lycra-Nikes in a spray-on mini-dress, giggled and gazed at one of the players braving the fishbowl of the tea tent, surrounded by a sea of pretty upturned, tuned-in young faces.

My host had been cornered on his way in by a young television journalist wielding a microphone and shoulder camera.

'Sir, can I snitch a few moments of your time?' asked the young reporter, trying to stand taller than he was.

His Highness, with the microphone thrust in his face, looked down on the reporter through the elegant parting of his beard.

'Snitch away,' he said in a voice of elastic vowels.

The white light of the camera flared.

'How much do you think royal patronage has to do with the promotion of the game?'

'Wee-e-ll.' A sound as long as a river, and then His Highness paused. 'It is only really in India and England that polo has been linked with the royal families because young men of the royal houses played. It is not the same in America or Australia. I suppose in the past the royal aspect has lent a kind of glamour. If this is promoting it now then it must be that we all need a bit of that sparkle to alleviate the grind.' He paused again, realizing that the young man was too busy worrying about his next set question to listen.

'Shall we?' His Highness waved graciously towards the tea and moved on, leaving the young journalist on the edge of the tent, his demarcation line.

Some people were beginning to pick their way back to their richly upholstered cars. Just beyond the spill of light from the tea tent the ponies were being led up ramps into the back of the lorries, their hooves crashing on the metal bottoms of the long-distance haulage trucks that would bump them back to their home lines. Along the dusty track where the big cars, windows black-ened, purred in departure, the ground staff lined up. They had spent the morning shovelling sand to flatten the bumpy road to the polo field. Now they were hunkered down beside the road for hot tea and oily samosas while the cars drove off over their day's labour in a cloud of dust.

The Delhi Polo Club was founded in 1916. It is a far cry from the glamour of the Jaipur Polo Ground and is kept alive by a core of passionate members. It was there that I used to go to ride, to escape for a couple of hours into the green. As it got dark, after the last ride of the day, it was possible to look up and actually see the stars above Delhi.

One evening a friend who had introduced me to the club tried to explain why he was a member.

'We Indians are not very physical. We are not very good at following the martial arts or going out for a jog, and not very many of us ride. But while we are not very good at taking exercise, we are world champions at sitting around and just watching our big bellies grow. See, mine is not exactly flat but it would be a good deal bigger if I did not come out and ride.' He patted his neat, rounded stomach, well protected by a fine English shooting jacket.

'Now take the expatriate diplomatic crowd. Many of them ride, a much higher percentage than Indians. What happened was that the club was becoming a place that some Indians were using to get their "in" with the diplomatic lot. It was and is used as a social ladder. When I came to join, the commandant asked me if I was going to ride regularly. I told him that I was. He replied that I better stick to that or my membership would be cancelled. It is a club that exists to promote a love of riding, of equestrian sports. It is not for chitty chatty.' He tapped his whip on the side of his riding boot and paused for thought.

'The problem lies in the fact that you can never really satisfactorily separate the two. If someone is set on climbing the social ladder they are not going to allow the small matter of learning to ride to get in their way.'

A group of us were sitting under a *kekar* tree in sagging wicker chairs. A cold evening mist snaked among the ponies' legs in the lines just next door.

'We have enough money at the club, you see, and people say "Why don't you build a nice club house where you can get snacks and drinks, have a phone and somewhere comfortable to sit?" And I say what will we see if we sit in this nice comfy club, sipping our nice expensive drinks? No more stars, no smell of manure, no horses being fed.'

The Sikh who ran the pony lines had been watching me pull my cardigan around me and over my crossed legs. He shouted something in Punjabi. A few minutes later an iron bucket appeared with a fire burning inside. It was placed in the centre of the circle of chairs and each of us bent forwards towards the heat.

'This is something rare, don't you agree? You show me a place in another city where you can sit out in the open, where you have just been out riding on the trails, where you can be beside the pony lines and watch them being groomed, where you can sit back and drink your tea and look up at all those stars with a bucket fire to keep you warm,' said a man in a good suit, his accent as well cut as the suit. He had played rugby for the English Universities team in the fifties.

He had just come from a meeting of the equestrian sports council and was filling the young men of the club in on the minutes of the meeting. There was an argument brewing about the new method of laser-beam timing for showjumping, a piece of technology much obstructed in India by those who found their way to glory by bribing the time-keepers.

The young men were all serious horsemen, two of them among India's top ten showjumpers, one a leading dressage rider and the fourth, a captain from the 61st Cavalry, the country's leading three-day eventer. They sat around the bucket fire talking with a passion now absent in so much amateur sport. I questioned one of the showjumpers about the quality of polo ponies in India.

'There is one big, big problem here. You see we are not having the kind of management that is going to give you horses and ponies that are going to be performing to the best of their ability. I have been lucky enough to compete and study all over the world. It has really shown me how weak we are when it comes to the way we are stabling and feeding our horses. Look, look how these animals are kept. By Indian standards these are good conditions.' He waved his hands towards the pony lines.

And lines they were, horses and ponies tethered in stalls not much bigger than they were, separated from their neighbours on either side by just a rope. Each time I returned a horse to the lines the other animals would flatten their ears, throw their heads up, lips rolled, teeth bared, ready to lash out.

'None of them ever get out into a paddock. They stand around in these stalls all day tied up or tethered. I couldn't stand that, could you? No one really understands their horses here.' He paused and then indicated the others around him.

'Well, very few of us. Most riders get on their horse and then throw it back at the *scyce* when they have finished riding. A lot of the *scyces* are really ignorant village-type people. I am not saying that they are stupid but they have just not been educated. Most of them are pretty rough with the animals, probably because of their village instinct that, underneath all that training, they are still dealing with something that is basically wild.

'I spend so much time with my horses, grooming them and just being around them in the pony lines. The whole psychology of working with them is very important to me but the polo players laugh at that. I really am not seeing anything in the way polo ponies are being trained that makes me think they are changing their methods. When they break a pony that is what they are doing, they are breaking its spirit so that they can dominate the animal. I cannot say that there is anyone in polo whose methods I can admire.'

'Can I quote you?' I asked.

'Of course, it is what I believe.'

A face appeared out of the darkness, first a Dali-esque moustache, then a thin body and legs bowed with east-west knees. He carried a polo stick and a ball. Dipping into the glow of the fire he was greeted by everyone with reverence. He returned the greetings and dipped back out into the darkness.

'That is our polo pony breaker here, a very great man. He has produced some of our best ponies,' said the showjumper.

The bucket fire had burnt down. The group began to fidget. One of them got up to leave. My older friend waved him back into his seat.

'Just one more thing. Gentlemen, why are we all here?'

There were a few confused mutters before the question was reiterated with a grand gesture towards the pony lines and the great sky above.

'I am a simple man. I make no pretence to know about the finer

The pony breaker: a Dali-esque moustache, a thin body and legs bowed east to west

details of polo but I go to the matches because I get a great feeling of pleasure from the thundering of the hooves. When I am standing there on the side and the horses come roaring past I am a little boy again, just carried away by the thrill of the sport. Sometimes I take my five-year-old grandson and I see the look in his eyes. I think I have that same look too and see, I am an old man, more than half a century on from my grandson, but we are excited by the sport in the same way.'

'No, surely not so old,' said one of the polite young men.

My friend gave a gracious smile and thanked him for his good manners. The young man smiled back and told him that it was not good manners but the truth.

As we drove back into the city he turned to me. 'It was Winston Churchill's great passion when he was here, you know. He did not have any love for other sports but polo really did something for him. If he managed to win a world war it must say something good about the sport.'

The Delhi Polo Club reflects the ideal of polo. There courtesy is traded with courtesy, smile with smile. These elegant exchanges made right beside the pony lines are a long way from the Sunday afternoon aspirations of Aarti and Anjuli and the sponsors' hoardings. When you look at a map of Delhi the Polo Club is only a couple of kilometres from the Jaipur Polo Ground but the two are worlds apart.

Sourish had given me another new hat to add to my confusing collection. Now I was to be a social commentator. It was not a hat that fitted. Yoga, fasting and sexual promiscuity I could cope with, but the social scene was a hat too far. However many parties and polo games I went to I was never going to catch all the nuances, recognize all the important faces, reach the right conclusions, though I had to admit that there was a vicarious pleasure in watching the Aartis and Anjulis pursuing their bankable dreams.

For once I felt Kipling had had it easier.

I'm here in Simla with Mother and Trix as Special
Correspondent for the *Civil and Military Gazette*. I try
to give my paper as near to £40 a month of editorial
notes; reviews; articles and social Simla letters. That in
itself is fairly lively work and – tho' this may sound
strange to you – entails as much riding, waltzing, dining
out and concerts in a week as I should get at home in a
lifetime.

In that hill station, with its reputation for gaiety and infidelity,
Kipling observed the court, the courtiers and the courtesans of a
colonial power at play. In their intrigues and games were actions
as important and telling as their deeds of governance down in the
plains. Here he saw every social ambition and every arch flirta-
tion. Simla also provided him with an outlet for the Englishness
in him that had been a little dented, a little softened by the late-
night bazaars and the sinuous figures that rose as 'sheeted ghosts'
from their roof-top pallets or brushed against him in the narrow
backstreets, speechless but eloquent in the movement of their
bodies and the rhythm of the bells around their ankles. On returning to Lahore he wrote:

The month was a round of picnics, dances, theatricals
and so on – and I flirted with the bottled-up energy of
a year on my lips.

From these light-hearted dalliances and observations came his
commentaries for the *Civil and Military Gazette*, and anything that
was not suitable for the paper was filed away for the books and
stories still to be written.

Not much has changed. The Anjulis and Aartis of the polo
scene mirror their own generation. But there is a difference.
Kipling had had the confidence to satirize his own people.
Though I was tempted towards satire these were not my people.

Satire is not something that the Indian press has taken to, but
it does have one great exponent of the art – Jug Suraiya. After ten

years as an assistant editor on *The Statesman* in Calcutta he and his wife Bunny packed their bags and came to Delhi. New to the capital he found plenty of fuel for satire in its doings and so his column was born. 'Jugular Vein' appears in the Sunday edition of *The Times of India*. Whether it be a politician, a film, a Hindi movie bimbette, the latest great Indian novel or just human frailty, Jug Suraiya covers it all:

> For years I have not been able to read the medium print on anything, let alone the fine. This includes my own articles, which might explain why they're indecipherable to so many; they're indecipherable to me when I am writing them.
>
> Why don't you get reading glasses? friends and colleagues would ask. Are you self-conscious about people seeing you in them? They missed the point entirely. Reading glasses are generally worn in private, and I wasn't worried about people seeing me in them.
>
> What I baulked at was my mental image of myself wearing them. It was like Peter Pan applying for an old age pension.

His column is much loved and constantly referred to by those worn down by the excessive coverage of the inconsequential or the horrific. Yet despite Jug's popularity among the decision-makers, the captains and lieutenants-in-waiting of industry, the women cracking through the glass ceiling, he is often criticized for not moving with the mainstream. He carries on regardless, drawing similarities between astronomy and politics, polo and sexual innuendo, the short-term effervescent effect of Eno Salts and the performance of the Indian Prime Minister, political sycophants and the little balls of spittle that gather in the corners of the mouth when people speak too fast.

His office at *The Times of India* was just a couple of minutes' away from the *Express* Building.

It was not a warm day when I went to call on the great man.

The streets were awash with the amazing woollies of India. Governments may fall, leaders may be assassinated in a hail of 'splattered body parts and parts of brains', but in India there is a perennial cool-season constant – bad woollen wear of every variety. The sensuous line of the sari is ignominiously cut by the lumpy folds of a toggle cardigan and street style breathes its last as the weather cools down.

Up in his eyrie Jug Saraiya, as always, was bucking the trend. He was wearing an anorak, his slight body hunched down into its brown folds, a shock of hair and his great swoop of a nose only just emerging from the collar. I could not pinpoint his age and it seemed irrelevant – mid-fifties perhaps. He did not shake my hand and as we spoke he twirled a pen between two fingers and flipped a packet of cigarettes open and closed with the other hand. Looking out over my shoulder to the offices beyond his door, he apologized for missing an earlier appointment. He did not seem comfortable about being interviewed and his mannerisms did not invite small talk. I asked him how much of his writing was curbed.

'Oh, they give me completely free rein. My column has only been stopped once in ten years and that was only on the Bombay edition.' An elegant finger stroked the curve of his nose. 'I came in the next morning and the editor called me. I had made an attack on a figure in Bombay, the man who was effectively running the city. He had started out as a cartoonist and I pointed out that he had now become a cartoon. The editor told me that it was all nice and fine for me sitting in Delhi. No one was going to come and picket our building here or throw stones in the street at me. Then he mentioned our colleagues in Bombay, some of my female friends, and asked me how I would like to take the responsibility of knowing that they had been beaten up by the Bombay mafia because of me. That was a salutary lesson. I have been my own censor since then.'

'But why is it that you alone have a satirical column in the English-language press? I don't understand why other people don't follow your example.'

'Oh, you know the journos here. They are a very earnest bunch and they do take themselves so very seriously. Unless they are making great crashing statements of national importance they do not feel that they are doing their job.'

'Yes, but your following should be an indicator to other newspapers.'

He laughed and hunched a little further into his anorak, making himself as small as possible.

'That may be as you see it, but when I am out and about or at a party people will come up to me to check if I am the columnist. The standard thing is some civil servant character. He will come up to say hello and then tell me that his wife and teenage daughter love my column and read it every week. He will not say that he or his sons read it because men look at the politics and the sport. My column is seen as lightweight stuff. What is it that you call it?'

'Fluffy stuff.'

He snorted, a sonorous blast through the great nose.

'That's about right.'

'You mean that by mixing the trivia of life with politics you are seen as being a columnist of no consequence?'

He snorted again but looked a little hurt.

'I was thinking about having a mild go myself but I'm a bit nervous about the reaction,' I offered.

'You can't be mild about it, subtlety is a thing that does not feature in the Indian lexicon. You have to hit them right in the teeth.' He took a cigarette out of its packet and examined it closely.

'Quite a lot of your stuff is subtle.'

'If you think that, you've been here too long.' He smiled and lit the cigarette.

'But don't you use subtlety as a way of protecting yourself from those you are satirizing?'

'I'm not sure if that is subtlety or cowardice. When one of those civil servant characters walks up to me I sometimes wonder whether he is going to hit me or give me the "wife and daughter" line. You must have realized that we really don't have much of a sense of humour about ourselves.' He flicked some ash off the sleeve of his anorak, continuing even after the ash had gone.

'If the character was to hit you, wouldn't that be an admission that he had read your articles?'

He laughed, then stopped abruptly to draw on his cigarette.

'Try it. The people you satirize will not notice. If they do they will blow up all hot and bothered but really be quite pleased. Fame of whatever variety is like a drug here.' He was looking out over my shoulder again. My slot was over. I left him in his brown anorak and headed out into the sea of fearsome woollies feeling more comfortable about having a small dig at Anjuli and Aarti, safe in the assurance of Jug Suraiya that they would not notice. And if they did it would be another step in their bid for their fifteen minutes.

Bushan was quiet on the way back to Hailey Road. He did not even respond to some of my criminal Hindustani pronunciations. I stopped taunting him and thanked him when he dropped me off. He did not reply.

Yashwant was back, newly returned from several weeks in the bosom of his family in Jodhpur and the painful process of sifting through several years' tax bills. Although he had been cleaned out by the government, he had come back laden with presents. There were Jodhpuri chiffon saris for all beautiful Mangay's womenfolk (especially his wife) and a particularly fine hairy tweed jacket for Dhan Singh, effective in keeping out the night and morning chill as it came down almost to his knees. He looked like a jolly elf as he paraded it proudly around the apartments. There were pearls for me, pearls from a gorgeous, gay, drunken prince, pearls to keep forever.

'You must wear them all the time or they will die,' he said as he put them around my neck. 'Dead pearls are a very sad thing and should not be allowed.'

Among his piles of luggage was an unnamed tortoise with star patterns on its shell. Its predecessor, whose demise was glossed over, had been called Ptolemy. This one was immediately christened Ozymandias just in case it succumbed to the fumes of Delhi

Ozymandias, king of kings, on a small stool

and ended up in a sad grave. The tortoise lasted but the name did not. He became simply Ozy.

Within a day of his return Yashwant was pacing the corridors, clasping his head and moaning about the high jinks filtering up from yet another wedding party in the garden below. Mangay was out on duty, on Black Cat patrol, slinking through the night to protect a politician with a few too many death threats to his name. Ozy the tortoise had wisely retreated to the security of his shell.

'The bugger! Bloody fish!' Yashwant shouted.

He banged on my door and stormed in, fins flying.

'*Four* of my fish have died. First the tin foil bard, now the silver dollar, the shad and the nigger barb. Look!' He produced a plate with the four dead fish on it, freshly frosted.

'Are you keeping those in the fridge?'

'Yes, of course.' He bent sadly over the four small corpses.

'But why?'

He laughed and one of the frozen fish fell off the plate, making a crispy sound as it hit the stone floor. 'Whoops. I froze them because I want you to click them so that I can take the picture to the shop to get new ones. I don't think people would be very happy if I wandered around with the poor little dead things in a bag, and imagine what might happen when they thaw.'

'Cryogenics?'

'You cannot do that here. I would have to send them to America and they would definitely thaw in the post.'

'If they can manage vital organs, four small fish shouldn't be too much of a problem. We could eat them *talā hua*, fried with butter and lemon.'

'And who do you propose will gut the things?'

'They're small enough to eat whole, like whitebait or sardines.'

'Even the tin foil barb?'

'I think so.'

'That is too much. You are suggesting that we eat my babies' hearts and eyes. How cruel, how disgusting.'

'While we are on the subject of food have you become addicted to powdered skimmed milk?' Yashwant was supposed to be on a diet.

'Why?'

'Well, you are motoring through mine. What do you do with half a jar a day?'

'You said I could and I have it with stewed plums, lots of it, but it's 99 per cent fat free so it doesn't matter.'

'Half a jar a day slightly defeats the point.'

Yashwant tied his dressing-gown more tightly and sucked in his cheeks. 'It makes me feel much better about my diet and it has added vitamin C, D and E so it is terribly good for me.'

'I will get a larger jar.'

'Thank you, dear.' He started to leave the room, bearing the frozen four aloft.

'So are you just going to leave them in the fridge?'

He paused in the doorway.

'When you have done with them I will feed them to the cat.'

'What cat?'

'I shall find one.' He set off again. 'They will be in the fridge when you wish to click them.'

And so they were, and so they stayed between the full-fat milk that Yashwant would not drink and the pot of curd.

That night I dreamt of dead fish. Next morning Dhan Singh, sprite-like in hairy tweed, banged on my door several times before getting any response. I was late for work even before I woke up. Bug-eyed and pillow pattern-faced I met the late morning on Hailey Road.

The usual crowd of rickshaw drivers was gathered by the *chai* stall. They looked up over their glasses of tea and said good morning, or was it good afternoon? How did the rickshaw drivers know that I had overslept? Ram Kumar could think of no better news to impart to the street than that the mad Mem had slept in. I searched among the unshaven faces and frightening woollies for the clean bright smile and well-ironed shirt of my king of the road. I asked the others where he was. They shrugged and smiled.

Bushan was not going to be coming that day.

The Foolish Man
Devours All He Has

POUF! BUSHAN, my knight of the road, had gone up in smoke. The gang of loafers around the *chai* stall gave me knowing grins as they scratched their stubble. Even gentle Mataji, the *chai* queen, could not help. Waving her hand in the air she spat some chewed cardamom pods into a bubbling pot and shook her head. He had disappeared and I stood in the road alone.

Bushan had a friend who ran a rather chic emporium on Connaught Place. He used to go there to talk and drink tea while I fussed over photographs and transparencies at a studio three doors away. The Chinese Arts Palace it was grandly called, a great cavern of a place, layered in dust, full of giant vases with the oily, opalescent finish of funfair prizes, and carvings of leering characters in dark teak, chortling over their fat polished bellies at glass paintings of tripping courtesans with secret smiles.

Here at last I found Bushan. He was wearing a smart green uniform to match the window of the shop. He had been appointed the official parcel-maker of the Chinese Arts Palace. His days of rickshaw-driving were over, his machine out on permanent loan to a strange Punjabi with a lazy eye. Bushan introduced the man. His eye, lazy or not, managed to roll, rest and remain on my bust. I thanked him but explained that I would not feel wholly confident with a driver whom I could not understand. My Hindi was weak but my Punjabi, well, I had none.

Bushan looked at my sad face and reached out and shook my hand. It was the first time that he had touched me in a year of

199

driving me in and out of the experiences of Delhi, a year of gently coaxing my fumbling pronunciation of his language. It was time for Bushan to move on – to a green uniform, a chair in a shop and a permanent place to drink his tea. Gone were his days as a rickshaw driver, gone the daily lungfuls of muck and the burden of hard-bargaining passengers. I smiled and tried to look pleased for him. It was not turning out to be a very good day.

This was the first time I felt lonely in Delhi. My safety net had gone, the buffer between the city and my vulnerability. I slouched around the corner to the optician's in search of someone to annoy. I had a pair of glasses to pick up that had broken three times in just a few weeks. They would do the trick.

The pretty girl behind the array of frames stopped smiling with her eyes, though her mouth stayed politely in place. My mood was obviously palpable. She was not sure whether my glasses were ready but she would go immediately and find out what was going on. Would Madam like a free eye-check while she waited? Why not, yes of course, how nice.

A nervous young man held up the test cards. N12 was for those beginning to have a problem:

> The old man could not remember
> how many generations of lotuses
> had bloomed and faded in the pond
> since he was born.
> He had lost track.

Then there was N24 for those who really did have a problem:

The foolish man devours all he has.

I was lucky, the young man told me, I could easily read N12 despite being a glasses-wearer. That was good. I was not so sure. N24 and the foolish man seemed more appropriate. I had lost Bushan. And as it was that kind of morning the glasses were naturally not ready.

There were many places to go before the end of the working day and the rickshaw drivers were lined up on Connaught Place outside the optician's window looking for prey. Out of the rabble shouting inflated prices appeared K.K. Chopra, almost a clone of Bushan, a champion of the dusty Ring Road, neat, clipped and clean, though with a bit more flesh on him than my angular former knight. His name was painted in flowery letters above where he sat, spine straight and shoulders back. Joy of joys, K.K. Chopra's rickshaw was more comfortable than Bushan's. My heart belonged to Bushan but K.K. Chopra rapidly filled another space. The day improved.

The subject allotted me by Sourish that week was the lavatories of Delhi, the smell of which caught in everyone's throats, climaxing in the hot season when the open urinals of the city poisoned the air. I set out to find three people whom I felt would have strong things to say on the sorry state of Delhi's loos: Madam Mayor, the officer in charge of the capital's conveniences and Mr E.P. Reddy of Hyderabad, a practitioner of Vastu Shastra, India's equivalent of the Chinese *feng-shui* method of putting things in the right place in your house or workplace. While the Chinese base their theory on the elements of wind and water, the Vedic Indian system goes three further, enlisting earth, air, fire, water and wind in the decision-making process of where best to put the lavatory in your home.

'A lavatory located in the north-east corner of a house can lead to fatal illness, you know,' said Mr Reddy as he bent over his book of cuttings. He was terribly neat. Everything about him was in the right place, as though the practice of his art extended to his wardrobe, the creases of his *kurta* pyjamas in sweet symmetry with the parting of his hair and the sharp lines of his black moustache. He pushed the clippings forward and sure enough on top of the pile was a piece from the Hyderabad edition of *The Indian Express*. 'Misplaced lavatory can cause cancer', it trumpeted.

'So where must a lavatory go?' I asked.

'Always in the south-west or north-west corner of the house.' He sat back and crossed his arms.

We were in the hall of Jodhpur Apartments. I had no idea where north was, let alone west. I grasped Mr Reddy by the hand. 'Would you mind telling me if my loo is in the right place?'

Mr Reddy seemed delighted to oblige. The bathroom was passable, the lavatory in almost the right place. He politely averted his gaze from the motley array of newly laundered knickers hanging out to dry but he did display a little concern as to whether my bowel movements were regular. I persuaded him that all was well and he seemed relieved that I was not showing any early symptoms of misplaced-lavatory cancer.

My bed, on the other hand, was problematic. It was in the south-east corner of the room resulting in a tendency, Mr Reddy declared, to make me quarrelsome or even inclined towards criminal activities. He quoted the recent case of an infamous Bombay swindler who had slept in the south-east corner of his lush apartment while running his scams. He had then changed his sleeping arrangements and had become an exemplary citizen. I did not see how I could move my bed but pointed out that I did not have a criminal record, though I admitted I could be a bit wilful when pushed. Mr Reddy shrugged. 'Who is telling where wilful might be leading,' he said in a grave tone.

We moved on to the lavatories of Delhi.

'How can you apply Vastu Shastra to a city? You can hardly put all the public lavatories in the north-west corner. What happens when you want to have a pee and you happen to be in the south-east?'

Mr Reddy was not enjoying himself. As Jug Suraiya had pointed out few Indians appreciate having their sense of self-importance nudged. He launched into a long diatribe on his success with international firms and referred me back to his book of cuttings. Then he rushed off to find Yashwant who always took his advice with the utmost seriousness.

Undeterred, I sought out another Vastu practitioner. Sitting cross-legged and comfortable on a large blue silk rug in an expensive part of town, he made no claims about important clients and did not produce a clippings file. I had already discovered that he looked after a number of film stars and characters who probably stalked Mr E.P. Reddy's financial dreams.

'No one can really say that they are a Vastu master now,' said Rajesh. 'Even my home is all the wrong way round.'

The room was simple and elegant in the extreme. It turned out not to be his home but that of a friend. Rajesh was from Bombay where he lived in quiet luxury in his discreetly un-Indian way.

'Vastu began with the principles of temple-building where everything was fixed and in place. We have to deal with reality now. Don't tell me that builders of high-rise apartment blocks today are really going to listen to some little guy like me.'

I told him about Chinese companies in Hong Kong that would not lay the first stone without the nannying of a *feng-shui* master.

Rajesh wiggled the end of his nose. 'We Indians may be mad most of the time but we are not quite as mad as that.'

I was silent.

'Okay, perhaps we are, but when it comes to big business, the guy calling the shots is usually not as wound up in hocus-pocus as the Chinese are.' The nose wiggled again.

I asked him what he was if not a Vastu master like the redoubtable E.P. Reddy of Hyderabad fame.

'I am a cosmic architect.' He laughed and spun round on the blue silk carpet. 'The two things are about as different as calcium carbonate and camembert.' Obviously a Bombay-*wallah*. Camembert was not on offer in Hyderabad.

We fell to talking about cheese. He was delighted with the news that there was somewhere in Delhi where he could buy fresh Italian Parmesan. We discussed the latest innovation in town, pizza *tikkā murg*, the favourite chicken of North India, cooked with yoghurt and spices in a tandoor oven, then plopped on a pizza base with the token authentic scattering of Parmesan cheese (neither fresh nor Italian), topped off with a good dose of chilli.

'And what would be your answer to the problem of Delhi's lavatories?' The good citizens would need them after a couple of pizzas *tikkā murg*.

'They have to be knocked down and rebuilt using space so that the energies can flow,' said the cosmic architect.

'But that is impossible.'

'Of course, but then India is all wrong if you go back to the ideals of Vastu. The mountains are in the north where the water should be, and the water is in the south. That's why it is all such a mess.' He gave a gnomic smile.

'Surely not.'

'Well, some of that is made up for by the fact that we are supported by three seas. Of course they are all in the wrong place, and we should have more roads up in the north-east to catch the energy flow of the rivers.'

'The whole country is perhaps a bit ambitious, but what about really doing something in Delhi?'

'This is not my town,' he said, stroking the silk rug.

So I went to talk to the mayor and the corporation and met a pretty girl on the way who was a guide for French tour groups.

Her gripe was that men refused to use the stinking public urinals and took to the open street instead. 'It is plain hell at times and very annoying. I have to move around with these groups and what am I supposed to say when they ask why the men are standing up against the wall? "Are they being shot?" someone joked last week and they should be, I say, except that they would be turning around the other way and then imagine what we would have to see. It's damn bad.' And she tossed her pretty head.

'But the French are fairly casual in their attitude about peeing in public. They are much more relaxed than the Americans or the British.'

She looked at me in horror. 'You mean they do it in Paris too?'

'Well, perhaps not quite so much, but certainly in desperation or when drunk.' I was not even sure whether it was illegal in Paris. It certainly was in London but somehow to make it a crime in the city of dreams seemed very un-French.

'The worst thing is if we are in the Old City and someone wants to go. The filth in that place! I would not even expect a beggar to go to one of those public urinals. You know I have to pile them back on to the bus and trip them up to Connaught Place. It's damn bad, damn bad.'

But she could offer no solution to the problem.

Madam Mayor was taken aback by my enquiry. She suspected a twist to the plot and was not convinced that a foreign journalist was following a story like this for *The Indian Express*. She turned the ubiquitous visiting-card over and over in her hand as if it might reveal the truth.

'It is not such a grave problem you must know. You see there is actually not so much I can do. *Yaar*, my hands are tied I think you say.' She drummed her long fingernails upon her imposing desk and added, 'Funds are a problem and then there is an acute shortage of cement.'

The fingernails drummed faster still and it was made quite clear that I was wasting her time. I withdrew without even having been offered a cup of tea. I had not been a popular appointment. As I left she was asking her secretary to check whether I was genuine.

The officer in charge of maintenance, public conveniences, New Delhi, felt that it was a 'public people's awareness lacking' problem.

'However much we are trying, Delhi is rising up against us,' he sighed.

How right he was. It was rising up in every way, from the main roads, the walls, the parks and the service lanes.

'The citizens of Delhi make it a point to steal the taps and use the lavatories for other shady activities. To come clean we are needing the co-operation of the police to ensure that this kind of misusage is being stopped.'

He stared sadly at the skin on his tea and explained that, in some parts of the city, it was a wise precaution to take to the streets to avoid the nefarious activities that took place in the public loos.

'The other problem we are having is of water. We do not have a regular supply. The water that is stored in the overhead tank is stolen by people to wash their person and by taximen to wash their cars.' He furrowed his brow over the conundrum. 'The maintenance is in the hands of private contractors you must know,' he added.

'Then couldn't you whip them into shape? After all, you are paying them.'

'I am just a government servant, you see.' The old chorus, the perennial excuse for inactivity in the corridors of power.

In the vacuum-sealed coffee shop of a five-star hotel I sought the opinion of a Delhiite friend who I felt would give a responsible answer. As I waited, I watched the comings and goings near the five-star loo where there were dancing attendants, fluffy white hand towels and moth balls in the drains to keep the silverfish at bay.

My friend was as late as you would expect a politician to be. He looked at me in disbelief when I asked him about Delhi's loos.

'Of course you are joking, aren't you?'

He was not the type to take to the streets to seek out the needs of his constituents, and he was certainly not the type to take to the streets to hunt for suitable urinal locations where there was a favourable flow of energy. The impending second election in as many years was occupying his mind. He was under the impression that I wanted to hear his opinion on the state of the nation rather than the nation's loos. 'How can you ask such a ridiculous question when this country is about to spend all these billions of rupees on another bloody election?'

The waiter overheard our conversation and suddenly realized who the speaker was. He began to hover with intent.

'Do you realize that leading up to the resignation of the Prime Minister we were kept up day and night, night and day in meetings. So of course you can imagine what happened; everyone was falling asleep, catnapping while the government fell in tatters around our nodding heads. And then I hear one of our great leaders say, "I haven't slept for thirty-six hours. Are we playing one-day cricket or ruling a huge country?" I am saying what is this, what does he mean by ruling? They have all gone mad. Ruling? No one gives a rupee damn that the government has fallen, and since when did a government rule? What a joke – the largest democracy in the world. And now you are asking me ridiculous questions about Delhi loos. Trust an Englishwoman to be out with the mad dogs.' He chortled into the folds of his neck.

'But it is just the sort of thing that the government should be applying themselves to if they want to make people listen or even care whether they are in power.'

'Come, you must be joking. How do you expect a bunch of people who have not set foot on a public street for years to give any thought to the when and how of improving public conveniences? If you feel so strongly why don't you put up a picket outside the Lok Sabha, suggesting that all politicians be forced to use public lavatories, to get back in touch with the country they like to think they are ruling?' He shouted at the waiter. His coffee was cold, weak and generally disgusting.

The waiter looked horrified and bowed low as he retrieved the offending cup.

'Just tell me what you think of Delhi's loos,' I begged, grabbing his hand across the table and holding it imploringly. He was an understanding friend.

The waiter looked on amazed, not knowing that this man had bounced me on his knee at an early age. He decided to replace my coffee too.

'They are disgusting, but then what do you expect of a people who regard their country and history as something that they can just urinate all over? Go out to some of the monuments, some of our great heritage, and see what the animals are up to.'

He left at speed, the waiter trailing after him, clutching another cup of coffee.

The tomb of Merza Muqion Abal Mahsur, Safdarjung to his friends, Governor of Oudh and favoured minister of the Mughal Emperor Mohamad Shah, lies on Aurobindo Road.

Amidst its intricate tracery, its domes, its secret corners and shaded doorways, lurk the smell of urine and the scrawl of graffiti. Young couples stand hand in hand by the walls, pen at the ready to make the first move in flowery words on the bird-shit streaked plaster. Here Sunday lovers can touch and smile – nervous young men with greased-back hair and skinny legs in drainpipe jeans and pretty, plump girls in *salwar kameez*. They walk among the pink stone, their flirtatious laughter bouncing off the domes. It is a simple kind of sexual liberty, purchased at the gate for just three rupees, to escape from the prying eyes of the police who stalk the public parks, stopping beside romantic couples and hitting them for a bribe. Pay up, cupid kids, or take a ride to the cop shop for indecent behaviour. All this lying with heads in laps and holding of hands, too, too much. And around the tomb the arid gardens stretch away to the trees where more couples lie, heads in laps, hearts in mouths. The elegant ornamental waterways are dry or clogged with rubbish and green sludge.

I sat and watched the afternoon crowd drift in and out, and beyond the outer wall the traffic of Aurobindo Road roared and screamed. Among the couples a small child hopped around her family as they picnicked on the parched grass. She danced, laughing, and then stopped, entranced by a flight of emerald parakeets that wheeled and circled above her among the domes.

But beyond the stench of urine, the graffiti, the roaring traffic and the litter, there was a kind of peace and the soft scent of rose petals.

I walked back to Jodhpur Apartments from the tomb past a small monument of sorts in Hailey Road. The *bowri*, a well, is tucked away in a side lane, just around the corner from No. 10. It is said that murderers dump their victims there. It also doubles as yet another unofficial public urinal. Though I saw no floating bodies as I crept to the edge of the well, there was a huddle of taxi, bus and rickshaw drivers lining up to take their ease. I had very little desire to get too close. It was not a place for women, even in the middle of the afternoon. The smell rose thick in the air. The stonework had been eaten away, more proof to back up the statement of my friend, the politician. I scuttled away but not before another driver had seen me and given half-hearted, playful chase, fortunately hampered by the obviously full state of his bladder.

A few days later I approached Dhan Singh on the subject as he was making my bed. I tiptoed around him, still embarrassed by the procedure. I wanted to make light conversation so stumbled into a question about public conveniences. Dhan Singh does not understand a word when I try to speak Hindustani. He looked at me blankly. I tried mime and he chortled as he returned to his task.

'What on earth are you doing?' Yashwant was standing in the corridor watching as I squatted for Dhan Singh's benefit.

'I was trying to ask Dhan Singh for his thoughts on Delhi's public loos.'

'He has none.' He came into the room and waved the old man away.

'Then what do you think of them?' I asked.

'Oh, now I see where I stand. I am asked after the servants.' He sat down on the spare bed and looked at me with raised eyebrows. I was swathed in blankets and shawls. It had been raining for three days and the average temperature was ten degrees below normal for the time of year.

'And you have to ask such disgusting questions. They are revolting in every way. You know the loo up in Palika Bazaar in the middle of Connaught Place. I needed to make the appropriate use of the place. I had to scream at some hideous pick-up scene using it for anything but.'

'So it is not surprising then that people go in the streets?'

'Oh, that is sheer laziness, of course, just a bunch of animals. What do you expect?' He lit a *biri* and coughed. 'God, I am so ill.'

'Are you being a snob?' I asked.

'I am not but if this is what education does for them, take it away.'

'Oh come on.'

'I am absolutely serious and I am afraid some of the blame lies at your great British door. You cannot educate the nigger natives, teach them to read and then put up signs saying "No natives or dogs allowed".' He blew the *biri* smoke politely away from me.

'But everyone has the right to education now.'

'Of course they do, but what kind of education is it if it doesn't stop them from pissing in the streets?'

The loo deadline was approaching. In other cities, in other countries, it is easy to slide into a café, to seek inspiration in other people's conversation, to find the lost words amongst the chatter of strangers. As long as there is a steady flow of coffee ordered, the waiters leave well alone. Sometimes, on wordless days, their familiarity, even a slight show of interest, acts as a catalyst.

The café craze of Europe has yet to reach Delhi but underneath the Moolchand flyover there is something close to the real thing, a coffee shop run by a sleepy, brown-eyed Moroccan from Fez. Unfortunately the waiters are not as supine as the man from Fez. They hover around, trying to grab any not quite empty cups and to slap down bills. *Jaldi karō*, hurry up. Order, drink and leave. But even they began to soften as the months passed.

That evening I sat there, bent over an empty page waiting for words to come to give cohesion to public urinals, misplaced mountains and cancerous lavatories.

A man in a tweed coat with a Rabindranath Tagore beard bumped down on the bench next to me. There were plenty of other empty tables available. I looked up but said nothing. He opened the *Evening News* with a flourish and started to read aloud. He stopped when he saw me hovering tentatively over a blank page.

'Where do you come from?' he asked. 'Ah, London, I have been there, and punting in Cambridge too. That is boating, you know. Which English writer was it who said "When a man is tired of London he is tired of life"?'

'Dr Johnson.'

He slapped his hand down on the page. 'When a man passes from youth to old age, he moves from passion to compassion.' He stared at me and repeated the phrase. He smelt of whisky, not too much, but enough to breach the code of good manners and my writing efforts.

A powercut intervened and the place was suddenly still. The tables around that had been occupied emptied. The waiters watched like hawks for anyone trying to leave without paying, one posted at each door, candle in hand, to check the faces of those departing. They knew who had and who had not coughed up. Tagore melted into the night. My waiter smashed his tray down on the table when he realized the man had slipped through the net without paying.

Somewhere in an inner pocket I had a tiny torch. I began to write by its pencil beam. If the waiters could carry on regardless, so could I. They still moved between the tables, not quite at the same speed, but with the trays piled just as high. One stopped and pushed his head into the small circle of light. 'Ich awr kafi?

The coffee-waiter

Another coffee?' He returned with a candle in a glass and a cup.

In the busy darkness no one seemed to mind how long I stayed. At last the article began to take shape. In a mood of grateful elation I paid bolting Tagore's bill as well as my own.

Even though it was almost the coldest time of year the fan was still whirling in Sourish's office. He was surrounded by a group of reporters being handed out assignments. I waited in the corner, leafing through the English newspapers from the weekend before. The country, or rather the media, had been absorbed in a round-up of the life of a rock star who had committed suicide in Sydney. I asked one of the reporters whether she had heard about it.

She shrugged. 'I think I know who you mean but he hadn't done anything really good for years. What is all the fuss about?'

'He had a love child with one of our media favourites. And, on the back of Princess Diana, we seem to have this obsession with only-the-good-die-young stories.'

'What?' she said, disbelievingly.

Sourish was singing a little song, weaving backwards and for-wards on his chair. He had the 'shock horror Delhi lavs' story on his desk.

'You quite like all this social issue stuff, don't you?' he said.

'Yes I do.' I changed the subject. 'How's the baby?'

'Oh, oh, still no name.'

'Any ideas?'

'Well, we have got it down to three and we just cannot decide. We might just stick all three together.'

'Then no one will remember his name.'

'Well, we call him Mike at the moment.'

'But you aren't Christian, are you?'

'No, no, but he's a damn good little fighter, you know, like the Tyson fella who bites ears and all.' He boxed the air with a Daddy smile and then he too changed the subject.

'Do you know about NGOs?'

I did not.

'They are Non-Government Organizations,' he explained.

'And what does that mean?'

'You surprise me, you really don't know? Hey, Karan, come in here, we've got something Justine doesn't know about.'

'Sourish . . .' I pleaded.

'NGOs, oh, oh, well I suppose they fight all the social issues, everything from AIDS to tree-planting. You would probably call them charities or voluntary thingies. They don't like that here, makes them feel as if they are members of the middle class just trying to justify their nice houses and their nice lives, which of course is exactly what they are. You know our consciences are being pricked all the time. We go off and spend *crores* of rupees buying houses in the most expensive colonies. But just around the corner there will be a slum, perhaps even an illegal one without water, proper sanitation or electricity.'

'And NGOs work in the slums?' What story was this going to be?

'Yes, and in the villages and all over the place.'

'And you want me to write about them?'

'No, no, not about them but you were talking about organic farms the other day and this might be something that you could have a look at. Organic farming is a very new thing in India. I know it is big and all in the West but it really has hardly even started here. See if you can find three or four of them and do a reportage on the situation and what is happening. I am sure you will find that you will be dealing with some NGOs.'

I couldn't see much connection between voluntary organizations working in slum areas and the increasingly lucrative branch of the giant health industry that organic produce has become in the West, but perhaps I was wrong. I went out to learn, starting with the monthly meeting of the NGO Club.

I walked into a stranger's garden at the address I had been given. A figure emerged and stretched out his hand to draw me into a lit room. There were not many people there and I knew very little about what they did. On the walls hung black-and-white photographs of mime actors, their faces whited out, their eyes dark and haunting.

'Are you part of this group?' I asked the man who had taken my hand in the garden.

'Yes, it is my mime group.'

'Where do you perform?'

'In the slums and shanty towns around the city.'

'And your group is an NGO?'

He bristled. 'We are not quite performing the *Ramayana* or Cinderella and the uglies. We mime stories about social issues: women's education, water and the slum dwellers' rights to facilities. Some are black-marketing parables, that sort of slightly less palatable thing.'

He offered me a whisky and I complimented him on his house.

'Perhaps you think that because we are working with the poor we should be wearing rags and living in slums? But here we are in our lovely house, as you put it, while just around the corner is one of Delhi's most famous slums.' He pushed his face up quite close to mine.

'And I suppose that because I am a journalist you think I should drink whisky until I fall flat on my face.'

The two eyes and the oily nose pressed against mine wrinkled up in a smile. 'Ah, the English sense of humour. I knew there was something about you that was worthwhile.'

I admitted I knew little about the background to NGOs.

'What you have to understand about volunteerism in poor countries is that it is not just an option for people with time sitting on their hands. It is our moral obligation, our duty.' He pressed his hands to his heart.

'But don't you think that all voluntary work starts out with the right intentions, but goes wrong in practice? You know, "many a slip 'twixt cup and lip".'

He threw back his head and laughed.

'*Acchā*, I have been saying that all my life, but hearing you now I have been getting it wrong all these years. I have been saying "There is many a drip between cup and lip" and no one ever put me right. That is our country for you, as long as it sounds about right it gets by.' He settled on the arm of a sofa. 'You know, in a way you are right. The charities and missions during the British time did very good things but they always wanted to change the poor natives, as they saw them, make them embrace their god, their dress, their morals. We are doing work in a different time. The first NGOs were the earliest freedom fighters here, trying to find a voice that would be heard by you British.' He winked.

More people started to arrive and he went out into the garden again, hands extended in charity. A Frenchwoman from the embassy with neat hair and neat hips announced as she walked through the door that she could not stay long. She had the air of a busy benefactress and spread her neat but gracious smile before placing her neat posterior on the very edge of a not-so-neat sofa, poised for a fast getaway.

The room was now almost full. A couple leant against the kitchen door, sipping vodka and Coca Cola, he staring deep into her eyes as he began a half-hearted rant about inner city water supplies. Others sat around the room on a cross-section of chairs in a cross-section of dress. Some wore variations on a theme of the voluntary workers' dress code – *kurta* pyjamas and *salwar kameez* in rural designs printed with vegetable dyes. They lived out in the villages and slums with those on whose behalf they now drew breath. The middle ground was held by those who were members of NGOs but realized that the life of residential Delhi was where they belonged. They wore jeans and soft blue denim shirts and went out on field trips to the slums and villages where their projects were based. At the top of the dress scale were the diplomatic set, emissaries from the embassies and high commissions that were the givers of funds to chosen NGOs, fitting their image of international munificence in a poor country. They dressed as they would in their home cities, their suits and expensive watches all part of the ex-pat package that went with the immunity of their diplomatic number plates. They did their best not to look uncomfortable among the vegetable dyes and heated debates.

There was to be a speaker that evening, his subject 'Rewriting the Constitution'. He got up and started to talk. Conversations continued around him. He believed that it was time for India to rewrite her constitution and shake off the one written by an out-dated colonial power. His speech lasted about two minutes. Then a man sitting next to the neat Frenchwoman leapt to his feet.

'Our kind of democracy comes down the barrel of a shotgun.'

There was a murmur of protest but he pressed on, undeterred.

'We will never have true democracy here. That is a luxury for the idle rich to talk of as they play with their stocks and shares. How can we have democracy in a country where every politician has his hand in someone else's pocket, while two-thirds of the electorate cannot even read or write enough to make tit or arse of a ballot paper?'

He trotted off to the bar to get himself a drink, ignoring the heated comments that pursued him from his small audience.

He returned with his drink and a plate. It was piled with two pieces of bread, something that looked like pâté, a couple of slices of *mooli*, the large white radish of India, some tomato sauce, two green chillis and a large pile of crisps. He settled himself back on the sofa a little too close to the neat French bottom. She fluttered off the edge and took her leave in a flurry of neat cuffs, card-case and click, click handbag. Undiscouraged, he spread himself across the sofa until he seemed, without moving, to have washed up against me.

A woman in a beige and brown kaftan and a tight blue cardigan began to talk heatedly about India being the largest democracy in the world. My neighbour nodded as she ranted, happy to let her talk, much more interested in the action on his plate. He spread one piece of bread with pâté and delicately applied a thin layer of tomato sauce on top.

'How can you resort to violence, the very thing that we deplored in colonial rule?' demanded the woman in the kaftan.

On top of the sauce went the *mooli* slices. Then the two chillis were carefully split, the seeds scraped out with the tip of a knife.

'Na, na, we are not talking about the definition of democracy here. It is all too much of a damn mess, and I suppose you think

India has been all peace and light since they left.' Another man had joined the fray.

My neighbour laid the chillis in tidy strips across the *mooli*. Then he added a generous pile of crisps. Finally he placed the second piece of bread on top. The *masala* sandwich was apparently now complete. He took a large bite and most of it fell on the floor, into his lap and into mine.

'Let us try and stick to the point,' said our host. 'We are talking about a constitution that was written by the British for a country that was under foreign rule and not a democracy.'

An ancient dog that had been lying in the centre of the room raised its filmy eyes, got up, farted and padded out to the garden where it began to bark with surprising energy.

'I would say Gandhi should never have opened his mouth,' said the woman in the kaftan.

'We have to look at the fact that a democracy must be able to feed itself and become literate from the grass roots up. With full bellies comes the freedom of speech that is real democracy,' countered another woman with a pock-marked face.

'Who said literacy is such a great thing?' asked my neighbour, making an over-extended effort to pick his sandwich out of my lap.

The discussion became an argument, the argument a row between the woman in the kaftan and my neighbour, who had by now finished fishing food from my lap. The dog returned from the garden, providing me with something to fondle nervously.

The original speaker stood up again. He called for silence but nobody heard. He said that there was going to be a round-table discussion on democracy and the constitution in a few weeks, in the middle of November. Two of the more elegant ladies politely took diaries from their purses, consulted them and then put them back again unmarked.

'The time of democracy is over,' said a man with a thin goatee beard, poet's eyes and artist's hands. He realized that the dog and I were the only ones listening. He lowered his voice.

'You see, the politics of India are run on full stomachs on behalf of those who will only ever have empty stomachs.' He offered me a bowl of cashew nuts.

Our host came back to perch on the arm of the sofa.

'You have to understand that this country is very fluid. We cannot qualify what we are so we just have to keep running like a river, hoping that it will all work out by the time it gets to the sea. What do you think?'

'I can only observe,' I said.

'Weak,' he said, patting my arm. 'Not how your great *sahibs* controlled this country. Try not to reinvent yourself as an Indian. You will not like it and then it will be too late.'

I could only smile in response. He patted my arm again. I got up and he let me go with just a quiet wave of his hand.

As I left I went to thank the man who had invited me to the NGO Club. His name was Gautam Vohra. He was going to set up an organic farming project. I wanted to talk to him.

He was standing in the kitchen chatting happily to some women, ignoring the din from the next-door room, his face alive as he studied each member of the conversation. He swung round when I touched his shoulder to try and get his attention.

'You can't go now, Justine, we have not even talked,' he said.

'Oh we will,' I replied.

Treading Lightly on Dreams

I HAD FIRST met Gautam Vohra on a veranda in the dark while mosquitoes were biting my ankles. He saw me scratching. 'You should wear socks,' he said.

It was a chance meeting. I had arrived late for a drink with a friend on the cusp of winter when all sensible people covered their ankles.

He was guarded when I was introduced as a journalist.

'This house is a house of habit so I am the bar-man for the night,' said our mutual friend, swinging through the mosquito screen to the whisky supplies.

'Why are you wary of me?' I asked Gautam.

'Because I was a journalist for fifteen years. Everything is another potential story for you.'

'And what are you doing now?'

'Having a whisky with a friend.'

'No, I mean what work do you do now?'

'I am starting an organic farm project.'

That was when my antennae went up. Oh Sourish, look what I have found. Gautam was right, he was going to become a story.

The bar-man for the night returned with the whiskies. The conversation reverted to travel, the dog's sore paw and the archetypal Indian man, the last two both very difficult to cure.

Gautam sent me the literature about his non-government organization. Here was another acronym, DRAG: Development

Research & Action Group. I flipped through, not really absorbing the enormity of the facts and figures. DRAG had come to life over coffee in Bombay in 1987, the hot air of idealism pinned down and put into practice. Its early work had been among tribal people in Maharashtra in the Western Ghats outside Bombay, implementing government poverty relief programmes. Now it had spread its wings to work among the urban poor of Delhi and had plans to diversify into an organic farming project. One thing did become clear; Sourish and I had been wrong. Organic farming was not returning to India. It had never left.

Ninety per cent of Indian farms comprise just two or three acres. Large-scale farming is made almost impossible by an agricultural land law which restricts the size of a holding to a standardized number of acres based on yield. In desert areas like Jodhpur in Rajasthan, officially referred to as an arid zone, the standard stretches up to 312 acres. In irrigated areas it drops down to as little as two.

Only in the Punjab and Haryana, where farms are larger, has there been a move away from traditional methods towards a system that resembles the high-yield, intensive farming of North America and Europe which produces crops and animals that conform to a particular size, shape and appearance, aided and abetted by the extensive use of chemical fertilizers and pesticides. Indian smallholders have always farmed organically because they have had no alternative. But now many of these same smallholders exist in a vicious circle of debt and desperation. When a harvest fails they have to borrow money. In order to repay the loan they need higher yields and so they mortgage themselves to buy chemical fertilizers. The increase in yield is marginal for the land is usually overworked even before the fertilizers have begun their own cycle of soil rape. It is hard to convince farmers whose lives have become governed by their creditors that returning to traditional organic methods is the way forward. They cannot believe that chemical fertilizers actually weaken their stock in the long term as well as robbing the soil of naturally occurring nutrients. The vicious circle spirals down. During a bad harvest the rate of suicide among smallholders in over-farmed belts of central India outstrips that of any other recorded farming community in the world.

It was among these people that Gautam Vohra was planning to ignite a green revolution of his own.

We met a couple of days after the club evening so that I could interview him about his organic farm project. He paced around his flat as I nosed through his bookshelves and admired his pictures. He seemed perturbed that I did not want a drink, at least not whisky. 'What kind of journalist are you?' he asked

'The Australian expression is a "one-pot screamer".'

He gave me a glass of water and some *mithai* instead, placing both neatly on a small stool at my feet before pouring himself a drink. He asked what other organic farms I had seen. I thought of the pretty farm and manor-house in the Kangra valley where Will and I had stopped on the way to Spiti for a taste of the rural idyll and exquisite home-made jam. I knew that an organic activist would think of it as hobby farming. Deflecting the question I asked him to explain his project.

To illustrate his idea he quoted the example of another NGO that had set up an organic farm on three and a half acres in Andhra Pradesh in the south-east of the country. There they did not till or plough the land. Produce was gathered from orchards and mixed forest, and crops were sown by hand on unturned soil. The farm was protected by a natural windbreak of trees and bushes, and subdivided by a live fence of thorny creepers. That experiment was worked by middle-class members of the NGO who integrated with the local people. Theoretically there was a constant exchange of information, the rural wisdom of the village farmers mixing with the influence and financial support of the NGO representatives.

Gautam himself was trying to buy a three-acre plot in Haryana on behalf of DRAG. He was being asked a high price for the land, 200,000 rupees an acre or about £3,000.

I asked whether produce from the farm would be sold to one of the very few organic outlets around the country.

'I am not interested in organic farming to produce food for middle-class sales. They can do what they bloody well like with their money. I want to prove to village people that they can make a damn good living from this kind of subsistence farming. I will show this with my farm.' He closed his eyes for a moment.

'If organic food for the middle classes is what you want to talk about I cannot help you. What you are doing in the West with your health shops and all is just nothing to do with what we are doing here.' He smacked his hand down hard.

I spilt my glass of water.

'The point of this project is that we go out and work with the community, not for them. We are not some middle-class voluntary set-up trying to make ourselves feel better. Those kind of people are not going to go out and work in the villages. Fifteen years as a journalist was a way of learning about my country. Now I am working for it.' He finished his drink. 'My journalism did not change people's lives. Perhaps organic farming can.'

'Isn't that rather an ambitious claim?'

He looked at me, his head on one side, his empty glass marking time in the air. 'Okay, I can't change lives but at least I can try and make a dent in the poverty level.'

'Are you going to live out in the village and work on the farm?' I was trying to mop up the spilt water with my shirt sleeve.

'What are you doing?'

He leapt up, wiped the water away and continued. 'I will live on the land, but I can never really belong. We are set apart from them by our background, our education, our whole lives. I will come back to Delhi at the weekends to see a movie, to see friends, have a drink.' He looked into his empty glass.

'That's quite a schizophrenic kind of life.'

'But I am not as idealistic as that. I'm no revolutionary, I'm no Che Guevara, I'm not trying to be a hero. I have friends who have done that. They have gone out to work in villages and stayed, declassed themselves. I suppose I am a hypocrite because I cannot do that. You know when it gets dark in the villages there is just nothing to do and not even really enough light to read by. Small doses, small doses, but then an injection of Delhi life.' He poured himself another drink, checked the amount of whisky against the light and smiled. 'I suppose you disapprove of someone who knocks back the pegs while shooting off his mouth about organic this and that?'

I had unconsciously been watching his glass.

'I may be a fake but I know that I operate better that way. I know I have the choice.' He topped up his whisky with water before carefully replacing the bottle at his feet.

'Do you think those people really achieve anything, really help by declassing themselves as you say?'

He looked at me with a sad smile, one that told me I was on territory that I did not understand. He shrugged. 'It is right for them.'

He talked about some of DRAG's other projects, about the move from the tribals of Maharashtra to the slums of Delhi. He was now involved in projects that used adult education as a way of entering the delicate hierarchy of slum life. At the start of each project he would work closely with the people. As it began to take root he would step back and let it grow at its own pace, organically. That was how DRAG worked, finding teachers and workers from within the slum communities and using the DRAG members as catalysts from the outside to sow the seeds. Once a project was underway they would slowly remove themselves from the scene. Gautam called it conscientization, a word coined by the Brazilian activist Paulo Freire to describe the way he worked with the Latin American poor. Let the people reflect on their situation, take action to change it and reflect on the results of that action. DRAG's adult education programmes were the touch-paper that would give the slum dwellers the tools for income generation, an understanding of the importance of hygiene and a voice to demand their right to vital utilities within the slums.

There was another voice that DRAG had turned to for its methodology:

I keep six honest serving men
They taught me all I know
Their names are What and Why and When
And Where and Who and How

Kipling's guidelines for his trade as a journalist have crossed
more boundaries than any of his books. They sit in offices across
the globe, plastered over the photocopier machine where the
office juniors of the world muse upon this four-line key to the
boardroom. Here it was back again in India. Kipling's code of survival during the Raj had become the scaffolding for working in the
slums of the millennium. 'Who' were the slum dwellers? 'Where'
did they come from? 'Why' had they been forced into slum conditions? 'What' could they offer in the way of skills? 'How' could
DRAG approach them with the idea of adult education? 'When'
could a programme be implemented in a given slum area? Would
Kipling have been glad of the interpretation? It was hard to tell
what a product of empire would have made of modern efforts to
empower the displaced and disenfranchised of India's slums. I like
to think he would have approved.

'Do you plan to spend a couple of years living out in the village
in Haryana when you start the farm?' I asked Gautam.

'No, it will be more than that, maybe five years, maybe eight
years. I will see.'

'But that is much longer than your other projects,' I queried.

At last his face was still. 'Oh well, that is because I want to
spend that much time there. I would like to steady the rush.'

'That's quite a romantic idea.'

'Of course it is, why would I embark on it otherwise?'

I trod with care now. I was in the territory of his dreams. 'And
after that, after the five or eight years, what then?'

'Oh, I will see.' This was a different Gautam, a poet with a
vision, not the cynical journalist who had seen so many shattered
and bandaged dreams.

'Are you still working on any of the Delhi slum projects?'

'Of course.'

'May I come on one of your trips with you?'

'You can come on as many as you like.' He showed me to the door. I had made my usual excuses at the beginning. Now I did not really want to leave.

In a booklet about DRAG that Gautam had given me, I found a diary of the progress made in one of the slum areas where an activity centre had been started for the children. Gautam told me that the centre had been based in several places around the slum but ended up under a *keekar* tree. The diary was entitled 'Blossoms under a *Keekar* Tree'. The blossoms were the children that flowered there. The piece had obviously been written by Gautam. It was about the walk from his home to where the slum was, less than a kilometre away:

> Territorial imperative: it is ingrained in dogs more strongly than in humans, or nearly so. As I walked through Vasant Vihar towards the Ridge and on to Bhagwan Singh Camp this view was driven home. *En route* a slender, long-eared mongrel attached herself to me, sidling next to me every time each locality's strays bared their teeth. I provided her with moral support, and once in a while even gave the persistent battle-scarred suitor the evil eye . . . but when the slum dogs approached her in growling packs, she finally abandoned me, beating a hasty retreat.

There were similar extracts throughout the diary but the slender mongrel moved me. She seemed to represent the transition in someone like Gautam as he crossed the shitting fields from his home to the slum, into territory where even a stray dog would not go.

I shouted at K.K. Chopra as we made our way through morning traffic to Gautam's house. He seemed to be taking a particularly roundabout route and it was beginning to get late. I had a feeling that Gautam would leave if I did not arrive on time.

'Where are we going?' I shrieked.

K.K. Chopra looked surprised. I had never shouted at him before.

We ground to yet another halt in one more traffic jam. He turned to me with his head on one side. 'Taking the road to Vasant Vihar.'

'Of course we are. *Maf kijiye*, I am sorry, KK. I am a bit late and probably a bit tired.'

'Too much of work, Mem, no problem.' He touched the picture of the blue-haired god next to the flowery lettering of his name above his head. Then he pressed his middle finger to the point between his eyebrows. Oh blue-rinsed god, deliver KK from the madness of over-excitable white women. We arrived at Vasant Vihar just in time. Gautam was already behind the wheel of his jeep.

We were going to Trilokpuri, trans-Yamuna, across the great Delhi river, to the western edge of the city. The slum had once had a high percentage of Sikhs in its community. In 1984 there had been riots there, triggered by the assassination of Mrs Gandhi by her Sikh bodyguard. The anger of the people had been directed towards the Sikh slum dwellers of Trilokpuri. As a result the government had recognized it as an area that needed attention and it had been declared a legal slum. It had water taps on every street, drainage, electricity and a government education plan. This was where DRAG came in, as Gautam explained.

'Because of the government's embarrassment after the riots in 1984 they provided all the necessary amenities. The irony is that now most of the Sikhs have moved away, although I think there are some still there. Someone saw a programme on the slum the other day. A woman was pointing at her son saying that he was the only one of her children not to have been slaughtered in the riots and yet the government had let the perpetrators of the murders get away.'

I was finding it almost impossible to concentrate on what he was saying. Gautam was one of those nerve-racking drivers who turn away from the road to look at their passenger while they are talking. He did not see all the near-collisions that were happening as he spoke. I did and winced each time. He did not seem to notice my reaction or perhaps he was being polite and thought it might be a nervous tic to which he should not draw attention. The traffic ducked and dived around us. I took off my glasses so that I would not be able to focus on the road.

'Today is a good day for the women,' he said, closing his eyes for a moment, drinking in the sun.

I kept mine wide open.

'Why a good day?'

'It is warm.' He opened his eyes and looked straight at me.

I clung to the seat.

'I will show you three faces of poverty. The first, Trilokpuri, you will find is a very pretty slum.'

We were passing the familiar postcard pieces of New Delhi, the government buildings and India Gate. A man drove a bullock pulling a lawnmower beside the great arch. Four other men followed, sweeping up the meagre cuttings. Five men and a bullock to trim grass that hardly grows.

Gautam parked the jeep a little way from the section that we were going to see. He was right, Trilokpuri had a prettiness of its own. The narrow streets were swept and either cobbled or

A cow, an Atco and Lutyens' Delhi

cemented. The *nalis*, the gulleys along which water and sewage run, had been sealed with cement so that the effluent would flow. Left to stagnate they would have become a breeding-ground for the aedes mosquito, the carrier of cerebral malaria, indiscriminate killer of the slums.

The winter sun was the first to break through the grey, dank run of December. The women of Trilokpuri were out on the streets washing furiously, themselves, their young families, their clothes, their pots and pans. Small children stood against the walls in the warmth as if they too had been hung out to dry beside the lines of laundry, their hair slicked down, their eyes kohl-rimmed, fingers in mouths, up noses, in ears, feet rolled on outer edges – the evocative, hip-jutting, belly-protruding stance of the slums, the pose of poverty and already tired bones.

We stopped at one house. Gautam called out to the women to find out what was going on. It was midday, the time the adult education class was supposed to begin. A *charpai* was pulled out for me. I perched on the edge of the frame on one buttock. I would have been happier to stand out of the way of the flow of the street, but to refuse the *charpai* would have implied that I did not wish to accept their hospitality, that it was not good enough for a foreigner.

Gautam was having a vociferous discussion with several of the women. Where was the class today? Why were they not there already? Where was the teacher from the community who had been chosen to run the class? His hands flew about.

A small boy edged up to the *charpai* to peer at me. He had a series of scabbed blisters across his face. They were undressed, left open to the sun to dry. I could think of no child that I knew who would leave those scabs alone. He stood silently by my side, examining my face, my hands, my shoes.

A girl appeared with a baby in her arms. Her name was Shabnam Begum and she was the appointed teacher. Gautam asked her what was happening. She gripped her baby's bare brown bottom hard so that the flesh dimpled. The government education guide had not been coming and she did not have the confidence to take the class alone.

'Come.' Gautam herded all before him. A small troop made its way along the street to a house where there was space for a class. Now it was clear why Gautam had thought it a good day for the women. The space was on an open roof, unprotected from the weather. It would have been miserable without the sun.

To start with there were only a few women. A mother and daughter from Aligarh arrived. They had been living in the slum since its inception in 1976. The mother was sixty, her daughter twenty-two. The daughter was called Namshree and she had an air of determination about her quite unlike the look of resignation in so many of the faces of the women of the slum. Then came a girl from Jaipur in Rajasthan. Another, Tara, from Sultanpur, had moved to Trilokpuri sixteen years before. She said that she was happy there because the bus stand was close by and water was available at all hours.

Again a *charpai* appeared. The boy with the scabs had followed us up on to the roof and he leant against the bed beside me, still silent and watching. A few others arrived and they settled cross-legged at a slight remove from the *charpai*. Gautam sat among them. He told Shabnam Begum to start the class. Her baby began to cry and was passed to a young girl in a blue school uniform. She too came to lean against the *charpai*, unconcerned by her proximity to me, unlike the older women who seemed to have marked out an invisible boundary around the old string bed.

The women were being taught the Hindi alphabet and word recognition so that they could learn to read and write, to enable them to question their rights as slum-dwellers instead of being cowed into silence by their lack of understanding. Hindi was not the vernacular of many of the women of Trilokpuri. Not only were they in a foreign city, they were having to live with another language beyond their native Tamil, Gujarati, Bengali or Punjabi.

The lesson of the day was a reading from a government adult education book about the benefits of the pomegranate tree and its fruit. Once every garden would have had a pomegranate tree because of its useful properties. Now there was too much over-crowding to allow for such planting. We heard about the gifts of the pomegranate: its juice for the alleviation of constipation, diarrhoea, fever and digestive disorders; the seeds for memory enhancement; the flesh for long life; the dried ground skin as a preventative against stomach cancer. Then came some strange advice. 'For women in the habit of getting repeatedly pregnant there is benefit of drinking each day for thirty days the juice of fresh pomegranate flowers ground down into paste and mixed with nine *tolas* of water and anything to sweeten to taste.' There was a certain practicality behind the wisdom. Anyone who knows the pomegranate will tell you that the flowers have a powerful diuretic effect. With all the running to and fro to find somewhere to pee, there would hardly be a moment for romance, let alone an opportunity for full-blown conception.

Maya, a tall, dark beauty from Etah, arrived, settling herself down, her exercise book and unsharpened pencil held tightly in her lap. There was no place made for her by the other women in their wash-worn working clothes. Maya stood apart in her elegant sari of pale silk, almost luminescent against the polished mahogany of her skin. Lift me up, take me away, I was not meant for this, said her dress. She sat at the back, still and erect, the slum swan with runaway eyes.

The little boy with the scabs plucked up the courage to come and sit on the *charpai*. He curled up against me in the afternoon sun, resting his open hand on my leg. It remained there, the small palm facing up to me, not begging, just lying on my leg.

The lesson turned into a discussion when one of the women pointed out that too many children in the house were a burden as there was never enough food. Others disagreed and said that poverty came not from the size of a family but from the lack of jobs. Even the educated of Trilokpuri could not find work. One of the women had a brother with a bachelor's degree. He had been offered the job of secretary in a government school, but if he was to take the job he had to pay an intermediary 25,000 rupees, about £400, the equivalent of almost a year's salary. To raise the money he would be forced to take out a loan at a high rate of interest.

Gautam wrote fast. This was news to him, another layer of corruption in the sticky web that DRAG was trying to pick its way through.

Namshree said that they were all very keen to have the classes but how could they when Shabnam Begum would not hold them?

Shabnam looked at Gautam with frightened eyes and said once more that she did not have the confidence to teach the class without the government guide. Namshree spoke again. She said that she could read some Hindi because her brother had taught her. She stopped for a moment and the other women looked at her. 'If I learn I will not be dependent on other people,' she said. She held her clasped hands out to Gautam in supplication.

He wrote down her words. He asked her if she felt she could help Shabnam with the class. Then he addressed the other women, asking them to remind Shabnam to give the class, to boost her confidence. They agreed to do so.

Namshree waved her finger at Gautam. This time there was no petition but a quick flex of her newly acquired authority. She told him not to address all the women as *mataji* as he had been doing. This was a term of respect for women older than he and yet he was throwing it around like so much chaff.

'Look, you are a white-headed one,' she said. 'We are nearly all younger than you, except my mother. Perhaps even she is younger than you. Call us *behanji* (sister) and save the respect for those who are older.'

A smile scuttled across Gautam's face but he turned to Namshree with a chastened expression. 'Thank you, sister.'

I caught his eye but the smile had gone.

Shabnam was now sitting beside me on the *charpai*, the baby wriggling on her lap. He happily ate one end of my pen while expertly inserting the lid into his ear.

A woman called Shanti, her name meaning peace, appeared with rumpled hair, her pencil and school book in hand, just as the class was coming to an end. Gautam greeted her and then turned to me. 'They all come in their own time. See, we now have ten.'

We rose to leave and I took out my camera. There was a group of men sitting over on the neighbouring roof. They were playing cards, making an earnest attempt to ignore the empowerment of their women from behind hands of three-card stud. With the appearance of a camera they put down their cards. This was a chance for a face in a photograph, one to put up next to all those of their children, rictus-faced, in financially crippling school uniforms.

A younger boy, who had been dancing attendance on the game, leapt across the gap between the two roofs, his arms thrown up to carry him over the divide. He elbowed his way to the front of the

Gautam Vohra and the women of the slums

small crowd that was pushing towards the camera. I was being pressed back further, right up against the edge of the roof. The crowd of children had swelled, new faces had just appeared. It was one o'clock. Lunch-break from school had become a photocall.

Some of the women were shy, pulling their *pallavs* across their unwashed hair. Not Maya, the tall, dark beauty with runaway eyes. She stood on the edge of the group, her school book tucked away. She shook her arms to bring all her gold bangles from under the folds of her *sari*.

Gautam loitered at the back of the group, always just melting from the edge of the frame that I was trying to take. The children pressed forward, as if by pushing their faces against the lens they could guarantee their place in the picture. I felt the low wall of the roof edge against my legs, my back arching away over the side.

As I lost my balance Shabnam Begum reached out her hand and caught mine. 'Come, photo the baby,' she said, holding on to me.

It was just a moment. The roof was quite high. I am not sure how bad the damage would have been if I had fallen. But Shabnam Begum's hand had reached out to catch me. I had been lucky. In these overcrowded places, these corners packed with life and death, it is all too easy to miss that moment when someone needs to be helped. Shabnam Begum had been my saviour on the edge of a roof in the winter sun of Trilokpuri.

I left the slum clutching her address so that I could send the picture of her earnest face and her baby's dimpled bottom.

*

'Why do you want to go poking around these slums?' asked Yashwant.

It was late morning and we were both still in our nightclothes, he in a rather elegant dressing-gown, me in unattractive layers topped by a hermaphrodite cardigan. I too had been forced by the cold to buy a shapeless but fairly harmless woolly. I was also clutching a hot-water bottle. It was the coldest, shortest day of the year. We stood at opposite ends of a grey corridor among the clouds made by our conversation in the cold air. Yashwant laughed.

'If the Rani could see us she would have a fit. Look, look, it is the middle of the day and we are wandering around in our night-clothes. Oh, she would be so horrified. Slums and nightclothes at midday, how uncivilized.'

'I am writing about NGOs. There was a beautiful girl yesterday. You could have put her anywhere in the world and she still would have held her own, head and shoulders above Miss India, Miss World or whatever she is.'

'We have some very beautiful peasants, you know.'

'Don't be sarcastic. I have a picture of her, I'll show you.'

'Well, let's go back and find her and turn her into a supermodel and make lots of lovely money.'

'Don't be ridiculous. She is married and has three children.'

'So?'

'She'd get dragged off by the fashion vampires who'd suck her dry and then what would happen to her family?'

'Oh, you are beginning to sound like an NGO.' He sailed off down the corridor, the dressing-gown swirling in his wake. 'I am going to see a doctor today somewhere out in the sticks. I shall be away for several days. There is some *nimish* in the fridge. Get the servants to make it for you, otherwise it will all have to be thrown away.'

Nimish is a little girl's fairytale concoction made of ground cuttlefish, milk and essence of rose, beaten into a froth of extravagance in unfired earthenware pots and set in morning dew. Yashwant had suddenly remembered his mother's *nimish* the night before. An edict had been issued to the kitchen that he wished to taste once more the stuff of his childhood. There had been a short, intense whirlwind of activity and shouting. As a result the cavernous fridge was full of untasted *nimish*.

'Have fun in the slums.' He waved as he disappeared into his room.

The second face of poverty that Gautam took me to see was in Uttam Nagar, off Pankha Road, past long rows of mechanics' shops where oil-smudged faces bent over engine parts. It is not a place where tourists generally go.

I did not shout at K.K. Chopra, though we were late and the traffic was bad. Once had been enough.

The sun made no appearance that day, and Uttam Nagar was not a pretty place.

'It is not a slum yet because it does not have the requisite over-crowding, but that will come. It is only because quite a few of the plots of land have not been sold and the vacant lots create space.' Gautam pointed at empty blocks through the grey mist. 'It really is not so bad, the houses are all built of concrete. It is more of a middle-class area at the moment.'

The place was called Mohan Gardens. A strange garden. Its flowers were piles of broken plastic chairs jutting from corners; its ornamental ponds were the *nalis*; its playground, half-finished houses with vacant, gap-toothed expressions; its children, rack-ribbed dogs with scabby, hairless bodies, howling through the fog that sat on the place.

We went to have tea with a teacher from the local secondary school who had been appointed to oversee the women's adult edu-cation class. Gautam's jeep was abandoned, the puddles being too deep. The teacher led the way as we sloshed through the mud. She wore strappy sandals and bright lipstick.

Tea was not so much a social thing but more a chance for the teacher's husband, a fancy glass-maker from the Punjab, to vet Gautam and the requirements of the part-time job for his wife. They had been living in Mohan Gardens for nearly five years but we sat on chairs against damp breeze-block walls in a room that looked as if it had only just been occupied. There were a couple of religious pictures stuck up on the wall, their edges peeling away in the cold. Most important of all, there was a television in the corner run off a car battery. This was proof that the teacher and her husband were on their way up the social ladder of Mohan Gardens.

Water was offered. Gautam declined, I accepted. He flicked his head, showing a concern that is almost a national trait. Ninety-five per cent of Indians suffer from amoebiasis, a constant diarrhoea-inflicting infection of the colon, picked up from the underground water pipes that run alongside the sewage pipes, the same pipes that had been laid by British engineers over a century before when Delhi's population was a thousandth of its current size. Now they are wearing out, the result a constant cross-seepage. The teacher was lucky, she had her own hand-pump outside the house. The water they got was not too bad, not too salty, she said. Most of the other water supplies in the area were only good for washing and cleaning. I tried some water from the pump. It tasted of bromide. Gautam laughed.

'Our over-population is awful but I don't think the government has started to put sexual suppressors in our water supplies yet.'

The couple looked on suspiciously, alerted by the word 'sexual' but unsure of the rest of the conversation. Gautam tried to explain. It did not improve the situation so the subject was changed and we drank hot, sweet tea, and a tiny puppy next to my feet watched with fascination as a puddle of his pee spread around him.

The class had started by the time we arrived at another grey house. There was a dog tied up outside. Inside a woman in a *salwar kameez* was taking the class from the same book that Shabnam Begum had read in the sun in Trilokpuri. The class asked my name and what I did, and stared as I stumbled a reply in Hindi. I doubt they understood what I'd said. The class was resumed.

They recited the Hindi vowel sounds, the song of Indian childhood, the mantra to conquer adult illiteracy. The dog howled in time.

It was not an inspiring place. I looked out through the doorway of that cold room and felt nothing but a creeping, self-indulgent sense of guilt that I was judging these slums against my notion of poverty, a notion of Indian poverty that was still associated with the overcrowded human throb of Trilokpuri rather than the less inspiring broken chairs and grey, vacant lots of Mohan Gardens. I heard the women laugh at something Gautam had said. I turned back into that room of women and saw the link between those faces from all over India, laughing with a man from a background almost as alien to them as my own. His face was alive as he watched and listened to the disparate group brought together by the class. He did not need images to motivate him. He was involved.

*

Sourish looked up from a pile of proof pages with a great smile. Karan and another journalist were bent over similar piles. It was almost the deadline for the paper but still Sourish could look up to smile. I was trying to trace some transparencies that had been used to illustrate the pieces I had been writing. Several hours of running around various departments talking to different picture editors had proved fruitless, but then my timing had been bad. The lunch hour was not the moment to go hunting for missing pictures. Fingers that had delved in rice, *dhal* and pickle were hastily wiped on grimy handkerchiefs. Perhaps it was a good thing that my transparencies were proving so elusive, I decided, as I watched other boxes of pictures being liberally smudged with the remnants of lunch.

'I've been trying to track down my pictures,' I said to Sourish.

He raised his eyebrows. 'Oh, oh, I think some of them have gone missing in the move from upstairs.'

'So they're lost?'

He shrugged and turned his attention back to the pages he was checking.

'If an English newspaper loses a transparency they have to pay £250. We are talking hundreds here, hundreds of my transparencies have just disappeared.'

Sourish looked up. I knew my face was going red.

'This is not an English newspaper.' This time he did not smile.

I flounced out in an ineffectual way. No one was watching. No point had been made. I back-pedalled and stuck my head around the door again.

'Any names yet? For the baby I mean.'

The smile came back. 'We have picked on one, I think, instead of the three that we couldn't choose between. I think it will be Samrat.'

'That's a pretty name.'

'You go and tell our parents that then, please. Can I have the travel piece on Seville by Monday? You know, bullfights and all.'

'I am doing research on adult education in the slums at the moment.'

'Oh, oh, of course. Yes, but we would still like Seville. The slums will not go away.'

The third face of poverty was shown to me on Christmas Day.

Gautam came to the door in his pyjamas. I was early this time. He left me in his sitting-room while he went to dress. There were books piled around the room – on Jung, Freud, psychology and organic farming. Each one had markers sticking out, flagging relevant pages, the tabs of an inveterate reader, a man caught up in his dreams. I opened one of them to see what kind of passages he'd marked just as he came back into the room. I snapped it shut, embarrassed that I had been caught snooping. Gautam laughed. 'See, you are still very English – why the blushing? They are there to read. Come.'

The grey fog was swirling and the slum was waiting. At home, five and a half hours behind Delhi time, parents were trying not to trip over sleeping dogs and children as they deposited lumpy stockings at the end of beds.

While shepherds watched their flocks by night we took to the shitting fields. There was no slender, long-eared mongrel to escort us on our trip through the mist, hopping over and around the piles of human faeces on the way. A boy squatting by the path watched as we passed, his face drained of expression to accompany the rapid, liquid evacuation of his bowels.

'Don't judge them, they have no choice,' Gautam said. He ducked down and touched the boy's cheek. The child's face remained impassive. 'I spent fifteen years as a journalist trying to understand my country, to wrap her flesh around me, rather than just standing on her shoulders to try and improve my view of the West. Perhaps this is what will happen to you too. Perhaps you will find yourself pulled into the heart, turning your head from West to East.' He walked on. 'Some people pretend to be indifferent to all this, some even are. I don't think you are.'

Even in the bitter morning cold a few boys were playing cricket on the *maidan,* the dusty open space on the edge of the slum. A wicket fell and a boy with knobbly knees yelled and punched the air, just as he had seen them do on Star Sport TV. His trousers had holes where once the back pockets had been and his bare bottom was exposed to the freezing cold.

The teacher stood under a *keekar* tree. The class had not started, though there were a few children sitting shivering on rush mats. None of them were wearing enough clothes and most of them were barefoot, their noses running free in the cold. Gautam shouted to encourage others emerging from the mist to hurry and join the group.

He waited until they were all seated on the ground before handing round paper, paints, crayons, pencils and coloured chalks. A boy on the edge of the group was quivering in just a shirt. Gautam bent down and wrapped an old shawl round him. He ruffled the boy's hair and moved on.

I sat down with them under the *keekar* tree. Fog dripped off the branches and down the backs of our necks. They were making greetings cards. Gautam had debated on the Christmas theme and then decided to be less specific – just cards for any old thing rather than scenes of Baby Jesus. One boy bent over his paper and began to draw a house with trees, some mountains in the background and a rising sun. The others looked on with troubled faces before beginning to copy. The first boy was struggling with a star. I drew one the way I had been taught, two triangles on top of each other, one pointing up, the other down. They all copied it perfectly and then repeated it over and over on their cards, triangular stars from a South Oxfordshire prep school. Gautam shouted over thirty young heads: 'Don't encourage them to copy. They refuse to use their imaginations. We have to try and kick-start them.'

I watched them draw and paint with tightly held pencils, crayons, chalks and brushes, tiny, congested pictures dwarfed even by the small pieces of paper that they drew on. As the lesson came to a close they placed their cards on a *charpai*. The fog from the *keekar* tree dripped down and smudged some of the tiny paintings. No one complained. Gautam looked on. He stroked a few faces and patted some of the older boys on the back. Now they smiled and laughed before rushing away to fight off the cold.

Gautam turned as we made our way back through the shitting fields again. 'I do not believe that one word that I wrote during those fifteen years of journalism changed a single life. But it did enable me to do this and now I think I am beginning finally to make a dent. Even if no one notices it or feels any change, something is happening.' He stopped as a cricket ball from the *maidan* sailed between his nose and my ear. 'At least something is happening to me.' He walked on, hands behind his back, the philosopher of the shitting fields. And the clergy of England were about to take to the pulpit and preach good tidings of great joy.

The blossoms under the keekar *tree*

Returned Empty

IT WAS RAINING on St Valentine's Day. The postman did not exactly stagger to the doors of Jodhpur Apartments laden with romantic missives. Equally depressing was the fact that the ballot box was back for the second general election in as many years. 'It is time for honest government,' said the beleaguered Prime Minister as he took a tired bow. More young men prepared to set fire to themselves at polling booths. The electorate shook its bemused head, too bored even to raise the subject. I had arrived during a general election and now I was leaving during another. There was a certain symmetry to it which I found oddly romantic, but perhaps that was St Valentine.

There was not much romance in the air at Hailey Road. My one card came in a box from New York, a 'Boyfriend in a Box', sent by a friend who knew what it was not to receive a Valentine. So I had Cowboy Hank in a stetson and bulging jeans, with all his vital statistics and a passport-sized photograph to keep in my wallet. I thought that perhaps Yashwant would appreciate Cowboy Hank more than me.

'Happy Valentine's Day.' And I handed over the Texan hunk.

He went through the box.

'He's not very handsome.'

He peered at the pictures.

'Well, that comes down to personal taste.'

'I suppose you're right, but look at this, he is losing his hair.'

'That's probably why he's got the stetson.'

'Will you sign it for me?' He pushed the photograph in front of me.

'What do you mean?'

'Sign it "with all my love Hank, kiss, kiss, kiss".'

'Why?'

'So that I can put it by my bed and cause a big jealousy performance. Come, come, it will be so much fun.' He passed me a pen.

'I'm not sure I want to be part of a big jealousy performance.'

'Enough, just sign. Come, do it for me.' He flung the *biri* that he had just lit out of my bedroom window.

I was hovering over the photograph.

'Please sign. I am so bored.'

I signed in the way I thought Texan Hank might sign, kind of big and illegible.

'Lovely.' He grabbed the picture and inspected the signature.

'It's not very convincing. It doesn't even look like a real photograph.'

'So what? This is going to be so much fun.' He stopped at the door. 'Ram Kumar tells me that you are going to be leaving soon. Is this true?'

'Not until well after the election.'

'Oh God, why do you want to wait for that?'

'Full circle maybe, election to election.'

'I shan't vote.'

'It's your moral obligation.'

'I never have.'

'Why not?'

'Who on earth would I vote for?'

Yashwant sniffed and left the room clutching 'Boyfriend in a Box' to his chest.

Amid the stress and strain of unseasonal rain and the ballot box, Delhi resorted to what it does best – eating. Huddled in corners under the dripping colonnades of Connaught Place, indistinct figures munched street-stall snacks; others peered out from inside over-priced, vacuum-sealed international fast-food joints;

poorer men crouched under tarpaulins at *chai* stalls over small glasses of sweet tea. The street politicians were drawn as magnets to the Bengali Sweet House at the end of Hailey Road. The waiters performed the dance of practical men at speed. If an elbow bumped, a knee bent to compensate, a shoulder dropped and the tray of sticky sweets continued on its way to table sixty-six. Plates of golden rolled rice *dosas* all landed as ordered, aluminium clattering on linoleum. Outside, the sky was black, a deep, dark sable washed by the rain. It was the end of the election but no one cared. As long as there were still stuffed *dosas* at the Bengali Sweet House everything would remain the same.

I was perched on the end of a bench, trying to be inconspicuous behind a very small paper cup of coffee. My large neighbour finished off his *dosa*, had a quick go at his small daughter's ice-cream, burped and turned to me as he wiped his fingers on a delicate white handkerchief.

'So you must be being English, *yaar*?'

I nodded.

He swiftly established that I was a journalist, that I was not married, that I did not live with a very good friend, that I was old enough to have had at least four children and that I was working for an Indian newspaper. He decided that I was a hangover from the Victorian era, one of those spinsters looking for salvation in good deeds in a dark land, all things that could be solved if I could find myself a good Indian husband. His wife looked on with a blank expression.

'You thought you had us all tied up, right under the colonial thumb, *yaar*? Now, show me what is English here.' He waved his hand at the bobbing crowd, *dosa*-covered fingers half in, half out of mouths, the hard ebb and flow of Hindustani shouted across the room, or just across a table, the volume always the same, loud and fast.

He had a point. I was still not quite letting go of the remnants of Englishness, clinging to the scaffolding of that finished time.

Just down the street, two minutes' walk through the driving rain, was an exhibition of photographs of the Delhi Durbar of

1911. There stood George, King-Emperor of all India, and his consort in full sail on a sea of subjects. Around their ermine trains, small princes of the royal houses waited in attendance: Jodhpur, Rewa, Bikaner and Kutch.

It was the opening night. What a to-do. What to do? And not a parking place in sight. Round and round the chauffeurs went, their electric windows whizzing up and down. The great-great-grandson of a former Viceroy was the star of the night with his wife by his side, so English, so Empire in taffeta and pearls. All Delhi was there, anxious to be seen and heard: 'Those were the days, shame, shame, all gone. What is this country coming to when we are about to hand ourselves over to some Italian butcher's daughter from Turin? Ah well. Champagne, yes, how nice.' And off they floated, glasses in hand, voicing their admiration for the tight taffeta frocks and tidy pearls of the token English crowd as they slid past in their fluid chiffons and gulls' egg jewels. On the walls magnificently moustached maharajas, inscrutable *sahibs* and exhausted *mems* gazed out from their sepia graves. In the glass between were reflected the social machinations of a very different age.

My Sweet House neighbour would have seen plenty that was English there but it seemed unlikely that he would be going to the exhibition.

'You still speak English,' I shrugged in response to his question.

He laughed, displaying the last of the *dosa* and his daughter's ice-cream.

'That is only as I am talking to you.'

*

The Opposition had won the election. *The Indian Express* had a front-page story: '*Sadhu* says PM elect must fast to succeed'. A Jain ascetic from Madhya Pradesh had announced to his enraptured coterie that the new prime minister was blocking his path to leadership of the nation by expending too much energy on his passion for food. Now he was facing the biggest hurdle of his life: not the achievement of his political ambitions but his greed. Readers of the article nodded their heads in all seriousness. The members of the prime minister designate's party listened to the ascetic's words gravely. After all, when their leader had won the general election two years before, he had managed to stay in power for only two and a half months before the lure of the lunch box dragged him down.

'Go vegetarian,' cried the learned Jain. 'Show some self-control, quit your favourite snack, ban the export of meat, and the premiership will be yours.'

A few minutes further on from the *dosa* politicians of the Bengali Sweet House, the international press gathered for their Friday night drink at the Foreign Correspondents' Club. The mood was buoyant after weeks of pre-election depression.

Through the crowd at the bar appeared a familiar face: the man from the NGO Club who had dropped his crisp sandwich into my lap. He lurched up to me.

'You shouldn't be here,' he whispered with about as much subtlety as Widow Twanky.

I did not respond.

'Gentlemen, we have a fraud among us,' he announced to the room.

No one took any notice. He smashed his hand down on the bar, pinched my cheek with his other hand, and announced, more loudly this time, 'Gentlemen, we have a fraud. She's not a foreign correspondent. She's in the local camp. Couldn't get a job back home so comes out here.' He pinched my cheek again with a big smile.

It was Friday night, drinking night for the boys, but even so the game was wearing thin. I bobbed away when he threatened to pinch my cheek a third time. He managed to get my ear instead. Not a very edifying spectacle.

A young journalist at the bar came to my rescue and offered a stool next to his.

'I would like to offer you a drink, but I think your friend has probably had enough. Do you really work for an Indian paper?' he asked incredulously.

'I really don't know him well. He just likes to tip crisps into my lap and pinch my cheek. I suppose that does make us friends in a broad sense and, yes, I do work for an Indian paper, *The Indian Express.*' I felt quite proud.

'How do you manage?' asked an American. 'You must be crazy. I know how much these guys earn. I know how much we pay the local guys, and that's oil company money, much more than you journos. How do you live?'

My friend in the broad sense, the cheek pincher, realizing that no one was going to buy him a drink or listen to him, swayed off towards another group. The young journalist had also lost interest and sat beside the American picking his fingernails with determined concentration.

'Delhi can be quite cheap. I walk a lot and eat at *dhabas.*' I tried to flick my shawl in an 'I belong' fashion. It fell off.

The American politely retrieved it for me from the floor. We bumped heads as he came up and I ducked down.

'So did you have the inside track on the elections then?' he asked.

'No, I'm not that heavyweight.'

'You mean you do all the Bollywood movie stars instead?'

'Yes, a few of them, and public loos, some sex, a bit of polo.'

'Let me get you a drink. What was your last story?' He settled in. 'Whisky, beer, what do you drink?'

'Fresh lime soda, please.'

'You don't drink?' He put his hands out in a beseeching fashion.

'Not much.'

'You're kidding me.' He fiddled with his cuffs.

'My most recent story was about the problem of bikinis in the *burqa*-wearing Muslim areas of Kerala.'

'Hey, I've just been down there. Well, come on, that's not so bad if they fly you off to do stuff like that.' He passed me the fresh lime soda and looked at his beer for a bit before pouring it into a glass.

'I took the train.'

'You mean the three-day hell ride?'

'Yup.'

'I guess the first-class sleepers are okay.' He was fiddling with his cuffs again.

'Third class had its moments.'

'Nah, come on, this really is bullshit. Are you on some Gandhi trip or something?'

'Third class is Rs. 2,000 cheaper than first class. It meant I could stay on for another four days at the end.'

'You mean you live on 500 rupees a day?'

'I try to.' God, I sounded so self-righteous.

'You're lying, aren't you?'

'Well, the man said I was a fraud.'

The American looked at me more closely: '500 rupees, that's what I tip the bell captain.'

'Lucky him. You must be very popular with bell captains.' I tried to smile warmly, realizing that I was making him still more uncomfortable.

He started to flap the jacket of his suit and fiddle with his tie knot. He looked around to see if there was anyone else he could draw into the conversation to dilute the social disquiet that was beginning to spoil the taste of his beer. Unable to find a suitable distraction he turned back.

'Can I ask you a kinda personal question? Why the hell do you do it?' He wiggled his shoulders, sensing that he was back in command as I looked out into the middle distance beyond his shoulder.

Voices swayed back and forth across the room. On the wall behind him were pictures taken by some of the great photographers working in the international press. There was one of ritual bathers on the *ghats* in Varanasi seen through the dawn mist: ripples of ancient skin sinking into the matching water beside spare, tight bodies; young women, their wet saris plastered and puckered against dark arches and angles, their mouths open as they poured the filthy, polluted waters of the Ganges over themselves, drinking in her diseases and pestilence. Next to it hung a photograph of Sunni Muslim self-flagellators during the festival of

Ramadan. The man with his back closest to the camera held his whip of chains in an arc over his head, the flat sides of the attached razor blades catching the light. Bright blood flowed from the wounds on his back. The sky was very blue, the blood very red. Next to that hung a portrait of a Bombay billionaire, one cowboy boot up on the front bumper of his Silver Shadow, a girl in a satin dress curled over the bonnet purring at the camera. The billionaire smiled the smile of acquisition.

They were a part of why I was here. The bathers in the Ganges, the blood of the Muslims, the billionaire's smile were all parts of liquid India. 'You have to understand that this country is very fluid,' the man at the NGO Club had said. I had been clinging to a structure that was no longer there except in memory and hyperbole. As India tried to reinvent herself I had to learn to swim instead of cling.

The American was waiting for an answer.

I shrugged. 'Hunting around for answers.'

He laughed. 'Did you find any?'

'Of course not, just lots more questions.'

'So you're having the standard Indian love affair?'

'I think I've been trying to let go of what India used to be.' And I knocked back the rest of my lime soda for all the world as if it was a whisky.

It shot up my nose and sprayed out liberally over the bar. The waiter politely passed me a pile of napkins.

'God, I'd hate to see what you do with a real drink,' said the American. He raised his beer. 'Here's to your letting go and finding some sanity.'

Sanity asserted itself on the Nicholson Ranges at five o'clock in the afternoon, just a twenty-minute ride from the mayhem of Delhi's newspaper world. Out on the ranges of the Ridge there was nothing but hillocks and scrub, circling Brahmini kites, a big mare called Kali Mem and the smell of her sweat. We cantered past the pony camps, the old British Army saddle creaking as we went, Kali Mem bucking and farting at the peafowl scratching in the scrub.

Out of the haze came the boys of the 61st Cavalry riding home from tent-pegging practice, their lances resting across the pommels of their saddles or daintily balanced on the tips of their flimsy brown regulation plimsolls, every man bolt upright in his seat. The officer leading them saluted.

'Good evening, ma'am.' He waved his hand and the troop dipped their lances as I passed.

Kali Mem shied and farted spectacularly. A peacock shrieked its applause.

Out beyond the last of the pony lines and the strutting peacocks was a wilderness where partridges scuttled in their dust baths and wild pigs exploded in and out of bushes. Here was a place to scream in silence and to whoop at the broad blue sky.

> I haven't been quite well and look on creation as through a glass darkly. My fellow had brought me opium and a pipe all complete and then and there insisted upon my smoking as much as I could. When I woke I found my man waiting at the bedside with a glass of milk and a stupendous grin. I must have looked queer, for Macdonald, my help from Allahabad, declares that I came into the office with every sign of advanced intoxication. This however has worn off and left me almost well – an evening ride will put me straight I trust.

Kipling rode his horse Joe to shake off the effects of a bout of cholera, to push away the questions that India raised. Kali Mem blew my frustrations out of her back end. Here was a symmetry of sorts, meeting in the evening pause when the day let go.

The last time I went out on the ranges Kali Mem bolted when a wild pig shot out from a bush between her hind legs. She is seventeen hands, a veritable war-horse. There was nothing I could do except hang on and wait for her to give up. Before she could do so we came to a *khud* and fell in a graceless heap to the bottom. We looked at each other in stunned silence. A peacock laughed from the lip of the ridge above.

Neither of us could get out the way we had come in. She was subdued, I was shaking. It was hard to tell whether either of us was injured. We were both standing. That seemed enough. Balancing uphill from her I tried to remount, but my leg was trembling too much to take the weight in the stirrup. There was blood on my hand that did not appear to come from anywhere in particular. There was no one to hear me cry, so I laughed. The peacock above laughed back.

The simplest way out was along the bottom of the *khud*. I led Kali Mem, hoping to find a stump or rock to use as a mounting-block. There was nothing. We walked on.

Above us were voices that followed. I stopped twice to try to establish where they were coming from. When we stopped, so did the voices. The afternoon changed its expression, the smile replaced by something not yet ominous but with the hint of a leer.

The mare was unabashed about having a good look at the strangers above. I did not want to acknowledge them. They might catch the scent of fear. The impression was of a group, perhaps nine or ten of them. I thought about what I was wearing – a cheap watch, a good pair of riding-boots, hand-made by Mr Minsen, the redoubtable Chinese bootmaker of Connaught Place, and the only pair of valuable earrings I possessed, stupidly worn at the wrong time.

We walked faster. The mare had recovered and she began to jog and sidestep, bored by the restrictions of the *khud*.

One of the group above shouted out. I walked on. Kali Mem danced on the toe of my boot and silent tears started. The voice shouted again, calling my name – *my* name.

I looked up. They were faces from the *chai* stall opposite Jodhpur Apartments, the two boys who made me glasses of tea, who always asked how I was, who laughed when I staggered through my Hindustani replies. They had never called me by name before.

Now there was no *chai* counter separating their role and mine. They jumped up and down on the lip above, waving me towards the end of the *khud*. Their shouts and laughter followed, bouncing around the mare and me. Kali Mem, sensing my relief, stomped on my foot again, just to keep things in perspective.

They were a gang of thirteen. Five of them held the mare's head and the rest went around the sharp end. There were hands everywhere, nervous, excited, unsure hands trying to help, doing all the wrong things. A halt was called by one of the older boys and they stood around me in a circle, smiling and shuffling about in the dust. There had been little conversation so far except the obvious realization that I needed to get back on top of the big black mare and that I could not do it without their help. A few orders were given by the boy who had obviously taken charge. Three of them gave me a leg-up with great enthusiasm, leaving me stranded across the saddle and scrambling to right myself while Kali Mem began to dance. Then I was towering above them. Conversation resumed, as if by my remounting the social order had been restored.

'*Chai*,' announced the boy in charge.

They all laughed. The balance had returned.

We had fallen into a *khud* and we had walked out of it. Now I had no idea how to get back. I asked the boy in charge. He waved his hand. 'Coming to my house to be drinking *chai*.'

The mare was gentle with the gaggle hopping and chattering around her hindquarters. As we came to the edge of the slum where the boys lived I dismounted. We walked in through the outskirts amidst the squatting figures. Twilight was skulking beyond the *maidan* where a loud game of cricket was in full swing. The *scyce* at the pony lines would be starting to fret. A search party would be sent out at dusk. There was half an hour to go. But we sat outside one of the boys' houses and drank hot, sweet tea. We talked about India's recent international cricket triumphs and Hindi pop music. They all asked me why I was not married. They tried to understand my Hindustani and, when it failed, they broke into English. They gave me *chai* and asked about my life in exchange.

The chai stall *on Hailey Road*

As the light began to fail the two boys from the *chai* stall guided me back to the pony lines through the dusk. We did not speak. It was a comfortable silence, not the kind of moment that is easy to let go.

Because of the *khud* I was a day late at the sparkling new *Indian Express Magazine* offices. Once again Sourish and his department had upped sticks. Now the newspaper was on one side of town, the magazine on the other. The late visit was to say goodbye to my part-time family. The election was over and another tenuous government was in place, so I was on my way back to England.

Sourish laughed when I poured out my excuses for being late.

'In the slums again, Justine? All this good doing on the quiet.' He looked at his newly acquired view out of his newly acquired windows. Sunlight flooded in.

'You know you will never fit in if you try to be more Indian than us,' he said, his round face smiling. 'Oh, oh, you English who fall for India. It is like you go blind to what makes India Indian. All that meditation and yoga, I am telling you, it does not get rid of the other billion people trying to get a bigger piece of the cake and such.'

Everyone crammed into his small office and we ate chocolate cake. Sourish waved as I left, chocolate cake in one hand, telephone hunched between his shoulder and ear, the other hand on the computer keyboard.

Yashwant was cool. I had upset his programme. I had not been there to convince a disbeliever that Texan Hank was a Valentine reality. And now I was leaving.

'Off you go, fly away to all your English friends. Don't think they understand you any better than we do. You just think they do because you all talk as quickly as each other and went to the same schools.'

When I held him before kissing him goodbye he stiffened in my arms like a child that has been let down.

253

As I took the lift down to the street, and then a taxi, a gulf opened.

> They were called the Hope Boats or the Empire Breeders; the ones that sailed from England to India carrying young women full to the brim with plans to find husbands and start the rest of their lives in a world away from their own.
>
> If they failed to make a match they came home on the R.E. Boat, the Returned Empties. They may not have found husbands but they had been in a place so extreme that it sucked away all the smallness that lurked in the Englishness of the English. To be an R.E. was not such a failure. For some it was devastating, a social disaster. For others it was a beginning, without husbands perhaps, without what was expected of them by their peers, but they were not empty.

The taxi slowed down for a cart clattering around the swoop of India Gate. The pony's hooves struck sparks off the road. Both animal and driver ignored the insistent hooting from the taxi. There were four other empty lanes. Yet in the quiet of pre-dawn the taxi and the cart fought for their right to that particular bit of road because that was the way in India. On my own in the back seat of the taxi I laughed. There was a gulf, a great *khud* in me, but it was filled with the sights and sounds of the life that I had moved into, the slap of Dhan Singh's bare brown feet along the passages of Jodhpur Apartments, the rustle of the Rani's chiffon sari floating around a corner, Bushan's shoulders thin and erect in the front of his rickshaw as we drove through the smog of Delhi, Sourish's laugh bubbling up from his belly, Gautam striding through the shitting fields and Yashwant, the Prince of Hailey Road, crushing out another *biri* with a brittle laugh.

A solitary hawker looked into the taxi as it passed. Seeing a white face in the back seat he waved his cane of bright balloons at the window. Beyond him nothing else stirred.

Black Oxfords and
Last Rites

OF COURSE I did not stay away. Just three months in London and I was back.

The city was holding its breath for the monsoon. It had been the hottest summer for over a hundred years and now that the thunderheads were flirting around the outskirts of town there was 95 per cent humidity to add to the record-breaking temperatures. Everything and everyone lolled and sweated.

It was four o'clock in the morning when I drummed on the door of Jodhpur Apartments. The bell had disappeared into a large hole that had been knocked through the wall. Ram Kumar's face appeared through a chink. We both stuck on a smile for effect.

'Welcome, sir.' He took the smallest from my pile of bags and lumbered off towards my room, the smell of old socks and armpits trailing behind him.

Yashwant did not appear until the following afternoon but his enthusiasm at my return made me reach out and kiss him.

'Thank God, some civilized conversation around here again. How was lovely sunny London?'

'Cold and wet.'

'But of course. And to what do we owe this return visit?'

There were various valid reasons, research to do, articles to write and an additional element that had taken everyone by surprise. The book I had written about the Spiti valley with Will's beautiful cover shot had just been published in India. The critics had outdone themselves and made it much more of a success than either the publisher or I had anticipated. Now I was going to talk to the press.

That made Sourish laugh when I went to see him a couple of days later.

'Oh, oh, that will teach you to write books.' He bounced on his chair.

'Thank you for the review that you did.'

'Did we?'

'The publisher told me you did.'

'Did they send us a copy of the book?'

'They must have done.'

He called through to one of the girls in the outer office and asked her to check. He seemed a bit embarrassed.

'Do you mean that you didn't review it?'

'I'm not so sure.' He fiddled with some papers on his desk.

'Thanks for the loyalty.'

'Oh, oh, whoops.' He tugged at one earlobe. 'So what are you going to write for us this time?'

'I really just came to say hello.'

'No, no, that won't do. Let's see now. What about a restaurant column?'

'I can't write a column about Indian food. I can't even spell most of it, let alone comment on the nuances of *masala*.'

'No, no, not reviews or anything. A weekly thingy about some of the places that you go to. Just give it your angle. You know, make it something good to read. None of these fancy five-star places. What about all those *dhabas* that you say you eat at all the time?'

'All right.'

'Okay, so we are back in business. About eight hundred words each and could you get the first one to me in the next couple of days?'

In return I made Sourish and his wife come down from the office to the garden so that I could take some photographs. As I saw them standing beside each other, each a little self-conscious, I realized how similar they looked.

'This garden is so pretty now. Someone must have worked hard.' It was just a comment to take their minds off the lens.

'Yes, Sourish has been overseeing it himself. Our *mali* has been coming to do it.' Kaveree patted Sourish's arm. He looked pleased.

'How lovely. So this is all because of you?'

Sourish mumbled something and fidgeted. Kaveree laughed.

'I suppose they don't really do that kind of thing in Wapping?' She put her hand on Sourish's shoulder and he stood still for a moment.

I took the pictures and released them. Sourish turned round as he walked away.

'Don't worry about pictures for the pieces. Just let me know where you are writing about and I'll send one of our people to take them.'

'Don't you like my pictures?'

But he was already back inside. He smiled from behind the glass door and waved.

All was not quite so fair in Hailey Road. An extended death-bed scene was being played out in Jodhpur Apartments and the clan had gathered to pay their respects to a chemotherapy-racked uncle. The Rani came back to town with Maharaj Sahib and a bevy of sisters, cousins and aunts. While the light flickered in the suffering uncle's eyes, family politics raged.

We were sitting in the day-room in a curious conversation piece. The afternoon was sagging under a fat, black sky that refused to deliver any rain. The Rani and another aunt were discussing the sensitive legal issue of some family property. The Rani was not enjoying herself, though she participated gracefully.

Yashwant's liver and sense of frustration were acute. He was in a dangerous mood. He sat in his worn dressing-gown at a desk beside the window. I was curled up on a small stool, almost at his feet, trying to make a telephone call. The Rani and the aunt were at the other end of the room facing each other on small sofas.

Yashwant passed me a piece of paper: 'I feel sick, do something.'

'Why? What's the matter?' I wrote back.

'I have a terrible stomach pain.'

'I'm not surprised after twenty-five years of vodka.'

'This whole thing is making me sick.' He waved his hand towards his mother and aunt as he passed the final note.

Dhan Singh appeared in a very dirty shirt but sporting a fresh short, back and sides. The Rani was wanted on the telephone in the other sitting-room, on the family line. She disappeared down the corridor in a cloud of chiffon, Dhan Singh padding behind her flat- and bare-footed.

'Onanism,' said Yashwant with a deep sigh as he stared out of the window.

The aunt and I both looked at him.

'What did you say, Yashwant Singh?' she asked.

'We have been discussing the definition of the word, Aunt.'

'What does it mean?'

'I am sure you have practised it, Aunt.' Yashwant was screwing our notes into small balls and firing them at the wastepaper basket.

She looked to me for an answer.

'Coitus interruptus?' I ventured.

'The Aunt does not know Latin.'

'What are you talking about?' demanded the aunt.

'Withdrawing before ejaculation. It can also mean masturbation. I imagine you probably have not practised the former.'

The aunt got up quickly. 'I think I will go and have a rest.'

'Good idea, Aunt.'

She scuttled away down the corridor.

'No one is any fun any more, except you of course.' He took a packet of *biris* from his dressing-gown pocket.

'That was not very kind.' I looked at him over my glasses.

'You look like a crotchety schoolmarm. What are you talking about? We have nothing to be kind about.' He tore a neat corner out of the *biri* packet. 'Are you in or out this evening?' He lit a *biri* and started to brush the ash from his sleeve even before he had drawn on it.

'Out.'

'With whom?'

'No one you know.'

'Does that mean you think I would not approve of him?' He raised an eyebrow.

'No, it means that it is no one you know.'

'Well, I hope he's very sexy and I hope you have lots of fun.' He stabbed out his *biri* in a neat pile of ash. 'And make sure that you come home with the milk delivery, swinging your dancing shoes over your shoulder.'

'I am going to a lecture on India's nuclear responsibility.'

'How very clever of you. Well, we will probably all be having much more fun here talking about hospital visits.' He lit another *biri*, his third in as many minutes.

The telephone rang. We both sat and looked at it until Dhan Singh shuffled back down the corridor. He listened for a moment with the receiver well away from his ear and then passed it to me. I asked him who was speaking and he shrugged.

It was an earnest-sounding young man from one of the news magazines. Could he do an interview about the book I had written on the Spiti valley? Actually he was much more interested in talking about the book he had heard I was writing on Indian newspapers.

But of course, what a nice idea.

And could I bring a mug shot of myself?

Put so charmingly, how could I refuse?

'Who was that?' asked Yashwant.

'A journalist asking for an interview.'

Yashwant rolled his eyes.

'My, we are famous now, aren't we?'

Even by the standards of the sparkling new *Indian Express* features offices, the magazine where the earnest young journalist worked was glamorous. I sat and waited on a leather sofa, conscious that I was probably going to leave a small pool of sweat behind me and make curious noises as I tried to get up. Having thought this one through I wriggled about, hoping my shirt would mop up the worst of it, then looked at the latest edition of the magazine which was prominently displayed on the table in front of me. The cover story was 'The Ugly Indian'.

> Fifty-one years after we came into our own we continue to defecate everywhere, pollute our rivers, empty garbage at our neighbour's door and jump traffic lights . . . we think only of our immediate convenience and hate it if someone tells us that we don't really lead that elevated an existence. But then, India has surpassed itself in rudeness.

There were large photographs of fermenting rubbish dumps, men peeing in public, policemen being paid bribes on the street and young children working in factories. This was the India I had chosen to live and work in. I read the article twice before realizing that I had been sitting on the squeaky leather sofa for over half an hour. That seemed quite normal, until I remembered that this time I was the one being interviewed. Why was I waiting? I went back to the rather superior girl in a pink sari at the reception desk. She waved me away, saying that I would not have to wait much longer. I sat down again, tempted to behave like a not-at-all-famous prima donna. Just in time the young journalist appeared clutching his head.

'Let's get out of here,' he said without introducing himself.

'Bad day?'

'The worst.'

Out of the office we went, into the thick humidity of the street, past the fruit-seller with a trail of red spittle on his chin, the silver jewellery hawker grabbing at the ankles of passing tourists, the man on the telephone at the *paan* shop screaming at someone about his telephone being out of order for two months, Ugly India, and straight into the cool darkness of one of the old-fashioned coffee houses of Connaught Place. The young man sat down and grabbed a handful of napkins from the glass on the table. Furiously mopping his neck and forehead, he waved a menu at one of the waiters.

'Have you had lunch?' he asked.

It was just after five o'clock.

'Yes, thank you.'

'Do you mind if I eat? I'm starving.'

'Of course not.'

He examined the menu, one hand held up to stop the waiter from leaving his side. He ordered, rearranged the cutlery that the waiter had put in front of him and then, after giving his brow one more wipe with the crumpled ball of napkins, seemed to settle.

'I'm from Calcutta, you see,' he said.

'I see.' I did not see at all.

'I don't like Delhi.' He rolled the napkin ball around his place setting.

'I love it.'

He stopped fidgeting. 'Are you mad? You come from the greatest country in the world with the best newspapers in the world and you love Delhi? Have you been to Cal?'

'Only for a couple of days.'

'It's much more civilized than Delhi, don't you think?'

'That's what everyone from Calcutta says.'

He shook his head and began to talk. His speech went on for the same amount of time that it took a couple to come in, sit down beside us, have two iced coffees and leave. He was a staunch monarchist. His favourite newspaper was the *Daily Telegraph*, his favourite magazine *The Spectator*. His heroes were the newspaper proprietor Conrad Black, the writer Bill Deedes, Oliver Cromwell and Harry Flashman.

'You mean the books?' I asked him about his last hero.

'Yes, so funny, so clever, so . . . ' He looked up at the fan above us to find the word.

'English?'

He smiled for the first time.

'Yes, I suppose so.'

'And Oliver Cromwell, that's unusual for a monarchist.'

'I know, but he was rather an important idealist, don't you think?' he said.

'Warts and all?'

'Whatever.' He rubbed at the dark shock of his high hairline.

'You should go and work for a paper like the *Telegraph*. You're their dream ticket – a right-wing monarchist who still thinks that Britain is great.'

The waiter came back with a chicken sandwich and coffee. My interviewer looked at them with distaste.

'And you are the Indian newspaper's dream ticket – a foreign journalist who thinks that India is wonderful in spite of the corruption, filth, pollution, government ineptitude and inherent national laziness.'

'Did you write "The Ugly Indian" cover story in your latest issue?' I asked.

He was half-way through the sandwich. A couple of strands of cabbage hung from his lip. He took the sandwich out but the cabbage stayed put. 'I didn't write it but my great friend did and I agree with every word he wrote.' The cabbage danced as he spoke.

'Peeing in public is illegal in Britain,' I said, waving towards his lip.

He got the cabbage in in one go. 'See, that's why I love it.'

'Have you ever been?'

'No.'

'So how do you know you will love it?'

There was a pause while he chewed and thought. 'That is the problem,' he said, wiping his mouth to check for more cabbage. 'You see, if I go to England I will probably destroy the whole thing.' He pushed the rest of the sandwich away.

'Destroy what?'

'The images of it that I have nurtured all my life – the dreaming spires, the writers, the general decency . . . ' He petered out.

'Well, I am afraid you are probably right not to go. Decency is a bit out of date now. We have political correctness instead. In the new Cool Britannia we seem to have decided to reverse the laws of nature. It is no longer survival of the fittest but the nurturing of the afflicted and the hard-done-by.'

'That sounds like Enoch Powell. He's another of my heroes. We are obviously going to be friends.' He clapped his hands.

'No, no, I didn't mean to sound so extreme. I meant it tongue-in-cheek rather than foot-in-mouth.' I saw the time on the waiter's watch as he retrieved the rejected sandwich with a sullen expression. We had been there for an hour and a half and still the journalist had not produced a notebook. 'I'm afraid I have to go in a minute,' I said.

'Oh, so soon? But we haven't really started.'

I shrugged.

'I don't really believe in the formal interview technique but I haven't asked you any of the things that I meant to. We will have to do this again, maybe lunch or something?'

I started to make an excuse but he interrupted.

'Just one question for the moment.' He got up as I started to gather my things. It was a polite gesture. 'Why an Indian paper?'

'Because I am involved and there comes a point when you just have to say "What the hell?" don't you think?' A great friend had said the same thing over lunch the previous day when I had asked him why he had so readily agreed to marry a virtual stranger. I felt flippant repeating him but I couldn't think of anything fresh to say.

'So do you think you understand India or are you involved in your image of India?'

'I love it warts and all.'

'How ironic,' he said. 'I mean you and India and me and England.'

We parted on the humid street outside his office and his shoulders tensed as he set off up the stairs to the leather sofas.

That evening I had dinner with another friend and he laughed as I described the conversation. He had been a journalist himself.

'I think we all just like to talk, especially when we are young and arrogant, especially when we are young, arrogant and Indian men,' he said.

'I'm not saying he was arrogant. It was just odd hearing someone talk about England in the way that I probably talk about India when I am back in England.' I was eating with my fingers, cross-legged on the floor.

'Ah, but the difference is that you have been living and working here, not sitting in London entertaining a fantasy about the India of the *Vedas* and the Raj.'

I spilt some *dhal* down my front. He laughed. 'See, you are even picking up our bad eating habits.'

I did not get back to Jodhpur Apartments until one o'clock in the morning. Yashwant was pacing the corridor, clean-shaven, wearing a good shirt and suit trousers, his feet shod in polished black Oxfords.

'He's died,' he announced.

'Oh, I'm so sorry.'

'Not at all, it is the best thing for everyone. He was having the most terrible time.' He trailed off without elaborating and began to pace again.

I ushered him into my room where he started to walk up and down beside the bed.

'We all have to troop off to Jodhpur at dawn for the cremation the day after.'

Outside the door Dhan Singh and Ram Kumar were arguing.

'How long will you be away?'

'Too long, maybe a week, maybe ten days. It all goes on far too long.' He pulled out the inevitable packet of *biris*, then dropped them on the windowsill. 'Bloody hell, I can't smoke. What if I burn a hole in this shirt?'

He went on pacing.

'I have to ask you to do some things if you wouldn't mind, and I am so sorry to inconvenience you.' With death and the black Oxfords came the formality of Yashwant Singh, the prince. 'Two of my finches were taken from their cages on the balcony by that bloody sparrowhawk today. I do not have a gun to shoot it so I have had a net made at enormous expense. Come, I will show you how it has to be put up on the balcony to protect the little things.' I trailed after him as he set off down the corridor.

At two o'clock in the morning we were standing out on the balcony waving around a huge white fisherman's net while Yashwant gave instructions as to how it should be put up. Next door his father was trying to sleep.

There were more edicts and proclamations to come.

'Now, for feeding the birds make sure that Dhan Singh blows the chaff off their grain very carefully and that their water is always topped up. If you think Ozy is lonely, please keep him in your room with you at night. He is very restless at the moment and I am rather worried about him.'

I had never slept with a tortoise before.

'The fish must have the tank filled right up to the top all the time and the air-conditioner in my room must stay on. I cannot deal with any more death.' He plucked at the sleeve of his shirt.

I reached out and touched his face. 'Are you all right?'

'Of course. I might be better if I had not had any vodka.' He paused.

'Travel safely, good luck with the cremation and please, don't worry about the birds, the fish or Ozy, they will all be fine. Just look after yourself.'

'Carry on regardless, never say die.' He set off from my room, one hand in the air in a farewell salute.

As I closed the door I could hear him issuing orders in the kitchen.

The family left at dawn to accompany the body to Jodhpur and I remained to watch over the menagerie. Dhan Singh and the other servants collapsed in corners to sleep off the frantic activity of the previous night. In the silence that descended on the apartments only Ozy moved, scuttling from room to room, a tortoise possessed.

In the late afternoon, while the bodies still lay draped in silence, I went out on to the balcony with the papers and watched parakeets circling the *neem* trees below in darts of green. Ozy finally gave up the chase and settled next to my left foot. On the front page of the paper was the rundown of the daily carnage of India – '17 wounded in city bomb blast' just five minutes' walk from Hailey Road, '35 killed in two train mishaps', 'Delhi on red alert after worst crime wave'. In England another pop group had broken up and a new model had been chosen for the Wonderbra advertising campaign. In the service lane below a flute player started a tune as he walked with a girl in a blue sari, jasmine in her hair. A black jeep cruised by, drowning out the flute player with the latest hit rocking Bollywood. The jeep passed and the sound of the flute returned. And then the Delhi dusk settled in around Ozy and me.